ReVision

A JOURNAL OF CONSCIOUSNESS AND TRANSFORMATION

CONTENTS

Shamanism and The Wounded West
Karen Jaenke, Editor

1 Editor's Introduction: Shamanism and The Wounded West
  Karen Jaenke

5 Poem: dreams of memory
  Nicolo Santilli

6 Wounded West: The Healing Potential of Shamanism in the Contemporary World
  Ana María Llamazares

24 Reality, Invisible World, and Shamanism: An Outlook from the Indigenous Worldview
  Carlos Martínez Sarasola

31 The Spirit Doctors of Nature
  Connie Grauds

40 Assessing a Quest to Heal HIV with Vegetalista Shamanism
  Robert Tindall

46 Walking in the Shaman's Shoes: A Transformational Walk with the Family Soul
  Francesco Mason Boring

54 The Contemporary Artist as Shaman
  Denita M. Benyshek

61 The Indigenous Spiritual Healing Tradition in Calabria Italy
  Stanley Krippner, Michael Bova, Ashwin Budden, and Roberto Galante

75 Fading Non-empirical Healing: The Reemergence of the Mending Mind
  Carl M. Hild

Current Issues

84 Julian Assange, WikiLeaks, and the Trickster: A Case Study of Archetypal Influence
  Niko Whitmire

Book Reviews

95 The Emergence of Somatic Psychology and Bodymind Psychotherapy
  Samuel Arthur Malkemus

96 The Street Corner Ching: The Ancient Chinese Oracle in Plain English
  Cristina Kaplan

Cover photo by Ana María Llamazares

Spring/Summer 2019 • Volume 32 • Numbers 2 & 3

What Is ReVision?

For over forty years ReVision has explored the transformative and consciousness-changing dimensions of leading-edge thinking. Since its inception ReVision has been a vital forum, especially in the North American context, for the articulation of contemporary spirituality, transpersonal studies, and related new models in such fields as education, medicine, organization, social transformation, work, psychology, ecology, and gender.

With a commitment to the future of humanity and the Earth, ReVision emphasizes the transformative dimensions of current and traditional thought and practice. ReVision advances inquiry and reflection especially focused on the fields presently identified as philosophy, religion, psychology, social theory, science, anthropology, education, frontier science, organizational transformation, and the arts. We seek to explore ancient ways of knowing as well as new models of transdisciplinary, interdisciplinary, multicultural, dialogical, and socially engaged inquiry. It is our intention to bring such work to bear on what appear to be the fundamental issues of our times through a variety of written and artistic modalities. In the interests of renewal and fresh vision, we strive to engage in conversation a diversity of perspectives and discourses which have often been kept separate, including those identified with terms such as Western and Eastern; indigenous and nonindigenous; Northern and Southern; feminine and masculine; intellectual; practical, and spiritual; local and global; young and old.

Memorial for the Shooting of Michael Brown in Ferguson, Missouri.

Volume 32, Nos. 2&3 (ISBN 978-0-9819706-8-4)

ReVision (ISSN 0275-6935) is published by *The Study of Shamanism, Healing, and Transformation.*

This issue was originally published electronically in Winter 2015

Copyright © 2020 ReVision Publishing.
Copyright retained by author when noted. The views expressed are not necessarily those of ReVision or its editors.

ReVision provides opportunities for publishing divergent opinions, ideas, or judgments.

Manuscript Submissions

We welcome manuscript submissions. Guidelines can be found on our webpage: http://revisionpublishing.org.

POSTMASTER: Send address changes to
ReVision Publishing,
P.O. Box 1855,
Sebastopol, CA 95473.

Subscriptions

For subscriptions mail a check to above address or go to www.revisionpublishing.org.

Individual Subscriptions

Subscription for one year: $36 online only,
$36 print only (international $72),
$48 print and on-line (international $84).

Subscription for two years: $60 online only,
$60 print only (international $96),
$79 print and online (international $115).

Subscription for three years: $72 online only,
$72 print only (international $108),
$96 print and online (international $132).

Institutional Subscriptions

$98 online only (international $134),
$134 print and online (international $191).

Please allow six weeks for delivery of first issue.

Editorial Board

Editor
Jürgen Werner Kremer, PhD
Santa Rosa Junior College, Santa Rosa, CA

Associate Editor
Karen Jaenke, PhD
John F. Kennedy University, Pleasant Hill, CA

Managing Editor
Marie Judson-Rosier

Editorial and Production Management Team

Denita M. Benyshek
Art Editor

Cristina Kaplan
Poetry Editor

Gary Newman
Book Designer/Production Specialist

Samuel A. Malkemus
Book Review Editor

Consulting Editors

John Adams, PhD
Saybrook University, San Francisco, CA

Sally Atkins, EdD
Appalachian University, Boone, NC

Caroline L. Bassett, PhD
The Wisdom Institute, Minneapolis, MN

Adam Blatner, MD
Senior University Georgetown, Georgetown, TX

Matthew C. Bronson, PhD
O'Reilly Scool of Technology, UC Davis, Davis, CA

Allan Combs, PhD
California Institute of Integral Studies, San Francisco, CA

Apela Colorado
Worldwide Indigenous Science Network

Jorge Ferrer, PhD
California Institute of Integral Studies, San Francisco, CA

Mary Gomes, PhD
Sonoma State University, Rohnert Park, CA

Stanislav Grof, MD
California Institute of Integral Studies, San Francisco, CA

Irene Karpiak, PhD
University of Oklahoma, Norman, OK

Nancy Kolenda
Center for Frontier Sciences, Philadelphia, PA

Stanley Krippner, PhD
Saybrook University, San Francisco, CA

Joan Marler, MA
California Institute of Integral Studies, San Francisco, CA

Laurel McCabe, PhD
Sonoma State University, Rohnert Park, CA

Alfonso Montuori, PhD
California Institute of Integral Studies, San Francisco, CA

Joseph Prabhu, PhD
California State University Los Angeles, CA

Donald Rothberg, PhD
Spirit Rock Meditation Center, Woodacre, CA

Meredith Sabini
The Dream Institute of Northern California, Berkeley, CA

Elenita Strobel, Ed.D
Sonoma State University, Rohnert Park, CA

Robin Voetterl, Ed.D
Portland State University, Portland, OR

ReVision Abstracts

Benyshek, D. M. (2014). The Contemporary Artist as Shaman. *ReVision, 32*(2&3), 54-60. doi:10.4298/REVN.32.2&3.54-60

This paper explores the relationship between art and shamanism, and proposes that certain aspects of an artist's life fulfill Heinze's definition of shaman. I was fortunate to attend the anthropologist Ruth-Inge Heinze's last seminar on shamanism at a Saybrook Graduate School residential conference, and it is from this seminar that the inspiration for this paper was born. During the course of her lectures and drumming rituals I began to recognize a number of distinct similarities between shamans and artists. Drawing on my experience as a professional visionary artist I share autobiographical evidence of shamanic experiences during artistic creativity. Research from psychology, anthropology, sociology, creative studies, art history, and religious studies, is also considered towards constructing an interdisciplinary and multicultural model of the artist as shaman.

Boring, F. C. (2010). Walking in the Shaman's Shoes: A Transformational Walk with the Family Soul. *ReVision, 32*(2&3), 46-53. doi:10.4298/REVN.32.2&3.46-53

Family, human and natural systems constellation and constellation as ceremony may again give the shaman a place in each of us. Walking in the "knowing field" of the family constellation, we are informed by the same clarity and humility that the shaman walked in. Incorporating the universal indigenous field, smudging, utilizing circle technology, honoring dream & synchronicity constitutes an effective approach to healing the scars of trans-generational trauma. Opening a new door to vision quests, nature constellations allow participants in constellations to experience animal and natural fields as a support to family systems and soul. Shamanic traditions of animal teaching may have fulfilled an ancestral and systemic need for including the natural world in the healing of the family soul.

Grauds, C. (2014). The Spirit Doctors of Nature. *ReVision, 32*(2&3), 31-39. doi:10.4298/REVN.32.2&3.31-39

A shaman's mysterious healing practices are a blend of medicine and spirit. The rainforest shamans are experts on the healing properties of the jungle's rich plant medicines. These shamans have an intimate relationship with the healing spirits of nature and of the plants, which they summon on behalf of the patient during the healing ritual. The author, a pharmacist by education, has spent 16 years apprenticing to an Amazonian shaman in the jungles of Peru. The author shares shamanic apprenticeship stories of the healing power of these spirit doctors of nature.

Hild, C. M. (2014). Fading non-empirical healing: The re-emergence of the mending mind. *ReVision, 32*(2), 74-82. doi:10.4298/REVN.32.2&3.74-82

Engaging Alaska Natives in discussions on traditional healing techniques and knowledge has provided a foundation for further investigation. The desire to document cultural-based skills led to a historic review of two centuries of ethnographic accounts. These observations were found to be similar to current medical practices of engaging the mental capacity of patient and healer in the act of improving well-being. There appears to be a broad spectrum of potential areas of mind/body healing that can be investigated that is firmly based in Alaska Native traditional practice. A community-based action research approach resulted in a process of multicultural engagement for learning and understanding (MELU) to utilize traditional healing techniques to complement and integrate with modern allopathic health services.

Krippner, S., Bova, M., Budden, A., & Gallante, R. (2014). The indigenous spiritual healing tradition in Calabria, Italy. *ReVision, 32*(2&3), 61-74. doi:10.4298/REVN.32.2&3.61-74

In 2003, the four of us spent several weeks in Calabria, Italy. We interviewed local people about folk healing remedies, attended a Feast Day honoring St. Cosma and St. Damian, and paid two visits to the Shrine of Madonna dello Scoglio, where we interviewed its founder, Fratel Cosimo. In this essay, we have provided our impressions of Calabria. Although it is one of the poorest areas in Italy, Calabria is one of the richest in its folk traditions and alternative modes of healing.

Llamazares, A. M. (2014). Wounded West: The healing potential of shamanism in the contemporary world. *ReVision, 34*(2&3), 6-23. doi:10.4298/REVN.32.2&3.6-23

By exploring the relationship between shamanism and the global contemporary crisis of a wounded Western culture, this article presents a general outlook of the main trans-cultural features of the shamanic worldview. It focuses on the process of shamanic healing by revisiting Lévi-Strauss' concept of "symbolic efficacy" in the light of healing conceptions found in new holistic science. It also provides epistemological elements to reflect upon the physical and psychological suffering that we endure in Western societies, as well as the possibilities of relief in the light of shamanic knowledge. Two classical mythological characters are evoked: Dionysus and Chiron. Both embody the initiation principle *par excellence* of shamanic fate, and thus remind us that this worldview is also rooted in our own Western tradition.

Sarasola, C. M. (2014). Reality, invisible world and shamanism: An outlook from the indigenous worldview. *ReVision, 32*(2&3), 24-30. doi:10.4298/REVN.32.2&3.24-30

If we challenge the Western rational idea of reality an avenue is opened to consider alternative forms of knowledge. The author recounts his experiences as an anthropologist with the indigenous peoples of Argentina and their concept of the "invisible world." This concept is brought into relation with shamanism without losing the perspective of the original worldview. This rests upon a different conception of reality, a great mythological corpus, and on several central ideas: totality, energy, communion, sacredness, and a communal sense of life. A path towards a cosmic consciousness is suggested, as well as the possibility that the indigenous worldview is a fruitful territory of encounter for Westerners.

Tindall, R. (2014). A quest to heal HIV with ayahuasca shamanism. *ReVision, 32*(2&3), 40-45. doi:10.4298/REVN.32.2&3.40-45

Amazonian shamanism is mainly associated with the visionary effects of the psychoactive vine ayahuasca, yet the practice of the Peruvian tradition of vegetalismo includes other factors such as diet (communing with the innate intelligence of healing plants) and purging (drawing disease out of the body), which allows healers to successfully treat serious disease such as cancer. In the process of undergoing such treatment, Westerners often begin to distinguish between the outcomes of a healing quest and being cured – and make their healing quest primary. This article documents one patient's quest to heal himself of HIV through apprenticeship with the Peruvian curandero Juan Flores..

Whitmire, N. (2014). Julian Assange, WikiLeaks, and The Trickster: A Case Study of Archetypal Influence. *ReVision, 32*(2&3), 84-94. doi:10.4298/REVN.32.2&3.84-94

Julian Assange has had a dramatic impact upon global society through his creation of the information leaking website WikiLeaks. This paper explores the cultural and social parallels between Julian Assange's character and the trickster archetype through the examination of his interviews, biographical information, and through the articles written about him as well as those he has written himself. This examination of archetypal influence shows how an individual psychology is contained within greater contexts and how that larger framework influences through unconscious means. Furthermore, archetypal case study shows how the individual taps into and impacts the culture by accessing archetypal images invoked by the greater community.

Editor's Introduction

Shamanism and the Wounded West

Karen Jaenke

Shamanism, humanity's oldest healing system, is today undergoing global resurgence. The origins of shamanism can be traced back to our ancestors some 60,000 to 200,000 years ago—who left evidence of their familiarity with two aspects of the shamanic cosmo-vision: the mastery of fire and the symbolic transcendence of death. Amid our current global crisis, there seems to be a need to investigate shamans, and this need reflects an emergent quest for *something*. Within these pages, that quest speaks to the unmet spiritual hunger of the West.

Shamans participate in a millenary tradition that involves the cultivation of relationships with "the invisible world". The shaman's power derives from spiritual or supernatural dimensions and entails mastery of hidden forces or energies, both positive and negative. Embracing a shamanic fate brings a life of ordeals and hardships, requires extensive training, and demands intimate acquaintance with pain, discipline, death and solitude, which become the shaman's true masters. The shaman engages the dynamics of life-death-rebirth, in which death is regarded not as a final end but a passage to a different state of consciousness or reality. The command of certain psychic and physical techniques endows shamans with the special ability to exit ordinary reality, enter extraordinary reality, and return bearing gifts from sacred dimensions. A special aspect of the shaman's training enables entry into the interiority of other beings, including plants, animals and stones; via this metamorphosis, wisdom is gathered from more- than-human forms of embodiment.

The shaman masters the art of transmutation—the ability to unite and connect, in order to transform. The shamanic task is always to transform something—an individual, community, or eco-niche that has become imbalanced and whose vitality is threatened. The shaman is a guardian of the traditions and the psycho-physical balance of the community, with an ability to restore balance through

Mexican shaman

profound knowledge of the laws of the universe. The shaman heals by becoming a master of imagination and the energetic world, capable of generating a harmonious reorganization of the energetic structure of living beings and systems.

Each of the above perspectives on the shaman is explored in this issue. Additionally, *Shamanism and the Wounded West* contextualizes shamanism within

---

Karen Ann Jaenke, M.Div, Ph.D. is Chair of the Consciousness and Transformative Studies program and former Director of the Ecotherapy Certificate program at John F. Kennedy University. From 2001-2008, she served as Dissertation Director and Core Faculty at the Institute of Imaginal Studies. Currently an Executive Editor of ReVision: Journal of Consciousness and Transformation, she has edited journals on the topics of Imaginal Psychology, Shamanism, and Earth Dreaming, as well as numerous articles. In 2000, she founded Dreamhut Consulting (www.dreamhut.org) to offer consulting services for dissertation and thesis writing, dreamwork, hypnotherapy and mentoring. Her creative vision synthesizes dreamwork, indigenous ways of knowing, the subtle body, and Gaian awareness.

a larger framework—the wounded West and our global contemporary crisis. Possibilities for addressing the alienation and anguish of our modern human condition are illuminated through shamanic modes of perception and healing, rooted in a holistic, interconnected and meaning-rich vision of the cosmos.

According to Ana Maria Llamazares, author of the lead article "Wounded West:

Fire dance during shamanic rite "Shandruu," outside Ulan-Ude, Buryatia, Siberia.

The Healing Potential of Shamanism in the Contemporary World", our greatest wound—the spiritual void of the West—can only be filled by genuine spirituality that reawakens our bonds "with Nature, with the vital, with one's own subjective and innermost self." "The deepest craving of the contemporary human soul," she maintains, "is to recover our lost spiritual connection to the cosmos, to heal the wounds of fragmentation, and to overcome the intellectual habit of turning opposites into antagonists." Llamazares first examines the epistemological and spiritual roots of the contemporary global crisis, identifying the various fragmentations that led the West "to lose its connection with Nature, with all that is vital, with human subjectivity..., and with all the subtle, sensitive and intangible dimensions of existence." Alienation is a natural consequence of the epistemological split between observer and observed, "a breach [that produced] a spiritual and emotional detachment from all living things." The loss of the feeling of belonging to an all-embracing Whole engenders an illusion of separateness and erodes the meaning of existence. Recovering consciousness of our natural participation in the web of life only becomes possible by transcending the material dimension and accessing subtle levels of reality and perception—which is the worldview of the shaman. This symbolic, multifaceted and magical quality of life, obscured by the cultural lenses of the West, permeates the entire shamanic world.

After deconstructing the modern Western scientistic paradigm, Llamazaeres constructs the essential elements common to trans-cultural shamanism: the Journey, the Trance, the Transformation and the Power. Then she turns to the Greek myths of Dionysus and Chiron, as exemplars of the initiatory pattern of shamanic fate, reminding us of shamanic roots in our own Western tradition. Dionysus embodies natural, instinctive energy within a socially accepted framework. Chiron teaches "about the conditions of healing based on learning to bear one's own pain, [and] informs us about the deepest roots of suffering: the break of loving ties between both natures, the divine and the human." Chiron, with his hybrid body, human top and animal bottom, offers an image of the integration of opposites, pointing to the reconciliation of all the Western schisms—between spirit and matter, subject and object, mind and matter, reason and emotion, masculine and feminine, and the human species and Nature.

A second, complementary article, "Reality, Invisible World and Shamanism: An Outlook from the Indigenous Worldview", elucidates key elements of a shamanic worldview, organized around the concept of the "invisible world". Carlos Martinez Sarasola distils the complex shamanic worldview into its essence. A handful of central ideas constitute the cosmic and spiritual consciousness of the indigenous world: totality, energy, communion, sacredness, a communal sense of life, and balance. *Totality* refers to a viewpoint that holds individual members of the cosmos in constant interrelationship as part of a whole, a whole infused with meaning, where integration is the rule. *Energy* is the main force that regulates the rhythm of the cosmos, generating vitality while possessing a creation-destruction dynamic. *Communion* reflects the deep link between the human person, nature and the cosmos, a special connection which intensely integrates relationships such as cosmos-home-body. *Sacredness* refers to a way of being in the world, an attitude full of feeling that links humans to the sacred and the different levels of reality in a profound manner. *Community sense of life* connotes that human life acquires meaning when collectively developed. *Balance* entails maintaining alignment with the universe through a constant search for harmony and through preserving the delicate interrelationship of each part of the whole.

These two opening articles, which paint trans-cultural shamanism in broad brush strokes, are followed by two personal accounts of engagement with Amazonian shamanism. Rainforest shamans are experts on the healing properties of the jungle's rich plant medicines, which are summoned and transmitted to the patient during healing rituals. Sacred plants bring about the possibility of provoking a state of extended consciousness in which perception is globally modified and supernatural dimensions or entities are contacted. According to Robert Tindall, "Amazonian shamanism is mainly associated with the visionary effects of the psychoactive vine ayahuasca, yet the practice of the Peruvian tradition of *vegetalismo* includes other factors such as diet (communing with the innate intelligence of healing plants) and purging (drawing disease out of the body), allowing healers to successfully treat serious disease." Amazonian medicine thus entails a complex synergy of plant medications, special diets verging on fasting undertaken in solitude, the shaman's *icaros* or sacred songs, and the ecology of the healing locale itself. Amazonian medicines are not easily removed from their matrix—the jungle and the shaman's intimate communication with the plant. Healing arises from re-embedding the patient in a living cosmology, a hierarchy of being that supports and gives meaning to the process of living and dying. This fulfills "one of the deepest needs of [the soul]: to live in a reciprocal universe, a benevolent order in which, when we call out, we are resoundingly heard" (Tindall, 2007).

Robert Tindall's article "Assessing a Quest to Heal HIV with Vegetalista Shamanism," follows the personal healing quest of a North American man with HIV. Tindall highlights the distinction between curing, the cessation of symptoms, and healing, from Old English *hælan* "to make whole, sound and well." Even when Western medicine brings a cure, there may be a deeper existential crisis of the soul and of meaning that Western medicine cannot touch. Accordingly, the healing quest can entail a soul-searching journey into the hidden psycho-somatic origins of disease. During a healing quest, whether or not a cure is found, the valence of the disease shifts as "the entire self... is engaged in unraveling a disease's enigma." Disease may be regarded as carrying an urgent life message to the patient, the body as a unique laboratory wherein a cure may be found, and the medicine as an ally to be won in a battle of the soul.

Connie Grauds, author of "The Spirit Doctors of Nature," writes with her feet firmly planted in two worlds. She is a pharmacist working in conventional Western medicine for nearly thirty years, and a shaman who apprenticed in the world of "nonrational" healing. Travelling to the Amazon in search of her own healing, she became a shaman's apprentice to find the magic missing from her own healing tradition. "There I was cooked in a cauldron of shamanic medicine rituals, *disciplinas* and unusual life-experiences, and blown apart by the magnitude and mystery of spirit." She discovered the encounter with Amazonian shamanism can entail walking "to the edges of madness" and wrestling with one's inner demons. "There is nothing like the jungle's intense heat, pesky mosquitoes and non-stop tickling sweat to wear you down. The jungle is the medicine: to merely show up the jungle guarantees a confrontation."

Grauds' vivid prose elicits the sheer, primal intensity of the jungle life force; the vibratory frequencies arising from the mass of surrounding vegetation; the cacophony of primal sounds that compose the music of the rainforest; the ceremony, in which outer jungle discomforts give way to internal phenomena of another order—dizziness, purging, visions and altered states; the Medicine in which pieces of one's life rearrange themselves; the shaman in his element, in deep communion with the spirits and full of ecstatic power, simultaneously surrendered and very much in control.

The next three articles in this double issue explore contemporary healing practices that suggest hybridizations of shamanism. Writing as a Shoshone and bicultural woman, Francesca Boring's article "Walking in the Shaman's Shoes" highlights striking parallels between shamanism and the contemporary healing approach of Family & Natural Systems Constellations. Family Constellation, a therapeutic method popular in Europe and elsewhere, draws upon a worldview and epistemology resonant with ancient shamanism. "Those who look to shamanism may really be searching for what already exists within their *own* family ancestry and field: the echo of a *universal indigenous* spiritual tradition." The shaman's gift of 'knowing' entails an ability to see ancestral influences and invoke conversations that put wandering souls to rest. Similarly, in Family Constellation, facilitators and individuals unravel barriers to experience life's vitality resulting from historical or trans-generational trauma. Family Constellations is based upon accessing a 'knowing field', a psychic reservoir of stories, accumulative traumas, and secrets of our ancestors. The therapeutic discipline of *Family Constellation* involves waiting, listening, and allowing an organic healing movement that comes from a field beyond the cognitive mind, known as a *movement of the soul*. Participants often have a stunning ability to "know" things about the family system that reveal the core of an individual's symptoms, including trauma from prior generations, a process that reflects the presence of *a family soul*. Boring demonstrates that "the soul can again journey to understand the interconnectedness and knowing that we have distanced our-

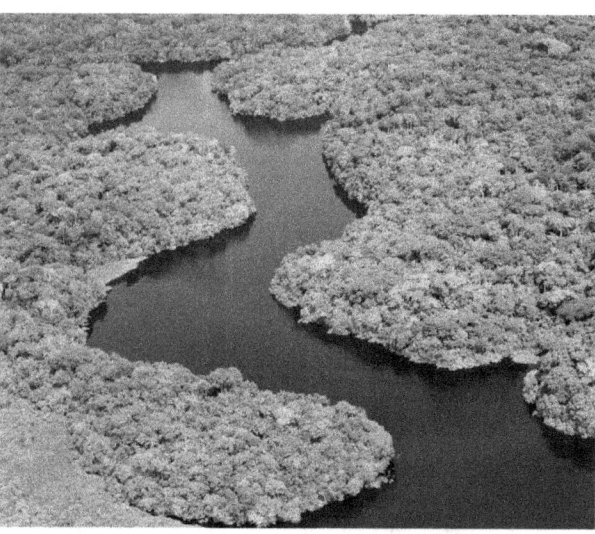
Aerial view of the Amazon Rainforest, near Manaus.

selves from to win the mantle of being modern."

Denita Benyshek, a visionary artist, asks the question: Do shamans and artists embark on comparable journeys, following analogous paths of descent, ascent and time-travel, thereby arriving at like destinations? This question leads to identification of the similarities between artists and shamans and to the contemporary category of artist-shaman.

Benyshek borrows Heinze's definition of a shaman to chart her inquiry: a shaman "forms community service in response to psychological, social, or spiritual needs, mediates between different states of consciousness, and creates connection to community in a meaningful and understood form."

Drawing upon her own intense experiences of the creative journey, Benyshek sees the travel of artists through levels of consciousness as the equivalent of shamanic flights to other worlds. She finds further parallels between the shamanic initiation that entails the deconstruction or dismemberment of identity, followed by reconstruction and rebirth. With Martha Graham, she recognized that to create, the artist must be destroyed. Both artist and shamans routinely draw illumination and power by entering liminal reality where boundaries are blurred, classification schemes upset, and ambiguity reigns.

By attempting to heal splits, unite opposites, and re-member society, shamans and artists provide community service.

Dancing Thunder, Chief of the Susquehannock tribe of Florida.

Benyshek justifiably concludes "The shaman-artist is recognized by the following actions: mediation between different states of consciousness, connection to higher powers, communication through understood forms, and service to community."

An article by Stanley Krippner and Michael Bova, et al. chronicles a field trip to Calabria, Italy to observe the region's traditional spiritual healing practices. Prior to Italy's introduction of free public medicine in the 1970s, folk medicine was the treatment of choice for the poor and those in rural areas. Although Western biomedicine is now the cornerstone of Italian healthcare, the "Calabrese maintain their cultural affinity for folk medicine, prayer, and the enactment of religious rituals for health and betterment." Calabrian traditional medicine fits within the category of complementary and alternative medicine, for which the world's population spends 60 billion dollars a year.

Due to both internal and external isolation, Calabria has proved more resistant to industrialization, allowing folk healing traditions to survive over the millennia. "Popular medicine in Calabria can be miraculous, medical, or magical." Calabrian popular medicine is a mixture of folk healing, sorcery, witchcraft, magical spells, and divine intervention, intended to bestow protection and survival amidst life's precarious enterprise. "Magical medicine is a collection of rituals, spells, elixirs, and potions that resemble cookbook recipes, [yet] their purported effectiveness results from an established and sequential methodology that activates their latent properties."

Akin to other shamanic worldviews, the Calabrian universe is an interconnected whole; tweaking one part of the fabric is likely to bring about changes in another part. Calabrians live in a cosmos inhabited by a variety of local spirits as well as by angels, demons, and saints, both benevolent and dangerous. An omnipresent "vital force" permeates the universe, conceived as a substance that can be lost or gained. While losses lead to weakness, illness, or death, gains can be catalyzed via certain external sources that transmit reinvigorating effects. This naturally-occurring vital force resides in medicinal plants and foods, and can be accessed through magical rituals or restored in miraculous healings.

Carl Hild, through 40 years of observation, reports on Inupiaq traditional healing practices that include a reliance upon of "other ways of knowing, spirit support, body manipulation, behavioral restrictions, and the extraction of bodily materials." Traditional healing is offered in a holistic manner, rather than the silos of care found in allopathic medicine.

Inupiaq healing practices emerge from a pervasive perception of oneness, known as Inua. Difficult for the fragmented Western mind to fathom, the concept of Inua transcends the notions of chi, spirit, or energy that permeate everything. "It is a well-grounded sense of oneness that goes beyond the concept of just being part of a whole." In other words, the perception of oneness is primary and fundamental, transcending a perception of separate things linked by a common element such as energy. Two types of Inupiaq healers, the anatguk and the ilisiilaq, enter a receptive and active state of non-local consciousness, enhanced at special places, thereby retrieving knowledge not regularly available through the five senses. Relying upon more than the empirical knowledge obtained by the senses, a more fluid and shape-shifting perception of the universe emerges.

Within shamanism, the true cause of illness is identified as a loss of balance, a recurrent theme found in these pages. The therapeutics of the shaman is energetic in nature, with a constant effort to restore balance. Balance is achieved through establishing a dynamic flow of energies—physical, mental and spiritual—in dialogue with forces or spirits that inhabit diverse dimensions or realities. Shamans understand that, in an interconnected universe, metaphysical patterns, depicted through symbolism, intersect and translate across different dimensions of existence. Physical, psychic and spiritual dimensions differ only in their density or intensity; thus it is completely feasible to operate—by way of structural correspondence—on the physical realm from the psychic realm and vice versa. Shamanism's presence provides living evidence that it is possible to live in more or less continuous contact with the non-ordinary and energetic dimensions of existence. Shamanic spirituality bestows authentic healing through reconnecting us with the experience of the sacred, restoring our trust in a meaningful order, and bringing assurance of belonging to a more comprehensive web of life.

References

Tindall, R. (2007). *Mark Plotkin, the Shaman's Apprentice, on Indigenous Healing and Western Medicine.* Retrieved July 10, 2009, from http://www.mariri.net/rainforest-blog/?p=14.

dreams of memory

Nicolo Santilli

fingered branches reaching for infinity
the slow dance of the manzanita
lends her curves to the mind
that spreads the spell of beauty

the sky is patient with its vast spaces
that open up awareness
in the soul that gazes
through the world

listen slowly to the vastness
whose speed is captured
by the still eye's movement

the world is a body of memory
awakening through the long sleep
of dreams that layer into darkness

we carry the smooth shyness of surfaces
beneath our protective bark
for those who move through many surfaces
have many skins

we long for the touch that nourishes what we love
through transparent boundaries of skin

we love the world of soul we live in

we must love the mountains
and the smooth tendriled fingers of the manzanita
to span the world that lives between us

in a perishing world
we cannot decide whether we are seed or plant
to seek the present spring of nourishment
or survive the long dark winter
with resolute silence

Tangled Branches.

the soul knows the seasons of its world
but we are children
who cannot see past many cycles

dream with the world
imagination is the flowering of earth
and what survives is what the landscape preserves
and takes into the subtle shape
our movements form

we are mobile creatures who have lost our roots
carrying seed pods waiting to explode
with blueprints for a world
where we can feel at home

when the great dreams of the world are forgotten
its species perish
and we who still live must gather the threads
and remember with vision

The Wounded West

The Healing Potential of Shamanism in the Contemporary World

Ana María Llamazares
Translated by Ana and Ramiro Morales

Shamanism is one of the oldest and most universal ways of accessing spiritual knowledge, extending from Paleolithic hunter-gatherers to complex sedentary and agricultural societies, maintaining its presence in most present-day indigenous communities, and persisting even in contemporary Western society, where it has given way to a phenomenon currently known as "neo-shamanism."

One of the core themes of shamanic knowledge is the capacity to heal both physical illnesses and spiritual disorders. In this sense, shamanism

---

Ana Llamazares, Argentine anthropologist and epistemologist, teaches about and researches shamanism and spirituality, the symbolism of pre-Columbian art and its relation to shamanism, holistic epistemology, and its correlations with indigenous cosmo-visions, especially South American. She is a researcher at the National Council of Scientific Research (CONICET), professor at the Universidad Nacional de Tres de Febrero (UNTREF) and Fundación Columbia, Buenos Aires. She has authored several books and specialized articles, including Del reloj a la flor de loto: Crisis contemporánea y cambio de paradigmas (Del Nuevo Extremo Editores, 2011) [From the Clock to the Lotus Blossom: The Contemporary Crisis and Paradigm Shift]. Contact: anallama@fibertel.com.ar www.delrelojalaflordeloto.blogspot.com

---

Uncertainty Rides.

is an ancestral healing practice based on an integral and multidimensional view of reality, human beings, and holistic health. Nowadays, this therapeutic quality motivates a widespread attraction toward shamanism, its potential healing and spiritual power. This phenomenon goes beyond academic circles and stirs the interest of a much larger public, since shamanism opens a rich space for intercultural dialogue and proves very helpful as a tool to reflect and act upon contemporary problems.

In the last few decades, shamanism has also become a subject of increasing anthropological interest, and I would like to contribute to its better understanding. With this purpose in mind, I will present a general outlook of the main trans-cultural features of the shamanic cosmovision and practices all over the world, ranging from its ancient forms to its present expressions. I will focus especially on the shamanic cure or healing process, revisiting Lévi-Strauss' classical concept of "symbolic efficacy" in the light of energetic conceptions about health and healing involved in the new paradigm of holistic science. At the same time I would like to place this subject in a larger scope, that of the global contemporary crisis and Western "wounds".

Due to the global process of westernization undergone by the whole planet during the last centuries, the sufferings and afflictions have reached us all, Westerners and non-Westerners alike. In different ways and degrees, we are all affected by this process. And just as it should be a global commitment to seek ways out of the environmental, socio-economic and ethical crisis, it is also necessary for each and every one of us to find ways to heal ourselves: to heal our planet and its biodiversity; to heal our societies and their economies; to heal our increasingly aching and ailing bodies; to heal our inexorably wounded souls.

Increasingly people today recognize that something about ancient shamanic wisdom can still be of great help to relieve the physical and psychological suffering that we endure as members of Western societies. I agree with this view, and it is my intention to explore and develop it throughout this article, providing epistemological elements to reflect upon the nature and origins of our wounds, as well as the possibilities of their relief and healing in the light of shamanic knowledge and its present projection. In line with this, I will also evoke two mythological characters that belong to our own Western tradition: Dionysus and Chiron.

Dionysus was the god of wine, drunkenness, irrationality, and joyful—if often violent—outburst, but above all, he was the great performer of ecstasy. The history and symbolism of this ancient pre-Olympian god show us the role that non-ordinary states of consciousness have played in the West and why it is that all that is Dionysian, in its broadest sense, has been almost eradicated from our lives. Chiron, for his part, is the wise centaur of Greek mythology, the perfect archetype of the wounded healer, of self-healing and of the wisdom potential involved in overcoming pain as well as in the integration of opposites.

Both Dionysus and Chiron embody the initiation principle par excellence of shamanic fate, and thus remind us that this worldview is also rooted in our own Western tradition. The time has come for us to re-discover and reclaim it. Indigenous peoples have cultivated this worldview for millennia, they have been in charge of enriching and preserving it ritually; and today, many of them are generously sharing this knowledge. The time has surely come to share, not only the pain that the process of modern westernization has provoked, but also the great healing power preserved as a treasure in shamanic knowledge, which to a certain extent belongs to humankind as whole.

The Wounds of the West

In speaking of wounds, I refer to a wide range of pain that extends from the planetary to the personal and intimate realms. As in a vertical arch, it spans from Gaia's suffocation –brought about by the constant cornering and destruction of animal and vegetal species, as well as the systematic manipulation of these species for massive consumption, scientific experimentation or collective entertainment; to wounds inflicted by death and violence of all kinds that scourge entire peoples through wars, guerrillas, organized crime, terrorism and the upkeep of the arms industry; to those wounds provoked by inequity and poverty, affecting growing sectors of the world's population; to the burden of educational, family, and personal wounds that each of us carry as a result of authoritarianism, discrimination, lack of affection, repression, punishment and so many other things that we may have had to endure, according to the diversity of our personal histories and stories.

In terms of the worldview of our indigenous peoples of the Andes, we could say that we are in the midst of a new Pachacuti, a cataclysm that involves great changes, both external—of the physical, energetic and climate environment—and internal—of the body, mind and spirit. In the Quechua language, Pacha means 'the Earth' —the Pachamama—as well as 'being here and now,' and Cutec refers to the idea of revolution, of a full turn and return to the origins.

Pachacuti is then synonymous with great transformation, a moment of profound change, in which everything becomes disarranged, turned upside down. Apart from an ecological transformation, with climate and telluric upheavals, it also implies a shift in collective consciousness, which will eventually express itself in significant social transformations. To some extent, it also means a return to the Earth, to the sources, as well as a recovery of original[1] values and energy. The current crisis may be interpreted then as a new Pachacuti of enormous magnitude, for, as we all know, the crisis is global.

Without sounding reductionistic, I do believe that it is possible to find a common element underlying all of our contemporary afflictions. If we look deeper inside, we can find it is all about one and the same pain, the same basic ablation suffered by the modern Western consciousness, almost as a price paid for its own existence, expressed in diverse ways.

A Comprehensive Look at the Contemporary Crisis

To enlarge this idea, I will resume the approach developed in my book *Del reloj a la flor de loto* (2011a), which proposes an interpretation of the Western crisis from a threefold perspective: epistemological, spiritual and evolutionary. These are three intertwined dimensions of the crisis.

This interpretation holds that, at the base of the multiple expressions of the Western crisis, we can find as a common root, a system of values that is implicit in the modern Western scientistic paradigm, developed in the West since the fourteenth century through the Renaissance, the Scientific Revolution, the Enlightenment, and the Industrial and Technological Revolution. In sum, it evolved through the socio-historical process known as Modernity, reaching Post-modernity as its present epigone. Such worldview or paradigm is based on the principles of exclusive opposition, competition and exploitation of human and natural resources for the benefit of the ideal of unlimited growth and prog-

> The West has suffered several fragmentations that led it to lose its connection with Nature, with all that is vital, with human subjectivity and, in general, with all the subtle, sensitive and intangible dimensions of existence.

---

1 Original here refers to the energy and values of the origins, and not to something unique and special.

ress. This value system determines a particular way of conceiving the world, of perceiving, feeling and acting in it.

It is from this point of view that we can state that the contemporary crisis has an epistemological basis, since what is actually undergoing a crisis is a way of thinking and conceiving reality, specifically the modern Western paradigm, the materialistic, mechanistic and rationalistic worldview derived from Cartesian-Newtonian science.

We can also look at the evolutionary dimension of this crisis. In these terms we may understand it as an instance of the unfolding of consciousness, whose goal has been the constitution of the identity of the human being as a subject, the self-assertion of a collective ego or self as an autonomous entity; although inevitably painful, this has been a highly transcendental stage within the macro-history of the human species. Modern consciousness has reached such extension because it has crossed cultural and ethnic boundaries, pervading the minds of millions around the world. Even though it was born in the West, the modern Western paradigm has become a common cognitive pattern at a global scale, which currently characterizes an evolutionary instance of Homo sapiens.

Beyond the epistemological commotion that the paradigm shift entails, the crisis that we are living has a deeper dimension, one of a spiritual kind. Throughout Modernity and almost as a condition for the existence of the scientistic[2] paradigm, the West has suffered several fragmentations that led it to lose its connection with Nature, with all that is vital, with human subjectivity and, in general, with all the subtle, sensitive and intangible dimensions of existence. The conception of reality that became established only accepts what is rational, material and measurable, and views scientific judgment as the ultimate court of certainty; it has made humans believe that their power is immeasurable and unlimited, that they are superior to everything else, that their needs are the first priority and that, in order to meet such needs, any outrage can be justified.

Above all, this conception has discarded as unnecessary the presence of the sacred and the supernatural and, together with this, of all that lies outside the narrow fringe of ordinary material reality. Thus, the everyday life of any regular person adapted to Western society usually passes by almost without any space for the deep experience of the spiritual, in a succession of profane linearity, after which the basic life experience that is left is the nonsense of the immediate, loneliness, lack of communication, emptiness, the most absolute state of abandonment, and consequently anguish and dissociation. So, we arrive at the deepest threshold of the contemporary crisis: its mental, spiritual and existential consequences.

At this point dwell the reasons that prompt the modern human being to search—many times in a desperate and compulsive way—for spiritual paths and psychotherapeutic resources and, we might also add, a certain eagerness to get to know the sacred plants and their effects. It is there, in the depths of the human heart and psyche where we find again, beyond the epistemological scale, the spiritual dimension of the crisis of paradigms.

Materialism and Fragmentation: Illusions of the Modern Mind

In order to understand this a little more thoroughly, let us consider with more detail how the breakdown of spirituality occurred in the West. To this end, it is necessary to acknowledge the profound ties that bind together the epistemological and the existential dimensions. This way we will be able to appreciate better the direct link that joins certain conceptions and epistemic resources—like fragmentation, materialistic reductionism and virtuality—and some of the most erosive contemporary experiences, such as helplessness, anguish, anxiety, competitive compulsion and thirst for power.

If we briefly examine the constituents of the modern Western paradigm, we can notice that pain lies in its very foundations. Each of the steps toward the autonomy of consciousness, from the inevitable loss of the state of mystical participation with Mother Nature and Cosmos to the constitution of a self-aware subject[3], brought about successive breaks and fragmentations that naturally have left overlapping wounds in collective memory, expressed and actualized in each of us at a particular level.

The main philosophical instrument of fragmentation was the Cartesian division between res extensa (matter) and res cogitans (mind), which led to the division between object and subject, between the world and the human being. From then on, the observer and the observed would be two independent entities: qualitatively different, opposed and autonomous.

Assuming as true the gap between subject and object, between man and the world, was the original sin of Western rationality. This breaking-off was the epistemological key of objectivity, philosophical materialism and the pragmatic neutrality of scientific ethics. It was also a very powerful instrument which paved the way for great discoveries and the unfolding of the modern world as we enjoy and suffer it today. Nevertheless, it was based on fictitious grounds. Sep-

---

2 Scientistic: Adj. derived from Scientism: the belief that the assumptions and methods of the natural sciences are appropriate and essential to all other disciplines, including the humanities and the social sciences. -Ologies & -Isms. Copyright 2008 The Gale Group, Inc. http://www.thefreedictionary.com/SCIENTISTIC

3 Kremer (1994), based on Owen Barfield's work, offers a very helpful framework for the ideas discussed in this section when they describe three modes of consciousness, 1) original participation or indigenous consciousness 2) unconscious participation or modern consciousness and 3) future participation or recovered indigenous consciousness. For a further discussion see also Llamazares, 2008, 2011a.

arateness is just a constructive illusion of our mind. Therefore, this assumption was also the root of much of our contemporary suffering.

The consequences of fragmentation affected both the object and the subject, leading to a double fracture or to what might be considered a double and simultaneous disenchantment. First, Nature has been exploited to the verge of ecological disaster. At the same time, life and the human mind itself have been reified (i.e. reduced to the condition of things) by being subjected to mechanistic principles. Alienation is a natural consequence of the epistemological discontinuity between the observer and the observed, which opened a breach that generated a spiritual and emotional detachment from all living things. By losing the connection with our environment and a feeling of belonging to a Whole that embraces us, we have fallen into the illusion of believing that we are alone in this world and, as a natural consequence, life has lost its value, and we seem to have forgotten what the meaning of our existence is.

Materialistic reductionism—i.e. the conviction that the world is only the narrow slice of material reality—has worsened our existential situation even more. As cognitive possibilities remain limited to sensory observation and mental lucubration, the illusion of separateness is nurtured, clouding our ability to notice that it is only in the material dimension that we perceive ourselves as isolated, individual and essentially separate beings. The consciousness of interconnectivity, of our natural participation in the web of life and in the cosmic order, is only possible if we transcend the immediate dimension of the material and access other subtler levels of reality and perception.

This epistemology of "objectivity," tied to the principle of neutrality, granted modern man an unprecedented operational freedom. The division between object and subject evolved into something more than a methodological resource—it became a fictitious antagonistic opposition. This in turn implied a hierarchization of scientific rationality over other forms of knowledge, of the Subject over the Object and consequently, of the Human Being over Nature, which resulted in an exploitable reservoir of raw materials.

In the process of construction and social adoption of this new form of rationality, science played a fundamental role: it was responsible for showing that it did work. With its pragmatic consciousness, it demonstrated immediate benefits and thus guaranteed legitimation. Eventually, science would become well established—and lasting, even in our contemporary collective imagining—as the only reliable and true knowledge, holding a position of seemingly natural and therefore undisputed power.

At the same time that the terms "rational" and "objective" were transformed into synonyms of "true knowledge," all other ways of being and knowing were banished and excluded, considered "irrational" and "non-objective" and, therefore, less reliable. This applied to whatever was subjective, philosophical, artistic, sensitive, intuitive, bodily, emotional, paradoxical, mystical, subtle, and of course, spiritual.

But the hegemony conquered by scientific rationality rests on its own epistemological blindness. In order to achieve the absolutist effect of objectivity, this rationality had to free itself from self-critical reflection and to preclude the possibility of regarding itself as one among other possible forms of knowledge. Finally, it fell under the spell of its own power, and it is not difficult to imagine the political and cultural implementation of this fundamentalist sense of superiority. Along a gradient of increasing violence, this meant the discrediting, repression and in some cases persecution or even annihilation of all that is different and strange, which one way or another was to occupy the disturbing place of the "other." In this way, a great ground of uncertainty has been forming gradually behind its back—a huge and ominous "shadow" that naturally, in time, began to seek paths to see the light of day again.

Mongolian Shaman

The Baconian aspiration expressed in "knowledge is power" achieved an effective instrumentation by means of mechanistic science, even if in the long run the price proved too high. Perhaps one root of the excesses lies in another nucleus of the modern paradigm: an aspiration to certainty and a search for the absolute boosted by the discovery of virtuality.

One of the factors that generated the epistemic conditions for the development of virtuality was the historical coincidence, at the dawn of Modernity, of the arithmetical use of zero, the invention of virtual money for commercial operations and the pictorial method of perspective based on a single vanishing point (Rotman, 1987[4]). The modern subject discovered a mechanism far more powerful than the single pulley, one which would make it possible to create illusions and reality effects by means of artificial resources.

---

[4] In his interesting essay called Signifying Nothing. The Semiotics of Zero (1987), Rotman holds that zero, the vanishing point, and virtual money are isomorphic manifestations, different but semiotically equivalent, of a single meaning or sense configuration. They all have in common the use of virtual resources to produce real effects. As regards zero, it is worth mentioning that we are considering its arithmetic use for calculation. The notion of zero was discovered and used in the ancient world by the Maya of Mesoamerica and the Babylonians of the Hellenistic Period. However, only by the end of the Middle Ages (14th c.) was it introduced in Europe, together with the Hindu-Arabic numeral systems and other contributions from the Arabian culture.

It shifted from iconicity to abstraction.

This epistemological fracture had been brought forward by Renaissance artists as early as the fifteenth century. The realistic mode of representation based on the geometric technique of linear perspective had implied an unprecedented cognitive transformation. This changing look opens a new space—absolute, uniform and mathematizable—and involves a distance between observer and object. The point of view of the observer—a single, fixed point outside the representation—generated a non-participatory way of knowing and relating to the world, based on confrontation and dissociation.

The modern subject is inevitably elided and also confused. Both realistic representation and the discourse of scientific objectivity entail a covertly contradictory message. On one hand, on a semantic level—the realistic mode of representation—we are explicitly told that there is a real, objective, solid world that can be manipulated and is independent from us. At the same time, on a syntactic level, the image-building technique reminds us implicitly that it is the subject who organizes the realistic world by means of a particular way of looking, which entails forgetting that one is looking and therefore erasing one's participation.

Thus, the perspective method marked the passage from a medieval semiotics of iconicity—in which it was possible to find a concrete referent for each sign—to a modern semiotics of abstraction, in which certain signs can be empty spaces and, by virtue of their essential ambiguity, be potentially occupied by infinite referents.

The arithmetical application of zero makes it possible to generate numbers ad infinitum, thus multiplying the possibilities of calculation. Similarly, by applying the rules of the perspective method, it is possible to create infinite images that copy reality and create an illusion of depth. Establishing a nominal exchange rate allows the possibility of performing infinite financial and economic transactions. These signs lack a specific concrete meaning because they represent nothing, and at the same time, as any vacuum, they can be filled with every possible meaning.

These empty signs or meta-signs are the key instruments on which virtuality operates with its infinite potentialities. Here lies one of the secrets of power in the modern world and also one of its greatest dangers. Given its purely mental and abstract condition, the semiotics of virtuality is dizzying and can easily lead to a loss of the notions of limit and balance.

And, in time, such a secret allowed modern man to reach the moon, develop cybernetic globalization, stuff wallets with plastic cards and so many other things that seem natural to us now and, yet, are really artificial. By casting off the shackles of the tangible, we discover the power of emptiness and absence: signs and meta-signs that can generate more and more signs ad infinitum, creating the deceptive illusion that the power of virtuality is unlimited.

Despite the fact that the twentieth century witnessed a host of dramatic experiences that have proved the opposite, the idea that our power has no limits is still one of the most firmly established convictions of Modernity. Let us think about the so frequent appeal of advertising resources. We are promised that together with the promoted product we will also acquire the possibility to defy any limit—of speed, of sports competitiveness, of seduction, of comfort, etc. Power based on virtuality is not concerned about limits, it does not take into account the environment; it follows the motto "the farther, the better," whatever the cost. And this is precisely where the ambivalent and paradoxical condition of this power opens up. Unless it is oriented by a firm ethical consciousness of balance, this kind of power can be carried away beyond reason, leading to a general destabilization of the whole system.

Perhaps this is the delicate point at which we, the human species, are standing. The risk of virtuality resides in the fact that such a great power is based only on our mental capacity for abstraction and lacks anchorage in the concrete. In this sense, recovering the direct experience of the real—basically through a re-connection with our bodies, our emotions, and Nature—may help us find our way along our search.[5]

The West and the Search for Ecstasy

So we reach the present time, when the most corrosive effects of that divorce of the human being from Nature, both at external and internal levels, can no longer be sustained. All those aspects that have been neglected, subdued, repressed, or eliminated from our consciousness—just like those sectors of society that embody and represent such aspects—making up an enormous "shadow" over the back of modern Western consciousness, tend to emerge, to resurface. They need to return, and at times even with considerable fury, they make their claim for recognition and reintegration.

As a final result from the process of psychic fracture to which fragmentation leads inevitably, one of the most widespread Western life experiences appears: anguish. A pleiades of other related states follow in chain: anxiety, depression, fear, abandonment, and a long list

> By losing the connection with our environment and a feeling of belonging to a Whole that embraces us, we have fallen into the illusion of believing that we are alone in this world and, as a natural consequence, life has lost its value, and we seem to have forgotten what the meaning of our existence is.

---

5 For a further discussion of this point, see the works of Charlene Spretnak (1991, 1997), especially the latter.

of psychophysical manifestations, from the now common stress to the increasingly frequent degenerative diseases and cardio-vascular conditions.

All this becomes crystal clear when considered from the point of view of frustrated spirituality. There is a profound interrelation among all these psychological experiences,[6] certain physical illnesses, addictive compulsion in its multiple variants—alcohol, tobacco, drugs, tranquilizers, work, speed, sex, etc.—and the search for spiritual and mystical ecstatic experiences.

According to psychologist Robert Johnson (1987):

> The great tragedy of contemporary Western society is having virtually lost its capacity to experience the transforming power of ecstasy and joy.... More than ever our spirits need to be nourished. But, having excluded from our lives the inner experience of the divine ecstasy, we can only look for its physical equivalents... This craving has led to the most characteristic symptom of our time: addictive behavior. (p.6)

It is important to be aware of this link between anguish and the need for ecstasy—so deep and so little known—because this may alert us and help us recognize a certain subtly compulsive tendency, often disguised as spiritual search, especially through an insatiable and varied reiteration of experiences with which one wants to unlock the contents of the unconscious or reach other dimensions of consciousness.

This link also appears in the conception of spirituality as an exclusively vertical and ascending movement whereas, in fact, spiritual opening is not achieved through an upward "evasion," but rather through a careful plunge into one's body and the earthly, in a balanced and paradoxical movement of simultaneous ascent and descent.

At an even deeper level we can notice a connection between insatiable spiritual hunger and an aspiration to unlimited power, discussed above. In modern consciousness both are also pulsing underneath the search for certainty and absolutes—the last of the faces that the patriarchal idea of "God the Father" has taken on in the West.

Perhaps one of the most important experiences of Modernity has been the definitive and systematic frustration of that frankly adolescent longing to verify the existence of that ever external, superior, transcendent, masculine seat of power. As long as we continue identifying power with the symbolic place of "the father," we will largely keep fearing or disputing it, as if an exclusive dynamics were the only way to deal with power: either subduing or being subdued. Our consciousness will only be able to overcome that old fallacy through a profound internalization of this frustration—which requires that we stop projecting authority outwards and upwards, and come to terms with our own personal power, conceiving it as a creative and positive inner force. This is the path to the fathomless dimension that can be unveiled by means of an authentic view of the holistic. To embrace uncertainty with confidence is indeed a remarkable achievement.

None of the above considerations inhibit the capital importance of genuinely seeking and integrating spirituality; they just make the search more complex and, at the same time, compel us to refine our instruments of navigation so as to be able to discern the illegitimate from the authentic. Precisely because of all that has been said, we must highlight the meaning of spirituality within the emergence of new forms of consciousness. As long as it is pursued as a tool of lucid freedom and a means to get in tune with the universe, spirituality has an enormous therapeutic power and great evolutionary potential.

Our postmodern society has corrupted spirituality by placing it in a big market of quick and easy sales. The same happens with the increasing attraction toward indigenous and shamanic resources. Such is the need to reestablish contact with original roots and the natural, that many people tend to adhere unconditionally to any proposal that sounds telluric: this ranges from harmless habits—such as adopting ethnic clothing—to truly dangerous ones—like taking part in ceremonies, exposing oneself to alleged healings or trials, using sacred plants out of mere psychedelic curiosity and then feeling "initiated" on the path of indigenous wisdom. The most

Haunts of solitude.

reckless go as far as to believe that they can acquire in a weekend workshop certain age-old pieces of wisdom that will enable them to perform afterwards as shamans or body and soul healers. And this occurs even among contemporary indigenous or 'mestizo' (mixed-blood) people who do not adhere clearly to the traditional values and worldview.

In any case, and precisely within this framework, we cannot but notice and emphasize the importance for the contemporary world of the healing potential of shamanism and, in particular, of the use of sacred plants, one of its main fields of knowledge.

Without lapsing into the simplicity of

---

6   For a detailed examination of addiction as a concealment of spiritual search, see also Grof & Grof, 1990.

suggesting that we should wait in line in front of modern "shamanic consulting rooms," what I find most inspiring when it comes to seeking ways to relieve the generalized sufferings of our time, along with sharing the cultural, concrete and physical phenomenon of shamanism, is the possibility of taking a fresh look at the shamanic cosmo-vision—this other way of viewing the world and acting on it, which is gradually converging with our own worldview. It is precisely this symbolic, multifaceted and "magical" quality of life that pervades the entire shamanic world, something that we Westerners have forgotten, immersed as we are in a culture of materiality and immediateness.

It is also necessary to frame all these issues within the worldwide process of philosophical and ethnic revival of indigenous peoples, who are recovering their sense of identity and unveiling their wisdom to contribute to collective awakening. This is happening particularly in the Americas, where the enormous wealth of native populations will surely lead our continents to play a key role in the coming years.

A central part of our mission as researchers, as anthropologists, but fundamentally as human beings fully committed to the new Pachacuti and the change of consciousness, is to pave the way for reflection and to provide respectful knowledge of this ancient wisdom for the good of everyone.

Shamanism: A Transcultural Phenomenon

Let us now focus again on shamanism so as to be able to fully appreciate what we propose as the spiritual and therapeutic potential of this ancestral wisdom in the context of the contemporary crisis.

Here I will aim to contribute some elements that will bring us closer to the difficult task of defining what shamanism is, certainly a complex but in any case necessary undertaking. To this end,

> At the same time that the terms "rational" and "objective" were transformed into synonyms of "true knowledge," all other ways of being and knowing were banished and excluded, considered "irrational" and "non-objective" and, therefore, less reliable.

I have gathered a series of features and concepts that characterize this phenomenon in its universality, beyond its particular cultural differences.

What is Shamanism?

In 1705, Nicolaas Witsen, a Dutch diplomat visiting the court of the Tsar Peter I of Russia, made a drawing that would become famous (see image below). During a journey across Siberian lands he had observed persons dressed in furs that made them look like bears, wearing big antlers on their heads, who danced and

Siberian shaman.

played their drums rhythmically until they fell in a profound trance. During that state, these men spoke, predicted the future, talked with spirits and with animals, and succeeded in healing ill people. They looked like lost "lunatics" that convulsed; yet they enjoyed great prestige in their communities. It was said that one of them, named Kököchi, had even encouraged with his prophecies the founder of the Mongolian Empire, Genghis Khan himself. Witsen had drawn a Siberian shaman of the Manchu Tungus group.

In the language of that group, this kind of individual was denominated xaman, or saman in Russian. This term comes from the root scha-, which means "knowledge," whence xaman is "the one who knows," "the wise". It also alludes to the idea of bodily movement or agitation (Narby, 1997, p.151), a very interesting etymology that we will meet again below. In time this term gained popularity and was then translated into English as "shaman," to refer to those persons who, in almost every known traditional culture, are in charge of communicating with different dimensions of reality. Thanks to the cultivation of their abilities to unfold their consciousness, they act as bridges between their communities and the supernatural, playing a wide range of roles—fortune-teller, healer, sage, ceremony celebrant or even chief, in charge of political decisions. What distinguishes and endows them with such special identity is their ability to "get out" of ordinary reality, to go to the extraordinary and know how to come back, bringing to this dimension something emanating from their connection with those other supernatural or sacred dimensions.

Shamans deal especially with maintaining communication with spiritual and natural forces. They talk to the spirits of animals, whom they ask permission before they go hunting or try to appease if they kill an animal by accident. They also seek advice from the spirits of plants, from whom they learn the art of healing illnesses of the body and the soul. Likewise, they talk to the spirits of the dead, whose souls sometimes refuse to leave. Shamans can operate on the elements of Nature in order to bring rain, conjure away a drought or subdue a fire, but above all they maintain the relationship with the deities, whom it is necessary to honor and heed permanently.

As formulated by Mircea Eliade and Ioan Couliano, shamanism cannot be considered a religion in the strict sense of the word, but more precisely:

> A collection of ecstatic methods organized in order to come into contact with the parallel, though invisible, universe of the spirits and to obtain their support for the man-

agement of human matters, very often in a wide sense of what today we would call therapeutic (Eliade and Couliano, 1992, quoted in Fericgla, 2000, p.82).

Nevertheless, we can also acknowledge that the role of the shaman transcends even the therapeutic.

The function of the shaman is of vital importance for the community. The shaman's role is not limited to seeing the human soul, getting to know its drama, healing, purifying houses and people, neutralizing or directing negative influences, foretelling and communicating with spirits, amongst other actions. The shaman, in the broadest sense of the word, is the true guardian of the traditions and the psycho-physical balance of the community. By renewing its myths and permanently reenacting its cosmo-vision, the shaman generates meaning to the group and thus becomes a foundation of the culture (Llamazares, 2004, p.107-108).

***The Main Shamanic Themes:
The Journey, the Trance, the Transformation and the Power***

Shamanism is a very ancient knowledge that was born alongside the basic needs of the way of life of hunter and gatherer societies. In Europe and Africa, Paleolithic paintings at least 35,000 years old already show human personages with animal features that can be interpreted as representations of shamans or sorcerers. However, we could trace the origins of shamanism further back, to a more remote period, perhaps to the times of our Neanderthal ancestors—some 60,000 and even 200,000 years ago—who left evidence of their familiarity with two central themes of the shamanic cosmo-vision: the mastery of fire and the symbolic transcendence of death (Eliade, 1964; Poveda Ed., 1997; Vitevsky, 1995).

Nevertheless, it is not only an age-old wisdom but also a universal phenomenon. With diverse names and traits but bearing an unmistakably distinct stamp, it has been present in hundreds of cultures throughout the five continents. We find shamanic traditions in Europe from the Paleolithic to pre-Christian times, and also in numerous indigenous groups of Africa, Oceania, Australia, Asia and the Americas.

This cultural diversity is still astonishing and favors the comparative study of the major shamanic features, those

The Sorcerer

recurring principles which, beyond specific cultural or local differences, are the common axes that maintain the universality of this lore. In a previous work (Llamazares, 2004) for which I carried out a transcultural study of the relation between cosmo-vision, ritual practices and shamanic art, I put forward a synthesis organized around four major themes:

- The journey and the communication between alternative worlds or dimensions of reality;
- The ecstatic trance as a way to access other realities;
- The transformation as a result and goal of the shamanic work; and
- The power as a force and an ethical challenge in the practice of the shaman.

The Journey

The central activity of the shaman is the journey between different worlds or dimensions of reality. At a cosmological level, the idea of the journey stems from a stratified and multiple conception of the universe, with the predominating idea of the tripartition into Upper world or Heaven (Supra-world), Earth (Intermediate or Middle World) and Underworld (Infra-world), communicated with one another through the vertical axis or axis mundi—axis of the world—often represented directly as stairs, dangling ropes, trees or trunks with steps, through which the passages occur.

Through the journey, shamans accomplish their prime mission: to connect the three cosmic dimensions, and thus maintain the balance between them. Only shamans are able to access such places, establish a communication with the spiritual forces that dwell there and bring their messages, the information and the knowledge that are needed here on Earth.

The journey theme is closely related to the presence and acquisition of the guiding animals or spirits. The usual way of traveling is flight, in the case of ascents, although there can also be descents achieved by means of different ways of falling; and generally, in order to perform the journey, shamans need to acquire the faculties of their protecting animals.

Together with the art of flight, shamans must develop their vision. Like the penetrating gaze of birds, this enhanced ability to scrutinize allows them to see through matter and know what is happening in other worlds. In a broader sense, the shamanic vision or the "strong eye" refers to the capacity to widen ordinary perception and have visions, or adjust one's sensitivity to receive and "see" subtle forces and energies (Ryen, 1999).

The Trance

In order to travel across different realms of reality, shamans must develop their main attribute: their ability to unfold their consciousness and enter ecstatic states. The trance is "the vehicle" of the journey and, so as to reach this trance, a variety of means are used, namely: music vibration, percussion, repetitive dancing and chanting, constant physical movement and especially the assimilation of psychoactive substances or plants, considered sacred because they are used exclusively for ritual and healing purposes.

In general, a number of power objects are also used to reach the trance, including staffs, scepters, knives or sharp elements, feathers, hooves or other animal parts and certain mineral substances such as different kinds of earth or semi-precious stones. An element that is sometimes disregarded in the technology of the trance is the use and production of icons and images such as statuettes, sculptures, decorated vessels or other items, and paintings, whether on the body or on other natural surfaces like bark, rock, or the ground itself. Finally, the command of certain psychic and physical techniques enables shamans to reach an absolute concentration and, therefore, extend their perception and direct their power at will.

The Transformation

As a result of the journey, the transformation occurs. It usually implies the symbolic death and resurrection of the shamans, as well as their becoming other beings, generally animals. This is possible thanks to their profound consubstantiation and connection with the animal and natural forces.

A special chapter in their training is the one that empowers them to enter the spirit of other beings—especially animals or plants—and via metamorphosis, to learn from such beings through the vivid experience of becoming and being them. Shamanic art, particularly from the pre-Columbian period, is rich in this kind of representation, in which animal and human traits are fused together and integrated, with a marked

Siberian shaman, Hivsu, summoning spirits.

emphasis on the symbiosis between the jaguar and the shaman, or the snake and the shaman. These images speak about the shamanic capacity for unfolding, transformation and access to other dimensions of reality.

The shamanic task is always to transform something: illness into health, drought into rain, signal into announcement. We could say that the shamanic art par excellence is the art of transmutation—the ability to unite and connect, in order to transform. For this, the shamans must necessarily go through the experience of their own personal transformation, which generally implies healing oneself in the first place.

The shamanic vocation or fate usually becomes apparent with some extraordinary event that acts as a "call," a clear signal that the person must take the path that leads to becoming a shaman. In general, the turning point is a serious illness, an accident, an attack of animals, insects or unknown spirits. The dilemma is extremely hard, for those who are called but fail to follow this path will surely worsen, die or cause serious damage to their families. On the other hand, by embracing their fate, they face a life fraught with ordeals and hardships. This long learning path implies becoming acquainted with pain, discipline, death and solitude, which become their true masters.

The most dramatic moment in the life of shaman is the initiation, and sometimes more than one is necessary. Initiation involves the shaman's withdrawing from his or her family and community, and undergoing severe psychic and physical trials. Some classical initiation themes include being dismembered, visiting the underworld, disincarnating and moving along one's own skeleton, and later assembling its parts again, to be reborn into a new life.

Thus, through successive initiations, shamans acquire their protecting animals and objects, which endow them with their distinct faculties, like the penetrating gaze, the ability to communicate with the spirits of the living and the dead, and the ability to control certain forces of nature.

It is through these limit-experiences that shamans learn the art of healing, which primarily consists in knowing how to transmute illnesses, defeat death, and regenerate life. These faculties enable them to leave their human condition and return to it. Their work pivots on the life-death-rebirth dialectics, based on a cosmo-vision that regards death not as a definitive end but as a passage to a different state of consciousness or reality.

The Power

Through this long process of learning, shamans gradually acquire their powers. The power of the shamans usually comes from spiritual or supernatural dimensions, and involves their mastery of the forces or hidden energies, both positive and negative. This confers on them a unique social status, which in certain circumstances becomes a way of legitimating their earthly power as religious-political leaders of their communities. In essence, their true power always emerges and is supported by their capacity to bring supernatural forces to Earth. The supernatural is ultimately what legitimates their earthly power. In shamanic societies, the sense of the sacred is a vital and fundamental trait.

Earthly power depends not only on the strength and the ability to prevail over other people, but rather on the wisdom to redress the relation between Heaven and Earth, and maintain that balance to the interests of the community.

Shamanic Healing: A Holistic View of Health and Illness

One of the main shamanic powers has to do with healing, both physical illnesses and spiritual disorders. In many cultures—e.g. among native peoples of the North American prairie—the term used as a synonym for "shaman" is "medicine-man" or "medicine-woman", which alludes to the condition of being a person of power as well as to the healing skills.[7] In Peru, shamans are also called curanderos (folk healers) or vegetalistas, due to their profound knowledge of the use and properties of plants, both medicinal and psychoactive. In the same cultural context, psychoactive plants, also considered master plants or plants of power, are generically designated as "the medicine."

This therapeutic faculty, which the shaman exercises through multiple resources, is the result of a long and harsh process of learning and self-healing. As mentioned, the shamanic vocation is usually linked to the onset of illnesses or near-death experiences that the person must overcome as proof of their courage and in order to take their first steps in the path of knowledge. Thus, self-healing becomes not only a trance of survival, but also the very condition that qualifies the shaman to help others by healing them.

Working upon themselves is a discipline that shamans must maintain throughout their life, as they will not be able to perform their functions as healer of others if they themselves are not in an adequate state of balance and in control of their powers. This is, perhaps, the most delicate of shamanic tasks, especially in the contemporary world, fraught with distractions and temptations that today's shamans usually come across, sometimes with fatal results.

Shamanic power, like all powers, has potential as well as danger, bright and beneficial sides as well as dark and potentially evil sides. This usually puts shamans in the position to choose toward which side they will direct their forces, so an enormous responsibility falls on them. Let us remember that the principle of complementary opposites is central in indigenous cosmo-visions (Llamazares, 2011b). It is well known that among shamans there are those who do good deeds and those who act in evil ways. Amongst the Guarani, for instance, the ipayé is the one who summons the rains and the mbaecuá, the one who stops them; usually both of them live in the same community, although not always at peace.

Don Juan, the legendary Yaqui man of wisdom portrayed in Carlos Castaneda's *The Teachings of Don Juan* (1977), originally published in English in 1974, said that power was the third and strongest of all enemies of the man of knowledge:

> And a moment will come when he will understand that his clarity was only a point before his eyes. And thus he will have overcome his second enemy... He will know at this point that the power he has been pursuing for so long is finally his. He can do with it whatever he pleases.... But he has also come across his third enemy: Power! Power is the strongest of all enemies. And naturally the easiest thing to do is to give in... and suddenly, without knowing, he will certainly have lost the battle. His enemy will have turned him into a cruel, capricious man… (p.110-111).

Attaining power compels the shaman to remain under a permanent tension between good and evil. But it is right there, on that edge of impeccability, where his or her therapeutic potential lies.

Let us now consider in greater detail

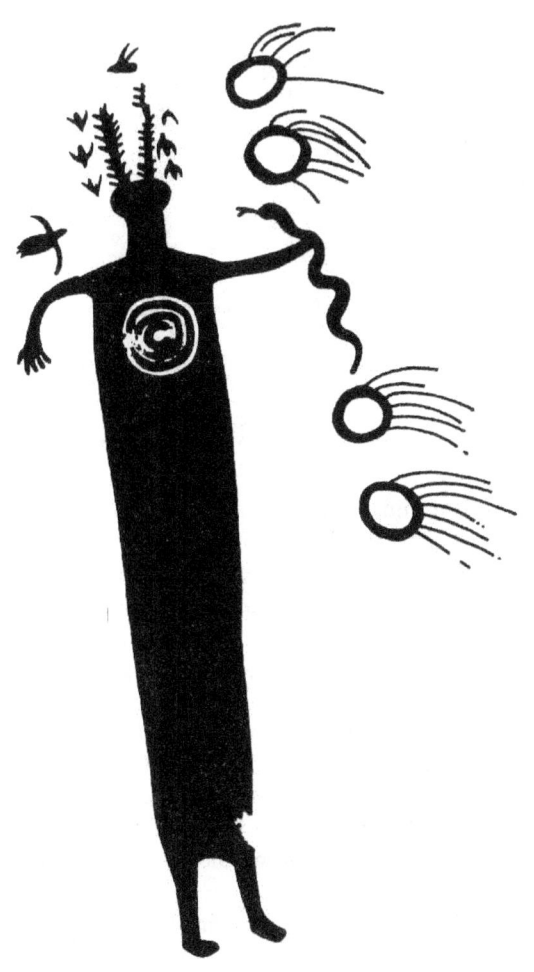

Shaman holding a snake.

how shamans heal and, if such thing is possible, what the phenomenon of shamanic healing consists of.

The Sacred Use of Psychoactive Plants

The ritual use of psychoactive plants is a fundamental element of the process of shamanic healing, totally complementary to the administering of strictly medicinal substances and plants.

In the indigenous conception, psychoactive plants are considered sacred and are distinguished from exclusively medicinal plants because apart from healing properties, sacred plants bring about the possibility of provoking in the person who takes them a state of extended consciousness comparable to an ecstatic

---

7 Ángeles Arrien, in her work *The Fourfold Way: Walking the Paths of the Warrior, Teacher, Healer, and Visionary*, presents another interesting equivalence in her description of the Way of the Warrior: "To the indigenous peoples of the American continent, the words power and medicine are synonyms. When an individual is fully expressing who they are, they are said to be 'full of power' and 'expressing their medicine'" (1998, p. 36).

seizure or trance. During this state, perception is globally modified and whether through bodily, auditory or visual means, it is possible to come into contact with supernatural dimensions or entities.

The state of consciousness produced by the sacred plants enhances sensitivity to such an extent that the person is capable of capturing energies and vibrations that ordinary consciousness cannot perceive. This has been compared with the emergence of a "sixth sense," a state of "hyperesthesia" (Castillo, 2001) in which sensitivity is overdeveloped. This is fundamental to the process of healing, for much of shamanic healing is of an energetic nature and is invisible to the regular eye. In most cases the shaman must take the plants so as to be able to perceive the bio-energetic state of the persons and also operate on them using such forces.

Individuals who seek healing do not always have to take the plants, although in many cases they do take them. At any rate, the person enters an energetic situation which is launched and intensified as a result of a meeting between the force of the plant and the consciousness of the person. The passages or shifts of consciousness that occur as one enters the trance (whether with plants or by other means) are healing per se, beyond the specific maneuvers that in turn the shaman may perform.

There is an inseparable link between sacred plants and shamanism, for these form part of the basic set of instruments of the shamans, of the resources that assist them in fulfilling their core activity: to reach the state of trance and thus access other dimensions of reality through their extended consciousness.

Most shamanic traditions throughout the world have used animal or plant substances to reach ecstatic trances. However our American continent, and particularly South America, due to its biodiversity, is especially rich in variety, age, and ongoing presence of traditional plant lore (Llamazares, Martínez Sarasola & Funes, 2008).

How Illnesses Are Produced

> The shamanic task is always to transform something: illness into health, drought into rain, signal into announcement. We could say that the shamanic art par excellence is the art of transmutation—the ability to unite and connect, in order to transform.

Shamans use various ways of healing according to the origin of the condition they have to treat. The most common causes of illness are:

I. Intrusion of evil spirits, subtle adherences or objects in the energetic or physical body of the afflicted person. In these cases one of the most traditional shamanic proceedings is administered, that of healing through suction.

Healing sessions are always accompanied by complex rituals that generally require the use of some kind of sacred plant, both by the shaman and, occasionally, by the patient. They usually include dancing, chanting, burning tobacco or other herbs, waving bunches of leaves or feathers ("venteo"), or small percussion instruments. Other objects are also used, for instance, the traditional statuettes modeled in wood or clay by the shaman and which play the role of the shaman's helping spirits or the patient's doubles. Part of the shamanic work involves "seeing" through the body of the person in order to find where the evil is lodged. Finally, the session culminates with a very strong inhalation or suction through which the shaman pulls out and removes the pathogenic substance.

II. Loss of the soul. This may affect the whole soul, parts of the soul or some of the souls, for amongst indigenous people it is conceivable that a person may be endowed with several souls. A series of hints tell the shaman that a loss of the soul has occurred. His or her task is to go to its rescue—if it so happens that it has been stolen by natural forces or other spirits that hold it captive—or convince it to return to the body of the person—if the soul fled voluntarily. Through the trance, the shaman has to begin a journey toward other dimensions in order to find it and then make it return, which sometimes implies having to fight with other spirits.

III. Breaking of a taboo or a rule of the group. In this case the task of the shaman is to restore the order that was broken or altered by the transgression. This is achieved through various means but in such cases the greatest force lies in the performance of rituals destined to appease the affected spirits, for example, through the narration of exemplary myths, and also through the creation of images, and the performance of chants or dancing forms that reestablish—in the fashion of cosmological icons—the structure and balance that are proper to cosmic order. It is in this aspect that the shaman becomes an artist whose art is the gift of being able to reestablish balance through his profound knowledge of the laws of the universe.

IV. Spells or witchcraft. These are considered actions of another shaman, witch or sorcerer devoted to do evil, sometimes for themselves, and other times, on behalf of someone else who wants to harm the affected person. These negative actions can cause illnesses by intrusion, damages, "eyeing" or evil eye, soul loss, or simply the energetic imbalance of the person; the used therapeutic techniques vary in each case. Amongst the Amazonian groups of Peru, one of the most serious dangers occurs through darts or "virotes" thrown by malicious sorcerers. Even today, this is a very common practice by which shamans attack one another; it is also very old on the Coast, judging by some representations of the darts which appear in pre-Columbian art, in some paintings of the Nazca culture (200-600 AD).

"Symbolic Efficacy" Revisited

Illness is usually conceived as something concrete that has occurred to the person, and shamans have to intervene concretely but their intervention always operates on multiple dimensions simultaneously—not only on the physical body, but primarily on the mental, spiritual dimension or, as we would say nowadays, the energetic dimension.

The conceptual framework within which illness and health are conceived in the shamanic cosmo-vision is openly multidimensional and basically spiritual. Although there may be an external agent, an attack, a trauma or any other violent event, the deepest root of a condition always lies in an imbalance or maladjustment of forces. The true cause of illness is a loss of balance. For this reason, the therapeutics of the shaman is clearly an energetic work, a constant effort to restore balance. The essence of the shamanic work is to ensure communication, the dynamic flow of energies—physical, mental and spiritual—through the dialogue and correspondence among the forces or the spirits that act in the diverse dimensions or realities.

There is a classical concept from the field of anthropology which has been used in attempts to explain how the therapeutic effect of shamanic healing takes place. It is the concept "symbolic efficacy," introduced in the 1950s by Claude Lévi-Strauss, the father of *Structural Anthropology*. He developed this notion in his book Structural Anthropology, in which he examines a case of shamanic healing amongst the Cuna Indians of Panama, based on chanting a mythological story, by which the shaman helped a parturient woman who could not give birth to her baby. In modern terms we would say that it was a case in which, although labor had begun, the woman did not reach enough dilation to have a natural delivery. It is an extremely interesting example, for the shaman at no time intervenes physically on the patient. His treatment is only "by word of mouth."

According to the description made by Lévi-Strauss, the first phase of the shamanic work consisted of making the nuchu, small figurines carved out of certain specific materials, to represent the protecting spirits that would assist the shaman on his journey to the abode of Muu, the power that had stolen the purba, or soul, of the future mother. The second phase of the work is the complete recitation of the chant that tells, in form of a myth, of the search and the recovery of the soul.

Lévi-Strauss (1968) points out that the exceptional interest of the story does not reside in its formal aspects, but rather in the

> discovery that to the native mind, Mu-Igala or `Muu's way´ and the abode of Muu are not simply a mythical itinerary and dwelling place. They represent literally the vagina and uterus of the pregnant woman, which are explored by the shaman and nuchu and in whose depths they wage their victorious combat (p. 170).

At first, when the labor is still difficult, the nuchu are lined up one behind the other; then, as the story progresses and we suppose that so does the dilation of the cervix, they advance side by side, moving in a much wider line.

We are clearly faced with the action of language and myth as symbolic operators or instruments. According to Lévi-Strauss, the narrated scene constitutes a purely psychological form of treatment that gives the patient a way to understand and express what is happening to her, so her body reacts as a consequence. And in this sense he holds that "the shamanic cure is half way between our organic medicine and psychological therapeutics such as psychoanalysis" (p. 179).

Fire ritual at Khurum day, Siberia.

The concept of "symbolic efficacy" is traditionally conceived as an instance of recovery of contents from the unconscious, which symbolism permits to surface in consciousness by provoking a vivid experience. Early in the twentieth century, the anthropologist Sir James George Frazer had advanced this interpretation in his classic *The Golden Bough* (1992) published originally between 1890-1922. In his work, he argues that the true healing power lies in the personal and collective unconscious, and that shamans are able to activate the healing by releasing people's psychic energy through mythical speech and ritual.

Perhaps the greatest difference between shamanic healing and psychoanalysis or Western exclusively verbal therapeutics, is that the shaman operates with all kinds of symbols based on an analogical methodology. And if we look at the efficacy of the symbol in the light of the new energetic conceptions, not only that of psychology, but also of physics and vibrational medicine, we will be able to recognize that the symbolic way of operating on reality goes far beyond the effects of a mere psychological or psychic "persuasion."

The symbol is "effective" when it successfully translates and expresses, into its own dimension of existence, metaphysical principles from a different dimension of existence. According to the old Hermetic maxim or law of correspondences ("as above so below"), the world or reality, is conceived as a whole full of meaning, which unfolds in a multidimensional continuum of successive, inclusive and interrelated, dimensions between which it is possible to find isomorphisms, analogies and linkages. The symbol operates as a mirror which, through perceptible forms in more immediate dimensions, brings us reflections from other more distant, less tangible and less visible dimensions.

Nevertheless, today this explanatory principle can be understood as a scientific statement rather than as a metaphysical one. From the vision inaugurated for us by relativity and quantum theory in the twentieth century, reality is conceived as a continuum of energy in different levels of density (Heisenberg, 1993; Briggs & Peat, 1990). Therefore, taking into account that the physical, psychic and spiritual dimensions differ only in intensity and in configuration of forces, it is completely feasible to operate—by way of a structural correspondence—on the physical realm from the psychic realm and vice versa. In fact, the interrelation and correspondence between the multiple dimensions happen all the time in all directions. It is just our ordinary—modern Western—way of fragmenting reality into separate levels that makes us think that the body must only be treated with physical resources—whether mechanical or chemical—and in turn that the mind only responds to verbal or psychic resources.

Lévi-Strauss (1968) himself already anticipated this explanatory expansion of the concept of "symbolic efficacy" when, by the end of the chapter, he refers once more to the parallel between psychoanalysis and shamanic healing:

> It is a matter of stimulating an organic transformation which would consist essentially in a structural reorganization by inducing a patient to live intensively out a myth whose structure would be, at the unconscious level, analogous to the structure whose genesis is sought on the organic level. The effectiveness of symbols would consist precisely in this 'inductive property,' by which formally homologous structures, built out of different materials and different levels of life—organic processes, unconscious mind, rational thought—are related to one another (p. 182).

Shamanic paraphernalia includes multiple instruments that are used to put into practice the same inductive procedure: not only poetic metaphors or myths, but also images, icons, visions, and all the vibrational resources—like music, percussion, movement, "venteos" and "sopladas" (i.e. the practice of smoking virgin tobacco and blowing the smoke forcefully over the head and the energetic centers of the patient), and most importantly, sacred plants, whose effects are also vibratory in a much subtler dimension.

Energy is vibration. And shamans seem to be great specialists in vibrational medicine, for they know how to achieve a harmonic reorganization of the energetic structure of the various —bodily, psychic and emotional—dimensions of living beings by means of vibrations — auditory, kinetic, chromatic, chemical, formal, geometrical, etc.

They are conscious of our being energy—says Colombian thinker Carlos Pinzón (2004). They already knew it before bioenergetic medicine existed. They know that thought is a form of energy; that what makes the circuits of the heart and circulation move are forms of energy, that verbal expression is a form of energetic existence. They knew that far before we did. (p. 244)

He further asserts "shamans are specialists in one of the body's most important systems of energy management: its immune system, which determines what must enter the body and what must not (p. 244)."

The healing and therapeutic potential of shamanism in the contemporary world intersects with one of the boundaries of scientific medicine, namely the treatment of addictions and the increasingly widespread and mutating illnesses caused by immune deficiencies.

Dionysus and Chiron: Western Shamanic Archetypes

Focusing back on the Western tradition, I also want to resort to analogical and symbolic thought in order to evoke two archetypal images that belong to our own mythology and can therefore help us understand the roots of our suffering as well give us guidance on how to "heal" the wounds of the West. These mythical figures are Dionysus and Centaur Chiron, both in profound harmony with shamanism. After learning about their stories, we will surely be able to appreciate them as two great Western "shamans."

Dionysus, Master of Ecstasy

When dealing with shamanism and the sacred plants in the context of the Western crisis, it is almost inevitable to refer to the archetypal figure of Dionysus, for the story and symbolism of this god—one of the oldest in Greek mythology—give us a very clear idea of the role that non-ordinary states of consciousness play in the West.

Dionysus—named Bacchus by the

> What distinguishes and endows shamans with such special identity is their ability to "get out" of ordinary reality, to go to the extraordinary and know how to come back, bringing to this dimension something emanating from their connection with those other supernatural or sacred dimensions.

Ancient Romans and finally demonized in the Middle Ages—is in fact the god of wine, drunkenness, illusion, irrationality, and often violent outburst. He is indeed the great demiurge of ecstasy. Under the influence of Dionysus, people transform themselves, just as this god was an artificer of transformation.

Amongst all Greek gods, Dionysus was the one who had the most varied manifestations or epiphanies. To begin with, his nature was double: half human, half divine. He was conceived by the unfaithful union between Zeus and Semele, daughter of King Cadmus, and had a very turbulent life, with many deaths, rebirths, and persecutions that led him to master the art of transfiguration. He had a changing image: he could appear as a man or a woman, as a god or in the shape of different animals, usually a lion, deer, ram, panther or bull.

These features portray a god of pre-Olympian origins, rooted in ancestral mystery cults, whose precedents date back to Mycenaean Crete and even to ancestral Siberian shamanism (Fericgla, 1999). His nature refers us to the pre-patriarchal feminine, the changing, the dynamic, and the power of death and resurrection. It also relates to the most basic forces of nature: the animal, the instinctive and the irrational, which act in the sphere of the human.

Ciénaga petroglyph

Because of their archetypal connotations, it is worthwhile to give an account of some episodes in the life of this god. First, there is his igneous origin, as he was the offspring of the amorous passion aroused between Zeus, the god of thunder, and Semele. Then, his triple birth is almost equivalent to a shamanic initiation process. He was initially gestated in the womb of his mother, who was consumed by the fire of lightning when she prayed to her beloved Zeus to let her behold him undisguised. Zeus rescued the fetus and sewed him up in his thigh, and thus, Dionysus was born as the young god of fire, only to be torn to pieces by the envy of his brothers, the Titans. It is said that only Dionysus' heart was left, and that from a drop of his blood a pomegranate tree—a symbol of fertility—was born, from which his grandmother Rhea—mother of Zeus—restored and cured him.

In order to prevent a new revenge from Hera, the jealous wife of Zeus, Rhea turned Dionysus into a ram. He spent his childhood in the form of this animal, fed by the nymphs of the forest, in absolute freedom, enjoying the pleasures of nature. He was brought up and instructed by Satyrs, Sileni and Centaurs. The first two, half men, half rams, introduced him to the secrets of dance and exuberant sexuality. The latter, half horses and half men, imbued him with virtue and wisdom. In his adulthood, Dionysus recovered his human shape and showed himself as a god. He discovered the

> The command of certain psychic and physical techniques enables shamans to reach an absolute concentration and, therefore, extend their perception and direct their power at will.

power of the vine and invented the art of winemaking. When Hera recognized him, she threw him into a state of madness. This gave way to a new phase of journeys across the world, in the company of his retinue of Satyrs, Sileni, Centaurs and spirits of the forest that danced and leaped, disseminating the cult and the pleasure of wine and drunkenness. He was also followed by the Maenades (possessed women), also known as Bacchants (women of Bacchus), a group of wild women of the mountain that worshipped him and performed bloody rituals in his honor, preceded by chants and dances that led them to exhaustion. This is the phase that earned Dionysus the "ill fame" that has followed him to this day.

Finally, his grandmother Rhea saved him again, redeeming him from madness and introducing him to the most secretive feminine mysteries of old women. His power became almost incomparable, and he gained more and more followers. Those who followed him experienced the divine ecstasy, those who opposed him, went mad. His last heroic deed was rescuing his mother from Hades, the world of the dead, and bringing her back to life under the name of Thyone, which is the Greek word for no less than "ecstasy."

Some of Dionysus' alternative names or surnames illustrate very aptly the archetypal characteristics that identify him with shamanism.

- Bromios, 'thundering' or 'he who roars.' This refers to the intervention of vibration as an essential element of ecstasy.

- Dimorphus (mo). He could appear as beautiful or awful, according to circumstances.
- Dithyramb, 'he of the double door.' This evokes his capacity for transformation and passage between different states and natures.
- Eleutherius (), 'the deliverer or liberator,' also applied to Eros.
- Lysios (Lysios), 'he who unleashes or loosens,' as a god of relaxation and liberation from worries.
- "Phallenus" or Phales (), 'he of the phallus,' guarantor of fecundity.
- Omadius () he who loves raw flesh, the flesh-eater, with reference to his instinctive character.

According to Josep Fericgla (1999), "this Greek god embodied what is now understood as the human unconscious mind in its different forms of expression" (p. 28).

Chiron, the "Wounded Healer"

Chiron, or Cheiron, is the wise centaur of Greek mythology, the archetype of the "wounded healer," of self-healing and the potential wisdom involved in overcoming pain and in the integration of opposites.

His sufferings began when he was forsaken by his parents, who could not bear the sight of his hybrid nature, half human and half equine. In fact, Chiron was not the offspring of a loving union but begotten as a result of the brutal, instinctive persecution of the nymph Philyra by Cronus. So as to escape from his harassment, Philyra had taken the shape of a mare but Cronus deceived her by turning into a horse himself. Compensation for the centaur's early abandonment came when Apollo adopted him and taught him many of his skills, thus enabling him to become the healer, tutor and guide of many heroes, among them the renowned Jason, Achilles, Hercules, and Asclepius. The latter was famous for his skill in the art of medicine, which he had certainly learned from Chiron.

Later began his everlasting agony, as he was accidentally wounded on a leg by Hercules, one of his disciples. The cut failed to heal because the arrow had been poisoned with the Hydra, causing him torturing pains that would accompany him for the rest of his life. This gave rise to his indefatigable quest to heal his wound, a journey that earned him not only great wisdom but also the development of his skills as a healer, enabling him to offer his help to others.

Chiron's history is almost a mythical version of the process of shamanic initiation. Its symbolism is very broad and complex. Not only does it teach us about the conditions of healing based on learning to bear one's own pain, but also informs us about the deepest roots of suffering: the break of loving ties between both natures, the divine and the human. On a different scale, this break brings to mind the prototypical wound of the western psyche: the disruption of the connection between the spiritual and the instinctive and all those overlapping fragmentations that came along—between subject and object, between mind and matter, between reason and emotion, between thought and body, between masculine and feminine, between the human species and Nature.

It is no coincidence either that in Chiron's history it was Hercules, one of his best disciples, who inflicted a wound in his lower, instinctive part: his rump. Hercules is the archetypal figure of the hero, a vivid image of the masculine rational inclination to achievement and self-improvement. Let us just think to what extent the history of the West has been dominated by this individualistic and hardworking heroic drive for success, "by conquest and domination as goals in themselves," as Melanie Reinhart (1991) says, "by a psychology of the 'right of force,' by a devaluation of the instinctive and feminine, and an overestimation of heroism at the expense of great human suffering" (p. 40).

Once again, the image of Chiron, with his hybrid body, his human top and animal bottom, provides a symbolic analogy of the integration of opposites, of the reconciliation and reparation of the fundamental schism between spirit and matter, as well as all other successive fragmentations; it is, indeed, a suitable metaphor of the journey to healing.

> The true cause of illness is a loss of balance. For this reason, the therapeutics of the shaman is clearly an energetic work, a constant effort to restore balance. The essence of the shamanic work is to ensure communication, the dynamic flow of energies—physical, mental and spiritual—through the dialogue and correspondence among the forces or the spirits that act in the diverse dimensions or realities.

To bear the simultaneous vision of opposites, that which Philyra was not able to tolerate, seems to be a master key to transcend the pain of fragmentation. And this is, once again, an integral element of shamanic wisdom. Joan Halifax (1988) tells us that "shamans are trained in the art of balance, in moving safely and confidently on the threshold of the opposites, in creating cosmos from chaos. Thus, the Middle Realm remains a dream that the dreamer can shape" (in Reinhart, 1991, p. 33).

Further Reflections About the Healing Potential of Shamanism in the Contemporary World

Both myths, Dionysus and Chiron, show clearly that in the West existed a deep shamanic-like tradition which in time was forgotten and degraded. Associated to all that had to be subdued to the order of reason, this tradition became stigmatized as a synonym of evil, craziness, sexual promiscuity and drunkenness.

In his book *Ecstasy, Understanding the Psychology of Joy* (1987), Jungian psychologist Robert Johnson analyzes the Dionysian myth in depth and argues that the loss of the Dionysian, particularly expressed in an inability to have a life experience of this natural, instinctive energy within a socially accepted framework, is one of the great tragedies of Western culture. Moreover, he warns that trying to fill a spiritual void with material things or physical sensations only increases the emptiness. And, worse still, it generates the vicious circle of compulsive search for satisfaction; a yearning that grows and grows as it cannot be fulfilled, showing clearly the direct relation between the spiritual void and addictive behavior.

It may be worthwhile to underscore that the spiritual void—one of the greatest wounds of the West, as we have seen—can only be fulfilled with genuine spirituality, and part of this spirituality lies in rediscovering and awakening the ability to re-establish a bond with Nature, with the vital, with one's own subjective and innermost self. Spirituality can be an authentic healing journey because it reconnects us with the experience of the sacred; it restores our trust in an order that includes us and our feeling of belonging to a more comprehensive web, thus dissipating fear and the ghosts of loneliness and anguish. This way, by integrating the parts of our fragmented consciousness that were repressed and neglected, other wounds could heal progressively too.

Fragmentation affects a very deep and delicate dimension of the human being, which claims to renovate the ties that have been cut, threads and connections that have weakened, becoming almost imperceptible. And this is a spiritual dimension because its approach demands to go beyond the cognitive as well as the exclusively sensory or somatic dimensions. It requires opening one's heart in order to arouse the loving capacity for acceptance, sine qua non condition of any healing.

Healing is a holistic, multidimensional and complex process that involves the whole of the person—body (physical

Centaurs.

and emotional), mind and spirit—and implies therefore, to relieve bodily, intellectual and spiritual afflictions. For this reason, true healing can only be achieved by means of the complementation and integration of physical, psycho-therapeutic and spiritual techniques, paths and resources.

True healing demands not only a positive synergy with an external agent (doctor, therapist, shaman, medicines) but also and fundamentally a participative commitment and surrender on the part of the being that is in need of healing. In fact, beyond anything that the external agent may do, there is an instance in which healing depends almost exclusively on the patient. We are, after all, the ones who permit or prevent our own healing by opening or shutting our hearts. And this is a basically spiritual process.

In order to start a healing process, it is essential to know the nature and origin of the wounds that cause pain, and explore with the aid of reason what might be the best ways to ease and surpass the problems. However, healing cannot be accomplished by means of an intellectual pursuit or through sensory and somatic paths alone. An integration of all these with the spiritual path must take place. All healing requires a loving reparation of inflicted wounds. And this takes patience, care, and confidence in the particular pace of natural processes, which is always slower than our mind and our desires.

We can see then that, when we discuss "healing" we are dealing with something that exceeds the scale of physical or psychological illnesses, for which we might apply more strictly the terms "cure" (for physical ailments) or "therapy" (for psychic or psychological disorders). It is not about eliminating symptoms or attacking pathogenic agents, but about something far more difficult. Healing is a complex process which involves re-establishing a balance—that we could call "energetic"—among the different dimensions of the person: somatic, emotional, intellectual and spiritual.

For this reason, when we talk about healing we are also alluding to a multidimensional and integral understanding of "health," a concept that leads us to conceive it as a state of dynamic balance of the different energetic dimensions, which produces a simultaneous alignment of the person both inward—with oneself—and outward—improving one's relation with the environment.

This is where the contemporary interest in shamanism reappears, for as we have seen, this ancestral wisdom is based precisely on a holistic and energetic conception of health and life. Several central aspects of the teachings and shamanic practice of the indigenous peoples can be most helpful to heal the "wounds of the West", for example:

• An understanding of the Cosmos

as a whole made up of multiple dimensions and realities, inhabited by a multiplicity of beings, forces and energies;
- the life experience of the human being as an integral part of such a cosmic order;
- an active and ongoing commitment to sustain balance;
- a social integration of the experience of ecstasy to maintain fluid contact with other dimensions of reality;
- a permanent bond of the human being with the Earth, which permits grounding these ascents and descents to different realms;
- the respectful interrelation of the human being with the other living species, vegetal and animal, as well as with the other elements of creation;
- in sum, the upkeep of a strong spiritual connection.

In this sense, shamanism—which has been ritually preserved by the indigenous peoples but, as discussed above, is also deeply rooted in our own mythical tradition—holds a great healing potential, as a wisdom that was restricted or reserved for ages and that is now being disclosed and disseminated.

By means of its concrete exercise, shamanism supports nowadays a way of conceiving and acting in the world, radically different from the one we have developed in the West. Thus, we could say that through its continued existence, shamanism has acquired an almost philosophical condition, since beyond its contribution to anthropology or to the history of religions, its presence provides living evidence that it is possible to live in a different way, in a constant familiarity with the "non-ordinary," with the multi-dimensional and the energetic, in an active search for the complementation of contraries.

This dimension of shamanism, which some authors call "shamanity" (Vitebsky, 1995), permits us nowadays to imagine a projection of this knowledge beyond the spheres of the indigenous communities and therapeutic practices, and also to think specifically about its connection with and approach to new forms of holistic and ecosophic consciousness that are emerging in the West, through a dialog that has only just begun.

> The deepest craving of the contemporary human soul—in which I include both indigenous and Western people—is to find that lost spiritual connection, to heal the wounds caused by fragmentation, and overcome the intellectual habit of turning opposites into antagonists.

I sincerely believe that the deepest craving of the contemporary human soul—in which I include both indigenous and Western people—is to find that lost spiritual connection, to heal the wounds caused by fragmentation, and overcome the intellectual habit of turning opposites into antagonists. The search for the holistic is a new awakening of that deep longing for understanding, meaning and integrity, which now is also renewed in the West in hand with shamanism.

References

Arrien, A. (1998). *Las cuatro sendas del chamán. El guerrero, el sanador, el vidente, el maestro.* Madrid: Gaia. [Orig. 1993. *The four-fold way.* Harpers Collins Pub.]

Berman, M. (1981). *The reenchantment of the world.* Ithaca: Cornell University Press.

Berman, M. (2000). *Wandering God. A study of nomadic spirituality.* Albany, NY: State University of New York Press.

Briggs, J. P. & Peat, D. (1990). *Turbulent mirror. An illustrated guide to chaos theory and the science of wholeness.* New York: Harper Collins Pub.

Castaneda, C. (1977). *Las enseñanzas de don Juan.* México: Fondo de cultura Económica. *The teachings of Don Juan: A Yaqui way of knowledge.* New York: Simon & Schuster.

Castillo, J. (2001). Chamanismo Piaroa. In Poveda, J.M. (Ed.) Chamanismo. *El arte natural de curar.* (pp.357-362). Madrid: Temas de Hoy.

Clottes, J. & Lewis-Wiliams, D. (1996). *Les chamanes de la préhistoire. Transe et magie dans les grottes ornées.* Paris: Le Seuil.

Costa, J.P. (2003). *Los chamanes ayer y hoy.* México: Siglo XXI Editores.

Doore, G. (Ed.) (1988). *Shaman's path. Healing, power and personal growth.* Boston: Shambhala.

Eliade, M. (1964). *Shamanism: Archaic techniques of ecstasy.* Bollingen Series LXXVI. New York: Pantheon.

Evans Schultes, R. & Hofmann, A. (1979). *Plants of the gods. Origins of hallucinogenic use.* New York: McGraw Hill.

Fericgla, J. (1999). *Apolo, Dionisos y el uso de enteógenos.* In Fericgla (Ed.) Los enteógenos y la ciencia. *Nuevas aportaciones científicas al estudio de las drogas.* Barcelona: Los libros de la liebre de marzo.

Fericgla, J. (2000). *Los chamanismos a revisión. De la vía del éxtasis a Internet.* Barcelona: Kairós.

Frazer, J. G. (1992). *The golden bough.* New York: Macmillan Co.

Furst, P. (1972). *Flesh of the gods. The ritual use of hallucinogens.* London: Allen & Unwin.

Furst, P. (1976). *Hallucinogens and culture.* San Francisco: Chandler & Sharp Pub.

Grof, C. & Grof, S. (1990). *The stormy search for the self.* Berkeley: The Putman Publishing Group.

Halifax, J. (1988). *The wounded healer.* London: Thames & Hudson.

Halifax, J. (1991). *Shamanic voices. A survey of visionary narratives.* New York: Arkana Books.

Harner, M. (1973). *Hallucinogens and shamanism.* New York: Oxford University Press.

Harner, M. (1980). *The way of the shaman: A guide to power and healing.* New York: Harper and Row.

Heisenberg, W. (1993). *La imagen de la naturaleza en la física actual.* Buenos Aires: Planeta.

James, A. & Jiménez, D. A. (Eds.) (2004). *Chamanismo. El otro hombre, la otra selva, el otro mundo. Entrevistas a especialistas sobre la magia y la filosofía amerindia.* Bogotá: Instituto Colombiano de Antropología e Historia.

Johnson, R. A. (1987). *Ecstasy. Understanding the psychology of joy.* San Francisco: Harper Collins Eds.

Kremer, J. (1994). *The past and future process of mythology.* In Kremer, J. Looking For Dame Yggdrasil. Red Bluff, CA: Falkenflug Press.

Levi-Strauss, C. (1968). *Antropología estructural.* Buenos Aires: Editorial Universitaria de Buenos Aires. [Orig. 1958 Anthopologie Structurale. Paris, Plon]

Lewis Williams, D. (2004). *The mind in the cave.* London: Thames & Hudson.

Llamazares, A. M. (2004). *Arte chamánico: visiones del universo.* In: Llamazares, A.M. & Martínez Sarasola, C. (Eds.). El lenguaje de los dioses. (pp. 67-125). Buenos Aires: Biblos.

Llamazares, A. M. (2008). *Conceptos básicos de epistemología holística.* In: www.delrelojalaflordeloto.blogspot.ar/search/label/Artículos

Llamazares, A. M. (2011a). *Del reloj a la flor de loto. Crisis contemporánea y cambio de paradigmas.* Buenos Aires: Del Nuevo Extremo Editores. (*From the Clock to the Lotus Blossom. The Contemporary Crisis and Paradigm Shift*).

Llamazares, A. M. (2011b). *Metáforas de la dualidad en los Andes: cosmovisión, arte, brillo y chamanismo.* In: Las imágenes precolombinas, reflejo de saberes. Victòria Solanilla Demestre & Carmen Valverde Valdés (Eds.). México: Universidad Nacional Autónoma de México.

Llamazares, A. M. & Martínez Sarasola, C. (Eds.). (2004). *El lenguaje de los dioses. Arte, chamanismo y cosmovisión indígena en Sudamérica.* Buenos Aires: Biblos.

Llamazares, A. M., Martínez Sarasola, C. & Funes, F. (2008). *Main sacred plants of South America.* Cft. Course Reader. San Francisco: CIIS.

Martínez Sarasola, C. (2004). *El círculo de la conciencia. Una introducción a la cosmovisión indígena americana.* In: Llamazares, A. & Martínez Sarasola, C. (Eds.). El lenguaje de los dioses. (pp.21-65). Buenos Aires: Biblos.

Narby, J. (1997). *La serpiente cósmica. El ADN y los orígenes del saber.* Lima: Takiwasi/Racimos de Ungurahui.

Narby, J. & Huxley, F. (Eds.). (2001). *Shamans through time: 500 years on the path to knowledge.* New York: Tarcher.

Neumann, E. (1995). *The origins and history of consciousness.* Princeton: Bollingen Paperbacks.

Pinzón, C. (2004). *Las prácticas chamánicas y el paradigma ecológico.* In: James & Jiménez (Comp.) Chamanismo. El otro hombre, la otra selva, el otro mundo. Entrevistas a especialistas sobre la magia y la filosofía amerindia. (pp. 233-257). Bogotá: Instituto Colombiano de Antropología e Historia.

Poveda, J. M. (Ed.) (1997). Chamanismo. *El arte natural de curar.* Madrid: Temas de Hoy.

Reinhart, M. (1991). *Significado y simbolismo de Quirón. Una dimensión psicológica de la astrología.* Barcelona: Urano. [Orig. 1989. *Chiron and the Healing Journey.* An Astrological and Psychological Perspective. England: Arkana Books].

Rotman, B. (1987). *Signifying nothing. The semiotics of zero.* Stanford: Stanford University Press.

Rutheford, W. (1986). *Shamanism. The foundations of magic.* Northans: Thorsons Pub. Group.

Ryen, R. E. (1999). *The strong eye of shamanism. A journey into the caves of consciousness.* Vermont: Inner Traditions.

Spretnak, C. (1991). *States of grace. The recovery of postmodern age.* San Francisco: Harper Collins Pub.

Spretnak, C. (1997). *The resurgence of the real. Body, nature and place in a hypermodern world.* Addison Wesley.

Tarnas, R. (1993). *The passion of the Western mind. Understanding the ideas that have shaped our world view.* New York: Ballantine Books.

Tarnas, R. (1994). *The Western mind at the threshold.* ReVision 16 (1), 2-7.

Vaughan, F. (1997). *Sombras de lo sagrado. Más allá de las trampas e ilusiones del camino espiritual.* Madrid: Gaia.

Vitebsky, P. (1995). *The shaman.* London: Duncan Baird Publishers.

Salish spindle whorl.

Reality, Invisible World and Shamanism

An Outlook from the Indigenous Worldview[1]

Carlos Martínez Sarasola
Pablo Figueroa, translator, Graciana Dutto, proofreader

The worldview of native peoples very often faces westerners with the problem of questioning our own beliefs about reality. In this clash of worldviews, important questions arise. Are there any other levels beyond the one known as "ordinary reality"? Is there an invisible world? What does it mean to "travel" through other realities?

Denying or excluding what cannot be understood is a common attitude in the western conception. It is also fairly common for uniformity of thought to be the rule. Things are one way or the other, and they can't be both ways at the same time. This dogmatic and narrow-minded perspective tends to exclude, deny, or in the best of circumstances discredit anything that is not easy to integrate into this frame. The dominant western worldview has difficulty handling elements that appear to be conflictive or opposite to each other except through simple dichotomies.

Mundara Koorang (Thunder Snake) of the Gamilaroi people of Moree, Australia.

Within an indigenous worldview, the search for harmony and balance is something natural. Thus, things, people and other living creatures are seen in a constant interrelationship where they are part of a whole and where integration is the rule. Dreams are incorporated into daily life and are not something separated from the person's "ordinary" world. The spirits in the woods live together with humans. Nature is magical and alive, and its creatures can talk with us.

Mutual openness is a necessary condition for trying to explore the territory between western and indigenous worldviews. In an interesting article, anthropologist Pablo Wright described a short time ago the difficulties he faced when interacting with a toba *(pi'ogonag)* shaman, and his efforts at trying to understand a view of the world different from the western one.

> I had never imagined being near a *pi'ogonag* who would make an everyday thing of relationships and entities that, in my mind, formed a set that wasn't linked with *real* life. There, in broad daylight, Alejandro was talking calmly and I was trying hard to understand what he was saying (1996, p. 173).

Carlos Martínez Sarasola is an anthropologist. Lecturer in the MA program in Cultural Diversity at the Universidad Nacional de Tres de Febrero, Buenos Aires, Argentina, and researcher in the Institute for Cultural Diversity at the same university. Member of the Editorial Board of the magazine Diversidad. Author of De manera sagrada y en celebración. Identidad, cosmovisión y espiritualidad en los pueblos indígenas (In a Sacred Way and in Celebration. Identity, Worldview and Spirituality in the Indigenous Peoples) Biblos, 2010 ; Nuestros paisanos los indios (Our Country Men, the Indians) [1992] Del Nuevo Extremo, 2013 –among others- and coauthor of El Lenguaje de los Dioses. Arte, chamanismo y cosmovisión indígena en Sudamérica (The Language of Gods. Art, Shamanism and Indigenous Worldview in South America) Biblos (2004). His work focuses on indigenous issues and ethnohistory of Argentina, comparative and cross-cultural approaches to indigenous worldviews and shamanism, and emerging processes of re-ethnization and spirituality in the Americas.

In one of his last works on the *shuar* groups from the jungle in Ecuador, anthropologist Josep M. Fericgla reflects on reality and the process of knowing it. He suggests that in light of the most recent findings in cognitive research, the early discarded perspective of some of the classic anthropologists should be reconsidered:

> Thinking reality—not "thinking about" reality—if it's possible to put it this way (doubtful), is closer to reality itself than to our abstract thinking. I start to see clearly that the *shuar* have a "primal thinking", that primitive humans are nature which became, to a certain extent, self awareness. We have created a symbolic-abstract reality remote from our own and we have swallowed it. The process through which the *shuar* elaborate thoughts is almost the opposite from our own. For them, the thought or mental conception itself makes the action happen: *I have thought this, so this must happen*" (1994, p.79).

In recent times, many philosophical debates, particularly epistemological ones (such as new scientific theories and paradigms), consider reality might be more complex than the one we are used to conceiving in the narrow perspective of materialism. However, the conventional scientific view remains a strong influence on perception.

The production of dissident knowledge is stigmatized and rejected because of its singularity. Any different option is transformed into an analogy of madness or perversion by the guards of the "official definitions" of reality. Alternative knowledge is annihilated because it constitutes the dark side which threatens the lucid reality that traditionally represented science.... science by and large has made all within its reach to state and reinforce the idea of a single and deterministic reality... the scientific vision of reality is based on certain mechanisms or formulas (particularly dualism in all its different forms) that, like black holes, devour differences or make them invisible, suppressing the emotions, the ability to perceive, to think, to dream. (Bergallo 2003, p.189-190).

It is then appropriate to seriously debate and reflect on the western "rational" idea of reality, while bearing in mind the existence of other forms of knowledge.

We are used to inquiring in only one direction: the one which is pointed out for us by the only criterion of reality that we use daily. This criterion is the result of traditional scientific conventions. But…is the reality we know the only possible one? Is the reality we know exactly as we experience and understand it? Is there anything beyond what we are used to perceiving? In general terms, science doesn't admit the possibility of discussing the existence of facts or phenomena that don't fit in its view of the world. This is a big flaw in the western perspective. (Martínez Sarasola, 2000a, p. 10).

Patrick Harpur's original and complete work recovers Jung's notions of the collective unconscious and "psychic reality." The concept of imagination is understood as "the realm halfway between mind and matter, the psychic realm of subtle bodies" and it comes from alchemical thought. Harpur also recovers the Neo-Platonic idea of *Anima Mundi*, which refers to a transitional world inhabited by *daimons* who act as intermediaries. Based on these concepts, he offers a definition of "daimonic reality". With it, he explains the ambiguous and mysterious spaces in which "a way of knowing and thinking, a way of seeing the world" navigates. This way of knowing has always been present in human beings, and it incorporates the direct experiences of encounters with entities, situations and phenomena belonging to other levels of reality (Harpur, 2003).

In a more recent essay, Harpur picks up Jung's crucial intuition about the psyche. "There are things in my psyche that I don't produce, but they have a life of their own … like animals in the woods or people in a room…" (Harpur, 2003, p. 34).

> The indigenous worldview stresses spirituality. It constitutes a way of being in the world, a particular attitude full of feeling that links humans to the sacred and the different levels of reality in a very profound manner.

Invisible World, Shamanistic Experiences and Worldview

From the beginning, my fieldwork experiences as an anthropologist brought me face to face with situations that conflicted with conventional logic. My fieldwork was carried out in the mid seventies in northwest Argentina in an area known as "Chaco-salteño". I was then surrounded by a very different universe. It was inhabited by stalking spirits, uncertainties, dangers, and unknown powers. For the first time these experiences brought about a serious questioning of my way of seeing the world and life.

In those early days, I witnessed a shamanic healing. It was the kind of healing that is known in anthropology as "suction healing".[1] Though shocking to my eyes, I realized –again, factually—that other forms of knowledge existed. The old shaman—an *ipayé*[2] of *ava-guaraní* or chiriguano origin—displayed his power of "seeing" the patient.

By means of this power, the shaman

---

[1] The person in charge of the healing literally "sucks" the patient in the area where he has detected the evil, which takes the form of an object, and he extracts it.

[2] *Ipayé* is the name that the *ava-guaraní* give to the "kindhearted" healers.

"saw" into the depths of the person, into his interior, in such a way that he was able to identify the illness. In his conception, the illness was an object lodged in some part of the body. Once detected through a set of techniques and with the aid of auxiliary spirits, he would extract the foreign object and thereby heal the patient. Indeed, all this is what happened.

In those years of my residence as a professor and researcher at Universidad Nacional de Salta, I had the good fortune of sharing fieldwork experiences with philosopher Rodolfo Kusch, a great expert on the Andean Peoples and their worldview. He also brought me closer to that multi-dimensional world which I began to appreciate in its real dimensions.

At the same time, I came across the early work of Carlos Castaneda, which generated a heated debate about its veracity. This debate eventually led to an even broader argument within anthropology. I was especially influenced by Castaneda's work, and although I had some questionings of my own, I wasn't so much concerned about the factual basis. What was attractive for me was not the issue of authenticity, but the notion of reality he put forth, conceived as something quite different from what I had until then considered valid. [3]

Some time later I explored Philosophical Anthropology when lecturing at Universidad del Salvador (Buenos Aires). I dove deeper into the quest of the concept of human person in the native thought of the peoples of the American Continent. I then surveyed sources, chronicles and codices. I also researched the work of religion historians such as Mircea Eliade, Rudolf Otto, Gerardus van der Leeuw, and anthropologists Paul Radin, Jacques Soustelle, Laurette Sejourné among others, who once again opened up my mind to other ways of being and conceiving the world and the universe.

Indigenous dancing.

Later on in the eighties, together with Ricardo Santillán Güemes, I started and co-directed the anthropological publication "Cultura Casa del Hombre". In this magazine, the topics mentioned above were examined and discussed. At the same time professor Abraham Haber introduced me to Jung's study of archetypes. I was also drawn to thinkers such as Eduardo A. Azcuy, a true pioneer in introducing in Argentina the confluence of the new scientific paradigms, hermetic traditions, symbolism and anomalous phenomena related to light. Azcuy's last book deals with reality and its multiple levels in a search he defined as "the metaphysic-real".

Towards 1996, along with some colleagues, I began more detailed research on shamanism and the "sacred" or "master" plants, also known as psychoactive plants or "entheogens". I was able to participate in ceremonies conducted by *curanderos*[4] or "vegetalist doctors" of the *shinipibo-conibo* and *ashánika* ethnic groups of the Peruvian Amazon. These experiences took me back to my first contacts with the depths of the indigenous world from the beginnings of my career as an anthropologist in that *chiriguano* community in the far north of my country. Being in physical contact with the shamanistic world, I realized once again its full importance. I got closer and closer to the essence of the foundations the native worldview was built on.

Only then I was able to start accepting the possibility of nature being in fact a sacred place to which we owe respect. What we traditionally understand by reality is something much more complex, with different levels and dimensions in which many entities and strange situations can be together. Through experiences of deepening awareness, one can access this world that the native Indians, especially shamans, know thoroughly. They are the inheritors of a millenary tradition and wisdom that some authors call "the invisible world" or simply "the Invisible":

> The gestures of a naked man in the equatorial jungle performing the immutable rites of his tribe next to his dead brother make the West face the first question, the first of all problems; because those gestures are being repeated in identical terms, and by putting into motion analogous symbols from one end of humanity to the other, the same faith in the same reality is implied.
>
> It is this person I wanted to talk about when I used the word *man*, because he has remained faithful to himself. He has kept his sense of place in the universe and the notion of the infinite value of the invisible principle he carries inside himself.
>
> It seems to me that the term *Invisible* defines more precisely what certain philosophers call the *Numinous* and others the *Sacred*. The Sacred can be created by human beings while

---

[3] Castaneda's work remains controversial to this day. This polemic arises from the narrow-mindedness of the so-called scientific approaches in anthropology, which oscillate between the author's disqualification and his blind acceptance. As a consequence, a deeper and richer debate about the nature of our world is obstructed.

[4] The meaning of the term "curandero" in Argentina (meaning deceitful) is different from the one given in other countries such as Peru. In Peru, "curandero" refers to a person of indigenous or mestizo origin who heals using ancestral techniques and wisdom, especially master plants.

the Invisible is imposed upon them. In the spirit of the members of traditional civilizations, the Invisible lacks the vagueness of a metaphysical concept. It is a reality, a dimension in which all those who make up humanity move. The Invisible is inside each person and it is more real, more present and more sensitive than any part of one's body. The Invisible is around humans as an environment that registers each of their earthly actions and reflects these in consequences that would be ineluctable without the action of mediators, invisible too (Servier, 1970, p. 9-10).

What I have understood after my years of experience and research in the fields of shamanism and sacred plants is that the ingestion of these plants, and the rituals associated with them, enable the shaman as well as the patient, to make contact with the invisible world and its beings and situations, and also journey through it and take from it the powers they need.

In the aforementioned Chiriguano community, the woods that surrounded it were inhabited by entities and spirits that one had to be careful of, especially at dusk. Among the Mocoví Indians in the Chaco region, there is a concept known as *nayic*, which refers to the paths going from the settlements to the woods: "They are trails that start from familiar ground and go deep into unknown, strange and dangerous regions. They allow people in the human world to cross towards a world that is not human, into the woods" (López & Campano, 2005, p. 5).

By conducting various seminars and doing research on "Cosmovisión Indígena Americana" (Indigenous Worldview in the American Continent), I was able to gather a set of materials that moved me closer to a new way of conceiving the world that native peoples carry. Finally, a change of perspective in the indigenous movement of the American continent due to a revaluation of their spirituality, along with my growing participation in ceremonies of different indigenous groups in Argentina and in other countries of the continent, contributed to my conviction of the importance of the native worldview, shamanism, and the invisible world. These are all interrelated fields that express a different way of knowing.

A broad theoretical frame that fully explains the native worldview of the American continent has yet to be developed. In fact, the word "worldview" itself doesn't always have the same meaning, and this is apparent when used in different languages. Nevertheless, there is a set of studies and authors from different disciplines that, from the end of the 19th century until now, assembled the pieces of a theoretical scaffolding that converge in the most recent research on this topic.

Although it is not possible here to thoroughly examine all the authors that have worked on this topic, some very important lines of research that have addressed the main ideas of the native worldview can be mentioned. They are the French ethnology (whose contributions come especially from its areas of work in Mesoamerica), the branch of American cultural anthropology, and the different currents in anthropology in Mesoamerica and South America.

It is also relevant to mention why I use the term "worldview" and not another one, as well as setting up some differences with other terms that may appear similar. It seems to me that the word "worldview" is comprehensive enough to explain the existential approach the native Indians have towards the whole that surrounds them, as well as the forms humans and community adopt to relate to that whole.

In this idea of a whole, the universe is included. For the indigenous person, his or her everyday life is a replica of the functioning of the cosmos and, both levels, everyday life and cosmos, are essential parts of the worldview.

For the time being, the term worldview fits perfectly into what I am trying to describe and analyze, and allows me to differentiate it from other terms such as "cosmology" (which is the branch of philosophy that deals with the origin, structure and laws of the universe, or a set of theories that state an image of the universe). I think it is also more precise than the term "cosmogony" which refers to the explanation of the creation or origin of the cosmos. Finally I prefer it to the term "religion", which is the set of beliefs and practices related to what a human group considers sacred, especially those practices linked to divinity. Many times this concept also alludes to the institutionalization of that set of beliefs and practices.

The aspects we could define as religious are part of the worldview because this term implies a more restricted meaning. Many indigenous societies have traditionally had a place specifically designated for religion, with their rituals, caste of priests, temples and other associated paraphernalia. Therefore, it

> The community sense of life, as a principle of the worldview, refers to one of the pillars of the native conception: human life acquires meaning when collectively developed.

seems more precise and comprehensive to use the term worldview because this peculiar indigenous conception (an all-inclusive and all-embracing conception) constitutes one of the pillars of their identity.[5]

It is also relevant to point out that the indigenous worldview stresses spirituality. It constitutes a way of being in the

---

[5] Some *mapuche* indigenous groups of southern Chile and Argentina refer to knowledge and wisdom as *kimun*. At the same time, this wisdom leads to *raquizuan* which is the collective way of thinking of this native people. *Raquizuan* is not individual thinking but the way all indigenous persons relate to *waj-mapu*: the Whole, the Universe, *Elchen*, of which they consider themselves a part. This series of relationships between knowledge, thought and a collective connection with the totality that surrounds the human (a totality of which one is a part), brings us closer to the conception of worldview that I use in this paper.

world, a particular attitude full of feeling that links humans to the sacred and the different levels of reality in a very profound manner. Spirituality is essentially practice, and it is done through concrete activities in everyday life, which is shaped by the celebration of rituals.

As expected, there is not only one definition of "worldview", but I think most of the authors have reached consensus to a certain extent implying a general agreement in the use of the term (Medina, 2000). All the definitions refer to human notions of the universe, to our place in it, and the analysis of life as an integral fact.[6]

The concept of worldview was originally developed in the end of the 19th century by German philosophers such as Wilhem Dilthey who would make the term *Weltanschauung* the core of his reflections (Medina, 2000). For this author, every person has an idea or conception of the world, a *Weltanschauung* that precedes the development of philosophy, religion, science or art. This *Weltanschauung*'s general principle is the "reality of life".

Mythological Corpus and Main Ideas

This way of being and understanding the world and life has a millenary tradition in which the indigenous peoples of the American continent have built up a complex system. This system has finally manifested itself in the native worldview, supported by a great mythological corpus and a profoundly interrelated set of ideas.

Regarding the mythological corpus, the native peoples (even though they did not have a writing system) possessed an extraordinary oral tradition, a way of transmitting their knowledge across generations through vocal utterance. An unlimited number of narrations about human existence's very diverse topics took shape throughout time.

Those stories tell us how the peoples were in the beginning, and of their deep relationship with the gods, with nature, with animals, with the universe. They express their worldview and show how the communities saw themselves in the world, what they thought and felt about life. Native Indians believe many of the stories to be true (for westerners they are myths, and for others, "tales" or legends). These essential narrations manifest also the fundamental values of the peoples, and from this point of view they are exemplary because they mostly are universal teachings.

The set of central ideas or principles are: *totality, energy, communion, sacredness* and the *community sense of life*. Although these ideas or principles are not the only ones (in fact they are a part of a broader conception of the world), it seems to me that they somehow summarize the native peoples' worldview.

The idea of *totality*, understood as an integrating view of the world and life, is expressed in different forms. Among them we can mention the complementary opposites (a notion tightly linked to duality), the multiformity of the gods (in a sense that they can adopt different meanings at the same time), the circle as a geometric form and circularity as an idea, the quaternity (time) and the quadrapartite system (space) as basic elements generally accompanied by the symbols of the Center and the World Axis *(Axis Mundi)*.

Energy, the main force that regulates the rhythm of the cosmos and generates vitality, and possesses a creation-destruction dynamic, is ever-present in the worldview of indigenous peoples. Often sacrifice (seen from an energetic perspective) plays a dominant role. In the same way, the relationship between energy and the human body, or energy and nature, is linked to the everyday vital-energetic consumption, as exemplified in the primal act of hunting.

In this context, *communion* is understood as a way of establishing a deep link between the human person, nature and the cosmos, and it goes a step further from what is usually referred as "participation". This particular union implies a special kind of connection which intensely integrates relationships such as cosmos-home-body, or cosmos-heaven-earth. The union is also strongly manifested in the ceremonies' different ritual elements, such as pipes, drums, clothing, or paintings. These ritual elements are full of symbolism that communicates with the transcendental levels.

The *sacredness* or the *sacred* is one of the crucial principles of the indigenous worldview. This idea (which refers to a space where a broader communication between humans and the gods exists) has a social value and is expressed through everyday life, dreams, shamanic practices, nature, sacred geography, social hierarchies and the animals.

The *community sense of life*, as a principle of the worldview, refers to one of the pillars of the native conception: human life acquires meaning when col-

Solid white female figure.

---

6   "By worldview we understand a structured view in which cosmologic notions were integrated into a coherent system that explained the cosmos and the situation of man within it" (Broda, 1991, p. 462). "In a people's worldview its main concepts of shape and quality of the universe, of its inhabitants, and the position of humanity within this system are synthesized in a structured way. Especially in traditional cultures the worldview serves as a model for various aspects of the culture, such as village settling patterns, the organization of society and rites of varied kinds. This is the reason why the worldview influences routine life in the village in many ways" (Köhler 1980:583)

lectively developed.

These five principles constitute a model to explain the complexity of the native worldview; they are not the worldview itself. The worldview is a never ending universe composed of multiple levels, which is constantly revealing itself. This model consists of three main points: first, the different native cultures in the American continent have worldviews with many elements in common. Second, those points in common can be summarized into the five principles I have mentioned above. The principles are also influenced by other vital concepts. Third, shamanism plays a very peculiar role in linking the communities with their own worldviews.

When I use the term "worldview" I do it in the singular form. Of course there are as many worldviews as indigenous groups, but I believe that from Alaska to Tierra del Fuego a common set of principles or main ideas characterize the indigenous peoples, shaping their identity and uniting them beyond whatever local and circumstantial differences they may have. The secrets of a native worldview bring them together, giving them a new collective sense that today, in the threshold of a different time, repositions them in the continent with renewed force.

The Way of a Cosmic Consciousness

Totality, energy, communion, sacredness and community sense of life are the five ideas that together constitute the expression of a cosmic and spiritual consciousness of the indigenous world. This consciousness could be depicted as a big circle because of the sense of completeness that constantly prevails in the native worldviews.

Shamanism plays a very special role in this system. Among the native Indians, it is one of the practices that allows understanding and communication of that cosmic consciousness with the community and vice versa. Shamanism "breaks through" the circle of consciousness, allowing communication with the different levels and dimensions of reality, navigating across the interstices of the invisible world.

Even though shamanism is not the only practice that allows "communication" with the cosmic consciousness, it may be the most important one. At the heart of the indigenous communities different members can play roles that offer the possibility of moving across the different levels of reality. Among other powers, leaders and chiefs traditionally had (in fact, some of them still do) the ability to connect with other dimensions and to achieve direct experience of them. In certain specific situations, old members or ceremony guides can also travel through the passages to the other dimensions.

In addition, many ceremonies and rituals in which most members of the community participate allow "passing" to other levels, therefore gaining access to a cosmic and spiritual consciousness. This is what some authors call "shamanity" which refers to a state of mind rather than an activity (Vitebsky 1995 in Costa 2003, p.10).

However, it is in shamanistic practices where the full possibilities of the native world are enhanced, because shamanism is able to guide the members of the community to the different levels of reality. Shamans are specialists. They have the power of healing. They are the inheritors of a millenary tradition. They were initiated and formed with a very rigorous discipline, and its observance is precisely one of the requisites to gain access to a genuine spirituality. Usually, transgression of the rules brings innumerable problems to the shaman, including a decrease in power and, as a consequence, a poor use of his capabilities. This point has special relevance today, especially in regard to the opening of the native world to westerners. In this process, the shaman's own balance is at risk and there are many cases of loss of the identity axis. The risk applies not only to shamans but also to all those native leaders who pass from their communities to the urban spheres and who are in contact with the western way of life. This process is part of the new challenges the native world has to face. Like the shaman, native Indians must travel through the worlds without losing their identity. They must be able to "go" but perhaps more importantly, they must know how to "get back."

Finally, there is one more element to the complex system of native worldview: balance. In his or her particular way of being in the world, the indigenous person tries to align with the universe with a constant search for harmony. Balance is a necessary condition.

Humanity must keep a delicate interrelationship with each part of the whole. Examples abound: from the sacrifices that hold up the cosmic order to the permission that is asked to start a journey, everything in the native world is regulated by this vital need of balance, which is the key to the organization of the worldview's different principles.

Rituals, dance and music in traditional ceremonies, the structure of sacred spaces, the symbols that are used, everything tends to reach the needed balance that regulates life and the different cosmic forces that are in constant interaction with human beings.

The practice of shamanism includes the idea of patient and healer "aligning" with spiritual entities whose aid is invited in the process of healing. Usually the shaman tries to "place" the patient, to balance him or her. There are many ways of achieving this. Some of them are: the use of tobacco which acts as a cleansing and restoring mechanism. This is done through a process known as *"la soplada"* (the blow). The *"mesa"* (table) the shaman uses with his different elements fol-

> It is in shamanistic practices where the full possibilities of the native world are enhanced, because shamanism is able to guide the members of the community to the different levels of reality.

lows an order related to the balance of the world. The search of the lost soul is a way of regaining the person's harmony. The chants, dances and performing of musical instruments during the healing aim to invoke benign spirits who will come to the aid of the shaman, or to expel the malefic spirits. Here too, the idea is to keep or restore the lost equilibrium.

Indigenous Cosmovision as a Territory of Encounter

Even though it is still being debated and elaborated, the concept of worldview has generated a certain consensus among many authors in regard to its range: it is a very fertile field to approach the sense of the path the native cultures have followed throughout time.

Even though the worldview retains and respects a central core of ideas and principles (what López Austin defines as "hard nucleus"), it is also important to notice that constant changes in native cultures bring about natural adaptations and recreations and, on the other hand, explain the worldview's vitality.

The theoretical view that is able to deal with this kind of research implies, from my point of view, not conceiving the native cultural forms as the uninterrupted and direct continuity of the pre-Hispanic past or as archaisms, but visualizing this culture in a constant process of transformation and re-elaboration that is nevertheless sustained in very ancient roots. The native culture must be studied in its process of constant transformation, in which ancient structures and beliefs have been articulated with new shapes and contents in a dynamic and creative way (Broda, 1995, p.14, in Medina 2000, p.261).

The native worldview nurtures a conception of life that is based on an integration of the different elements that surround humans. Dialogue with native cultures, and more specifically with men and women of wisdom (may they be spiritual leaders, shamans, the elders, advisers or artists) who treasure a very ancient knowledge, is indispensable not only for anthropologists but also for all those who perceive that we are entering into a new stage in the encounter of westerners and native Indians.

Slowly and subtly but growing steadier with time, a mutual opening is happening. Perhaps, diving deeper into the vast territory of the native worldview will contribute to finding and discovering the still mysterious common points of the human condition. This condition passes through the visible world, which is connected with the invisible one, making it possible for us to get together in a sacred and spiritual dimension essential for the new times.

References

Azcuy, E. A. (1999). *Asedios a la otra realidad. Una búsqueda de lo metafísico-real.* Buenos Aires, Argentina: Kier.

Azcuy, Eduardo A. (1976). *Arquetipos y símbolos celestes.* Buenos Aires, Argentina: Fernando García Cambeiro.

Bergallo, G. E. (2003). *Las bases interpretativas de la cultura: Estética cuántica y antropología.* In M. J. Caro & J. W. Murphy (Eds). *El mundo de la cultura cuántica.* Granada, Spain: Port-Royal Ediciones, pp.189-212.

Broda, J. (1991). *Cosmovision y observación de la naturaleza: El ejemplo del culto de los cerros en Mesoamérica.* In J. Broda, S. Iwaniszewski y L.Maupomé (Eds). Arqueoastronomía y Etnoastronomía en Mesoamérica. México: UNAM, pp. 461-500.

Castenada, C. (1968). *The Teachings of Don Juan: A Yaqui Way of Knowledge.* Berkeley, CA: University of California Press.

Costa, J-P. (2003). *Los chamanes ayer y hoy. México:* Siglo XXI Editores.

Eliade, M. (1979). *Lo sagrado y lo profano.* Barcelona, Spain: Guadarrama/Punto Omega.

Eliade, M. (1993). *El chamanismo y las técnicas arcaicas del éxtasis.* México: Fondo de Cultura Económica. (1964. Shamanism: Archaic Techniques of 'Ecstasy. Bollingen Series LXXVI. New York, Pantheon.)

Fericgla, J. M. (1994). *Los jíbaros, cazadores de sueños. Diario de un antropólogo entre los shuar. Experimentos con la ayahuasca.* Barcelona, Spain: Integral.

Haber, A. (1969). *Un símbolo vivo. Arquetipos, historia y sociedad.* Buenos Aires: Paidós.

Haber, A. (1976). *Símbolos, héroes y estructuras.* Buenos Aires: Hachette.

Harpur, P. (2003a). *Daimonic reality. A field guide to the otherworld.* Pine Winds: Idyll Arbor Inc.

Harpur, P. (2003b). *The philosophers' secret fire: A history of the imagination.* Ivan R. Dee.

Kohler, U. (1980). *Cosmovisión indígena e interpretación europea en estudios mesoamericanistas. In La Antropología americanista en la actualidad.* Homenaje a Raphael Girard. México: Editores mexicanos Unidos, Tomo I, p. 583-596.

Kusch, R. (1973). *El pensamiento indígena y popular en América.* Buenos Aires, Argentina ICA.

Kusch, R. (1975). *América profunda.* Buenos Aires, Argentina: Bonum.

Llamazares, A. M. & Martinez Sarasola, C. (2004). *El Lenguaje de los dioses: Arte, chamanismo y cosmovisión indígena de Sudamérica.* Buenos Aires, Argentina: Editorial Biblos.

Martinez Sarasola, C. (2000a). *Palabras Previas.* In Acevedo, Juan & Néstor Berlanda. Los extraños. Buenos Aires: Emecé.

Martinez Sarasola, C. (2000b). *Carlos Castaneda: A través del infinito.* Lea, 7: 18-20, Buenos Aires, Argentina.

Martinez Sarasola, C. (2004). *El círculo de la conciencia. Una introducción a la cosmovisión indígena americana.* In A. Llamazares & C. Martinez Sarasola (Eds). 2004: 21-65.

Martinez Sarasola, C. (2010). *De manera sagrada y en celebración. Cosmovisión y espiritualidad en los pueblos indígenas de la Argentina.* Buenos Aires, Argentina: Editorial Biblos.

Medina, A. (2000.) *En las cuatro esquinas, en el centro.* Etnografía de la cosmovisión mesoamericana. México: UNAM.

Sandner, D. F. & Wong, S. H. (1997). *The sacred heritage: The influence of shamanism on analytical psychology.* New York, NY: Routledge.

Servier, J. (1964). *El hombre y lo invisible.* Caracas, Venzuala: Monte Avila Editores.

Wright, P. G. (1996).*Crónicas de un encuentro shamánico: Alejandro el "silbador" y el Antropólogo.* In I. Lagarriga, J. Galinier & M. Perrin (Coord). Chamanismo en Latinoamérica. Una revisión conceptual. México: Plaza y Valdés Editores.

The Spirit Doctors of Nature

Connie Grauds

"A shaman's mysterious healing practices are a blend of medicine and spirit," says pharmacist Connie Grauds. *"The rainforest shamans are experts on the healing properties of the jungle's rich plant medicines. These shamans have an intimate relationship with the healing spirits of nature and of the plants, which they summon on behalf of the patient during the healing.* Connie, as a shamama of the Amazonian jungle tradition, shares the secret of the shamans, *"Shamans summon these healing forces and transfer these healing plant spirit energies to their patients during the healing."*

These are just such stories of the healing power of the spirit doctors of nature.

The Calling

Today, I stand with my feet firmly planted in two very different worlds. I am a pharmacist who has worked in the world of conventional Western medicine for nearly thirty years, and I'm also a shamana who has apprenticed in the world of "nonrational" healing for over fifteen years.

Connie Grauds, RPh, MNPA, is President of the Association of Natural Medicine Pharmacists; Adjunct Faculty at the University of Minnesota, Center for Spirituality and Healing; and is author of Jungle Medicine, and The Energy Prescription. Connie is Executive Director of the Living Shaman Museum.

Head-to-Head: The Maestro and The Apprentice, don Antonio (shaman) and Connie Grauds.

Through a series of seemingly random events, I ended up in the Amazon jungle on a continuing education trip. There, I met a powerful shaman, don Antonio, and took an unexpected, disorienting plunge into the world of the irrational—a realm of inner visions and voices, powerful energies, and strange experiences. At that time, I knew practically nothing about shamanism, nor did I imagine my ordeal to be anything like an initiation. During my first encounters with Amazonian shamans, I found myself talking to plants and seeing visions I couldn't explain. One shaman told me I had a block in my neck, whatever that meant. I was confronted with the terror that I might be going mad—a fear buried deep within me since my childhood.

I had been taught early in my life that hearing extraordinary voices and seeing visions were signs of pathology. During my early childhood, I had seen my mother hospitalized and diagnosed as psychotic—precisely for hearing unusual voices and seeing other-worldly visions. I had seen what the Western medical system had done to my mother for not being normal, and I was determined to do everything within my power to make sure that my life was grounded, rational, and, above all, sane.

After I graduated from the University of Minnesota's College of Pharmacy, my life and career were set. I became a pharmacist—a respected member of the Western medical establishment. Ironically, my mother's madness had driven me into the arms of the medical profession that had virtually destroyed her because it didn't understand the spiritual roots of her disease. In time, I would come to realize that the medical profession itself was in need of spiritual healing.

In my early forties, nearly two decades into my career, my life took a turn. I discovered a lump on my neck, which was diagnosed as thyroid cancer. The surgeon removed the cancerous thyroid. While Western medicine told me I was cured, I knew that there was something deep inside my being that was in crisis beyond the cancerous thyroid… some kind of deep existential crisis that I intuitively knew that Western medicine couldn't cure.

During my recovery from surgery, I remembered one of the Amazonian shamans who said I had a block in my neck. Could this be the same thing? How did the shaman know this? In a dream, I saw the Amazonian shaman don Antonio uttering the words he had spoken to me during my first trip to the rainforest, "You have enough energy to be a shaman yourself." Now I wanted to see him again. I wasn't sure what I would do if I found him, and I didn't even know if I would be able to find him, but I decided to return to Peru as soon as possible.

Soon after I arrived in Iquitos, the jungle-drums of gossip eventually led me to find don Antonio. He was about to begin planting a medicinal plant garden powers from which indigenous shamans have drawn their healing wisdom and spiritual gifts. In doing so, he initiated me into ancient mysteries of healing upon which modern medicine had turned its back.

After many moons of getting to know each other and working together in the primal depths of the jungle, don Antonio finally took me on as his apprentice. During my apprenticeship, I would learn of the awesomely powerful healing forces that are nature itself. I offer here the spirited stories of two healings during deep shamanic ceremony in the jungles of Peru that exemplify the importance of the inclusion of the powerful nature spirits into the healing equation.

Two Stories of Nature Spirit Healings

I left for Peru with the usual stopover in Miami to change planes. While waiting in the Miami airport between flights, I struck up a conversation with Kay, an interesting and friendly American woman in her fifties who was also on her way to Iquitos. Kay had a passion for pottery, and had studied with indigenous potters in Ecuador twenty years before. But she had mostly given up her craft to become a respiratory therapist in the United States. a healing herself. I told her we could consider it further in Iquitos.

When we arrived in Iquitos, we both checked into the El Dorado hotel, located near the Plaza de Armas in the center of town. That night, while dining in the hotel restaurant, we struck up a lively conversation with a Canadian woman, a high-spirited family therapist in her mid-forties named Marcie who told us she'd come to Peru in search of a "spiritual adventure". As we shared stories, Marcie revealed that she was also looking for ways to integrate spiritual perspectives into her personal and professional life.

To make a long story short, by the end of the evening we were comrades in adventure, and they were both asking me to let them meet don Antonio. I agreed, wondering what don Antonio would say when I showed up with two unexpected guests.

Our *rapido*, the speed boat, wound along the Napo River, past the familiar, progressively rising skyline of foliage and trees, deeper into the primal jungle. I now knew the route by heart. Shaman don Antonio met us at the docks near the camp, and did not seem surprised to see *Los Tres Mosqueteros*, as we were now calling our adventuresome threesome. He told me later he'd seen himself in a dream several weeks ago, performing a healing with three white women. But he hadn't known what the dream meant until we arrived that afternoon.

> Today, I stand with my feet firmly planted in two very different worlds. I am a pharmacist who has worked in the world of conventional Western medicine for nearly thirty years, and I'm also a shamana who has apprenticed in the world of "nonrational" healing.

in a village on the Yanayaco River, and he needed volunteers to help tend his new garden. As I worked the gardens in the day, the nights were saved for healing rituals. Don Antonio had taken me on as his patient. He knew I needed the help that only a shaman can provide.

Don Antonio understood what was happening to me, and helped me to see it as a transformational, rather than a pathological, process. He walked with me to the edges of madness where I wrestled with my inner demons. He helped me to understand and relate directly to these

She also told me that a childhood bout with polio had left her lame in one leg, and that recurring bouts of post-polio syndrome over the past few years had left her exhausted and depleted. She was on her way to the Amazon's lush tropical jungles to find rest and rejuvenation. We sat together on the plane to continue our conversation. When I told her a little about my apprenticeship as a healer with don Antonio, she expressed a strong interest in spiritual healing. Then she asked me outright if she could come with me to meet don Antonio and perhaps get

During these first several days near don Antonio's childhood village on the Yanayacu River, he put us all to work in the medicinal plant garden. I had grown to love this place like home, I accepted shamanism on its own terms, and don Antonio was now like family to me, a loving taskmaster of spirit. But all of this was new for Kay and Marcie.

Don Antonio had announced his requirements for our working with him on the first afternoon, when I explained to him Kay and Marcie's reasons for coming. "If you want to work with me, I will need a little work from you," he said, mincing no words. "If you want the spirits of the jungle and its plants to provide some healing for you, you must provide something for them in return. Working with spirit is always a reciprocal arrangement."

The next morning he handed each of us, respectively, a wheelbarrow, a shovel, and a machete for our first full day's work. His own trusty machete, as always, hung loosely in the belt around his waist.

"Tilling the soil is tilling your substance, too," he said. He pointed to a newly cleared section of land. "Prepare the land there to accept the new plant seeds I have collected from the jungle." He handed me a calabash full of tiny black seeds. "Connie will show you what to do." Then he added, "The jungle itself will prepare you and humble you." Then he turned and walked off to work in another part of the gardens.

Yes, there is nothing like the jungle's intense heat, pesky mosquitoes and nonstop tickling sweat to wear you down. The jungle is the medicine: to merely show up the jungle guarantees a confrontation. And performing intense physical labor there forces a deeper level of surrender. This was no tourist safari from the safety of a boat or cleared jungle path. This would be a dirty-up-to-the-elbows, sing-for-your-supper complete immersion experience. I wondered how Kay and Marcie would take to it.

In the first few days of work in the gardens, full of grumbling and sore muscles, Marcie and Kay began to fall into the rhythm of the jungle. The animal sounds, the afternoon rains, the spectacular beauty of the flora and fauna all worked their magic and medicine upon them. As the week wore on, we began to fall into rhythm with each other. Working together gave us an opportunity to talk at a deeper level and get to know each other better. Marcie and Kay got to know don Antonio better, too. And after each hard day's work, a *limpia* (sacred healing herbal bath) at dusk in a nearby stream with don Antonio deepened their connection to him. After our limpias by

Irridescent Blue Morpho Butterfly.

the river's edge at the end of the week, don Antonio spoke to us.

"I am pleased with your work," he announced. "The spirits told me in my dream that you would come for a healing. You are all now ready. Tomorrow night, if you are willing, there will be an all-night ayahuasca healing ceremony."

Kay's Healing Ceremony

Both Kay and Marcie expressed a strong desire to undergo the ceremony, which they knew would include drinking the Medicine (with a capital "M", as don Antonio best describes it.). Don Antonio was pleased. "To prepare yourselves, do not eat anything tomorrow and spend the day in silent communion with nature. Kay, this first healing is for you. We will all come prepared and drink ayahuasca together. Remember," he concluded, "healing is a community effort. There are no observers. We will all participate in Kay's healing."

The symptoms of Kay's recurring post-polio syndrome flare-ups included chronic fatigue, increasing motor difficulties, and pain in her lame left leg. Being a healthcare professional, she had tried every conventional treatment available. Now, having reached a dead end, she was willing to try anything…even the ayahuasca healing ceremony that shaman don Antonio was now preparing on her behalf.

Kay intuitively knew she needed a deeper healing than conventional medicine offered, and which it had already failed to provide. She needed to reach into the spiritual depths where both illness and healing have their roots. And while grateful and excited at being allowed to participate in this shamanic healing ritual with don Antonio, she also had a case of the jitters at the prospect of drinking ayahuasca, the sacred Medicine don Antonio and I had, through rituals and words, been preparing her to meet.

During the day of preparation and ceremonial fasting, my body and mind began quieting down. I chose to spend my reflecting time swaying lazily in the arms of nature in a hammock strung in the shade of the jungle foliage, between a breadfruit tree and a giant *cecropia*. Toward the end of the day the heat, the sense of weightlessness and the swaying, and the late afternoon shadows flickering across my half-closed eyes, lulled me into a deep, peaceful trance.

Early evening is the in-between time, the intersection of light and darkness when don Antonio says the spirits reveal themselves. Now, after a day of fasting, contemplation and invoking the spirits for the evening ceremony, I began to notice faint milky silhouettes in the play of the shadows, against a distant background of dark-green jungle foliage. Some soared amidst a group of hanging lianas, flickering in and out of visibility the way fireflies do. Was I dreaming? Imagining? Perceiving reality beyond my "normal" senses? It didn't matter. I wasn't concerned. Their simple presence felt comforting.

As the sun set, and the awaited ayahuasca hour approached, I experienced the familiar pre-Medicine tension, a mixture of anticipation, excitement, anxiety, fear of the unknown, and a peculiar heightening of the senses, almost like a shadow cast by the Medicine's approach. I was soon drenched in sweat. The body/mind of an *ayahuasquero* always feels this peculiar anticipatory dread and respect which the medicine commands. Ayahuasca healing ceremonies are intense ordeals on every level, physical, mental, emotional and spiritual. Like the jungle itself, they are not for the faint of heart.

We were to meet don Antonio at the ceremonial hut at 9 p.m. sharp. At 8:30 p.m. we gathered in my room, said a last round of prayers together, and started down the path away from the camp toward don Antonio's ceremonial hut in the depths of the jungle. The sky was cloudy and the night was dark. Our ears rang with the nocturnal cacophony, the cries of animals searching for food, calling for mates, or simply bursting with the sheer, primal intensity of the jungle life force. I heard far off the powerful, unmistakable growl of a jaguar announcing an evening's hunt, and the disturbing phrase "eat or be eaten" popped uninvited into my mind.

As we walked along the path, the pitch dark jungle night seemed to absorb our flashlight beams the way black holes are said to devour the light of stars. Somehow we lost our way…the slippery clay path turned to mud, then to an ankle-deep swamp, and we soon found ourselves floundering, legs tangled in the thickly growing *camu camu* plants that thrive in these common low-lying swamps. We walked in circles, bumping into each other, seeking a way out of the watery bog. The *Tres Mosqueteros* had become the *Tres Stooges*. I didn't know whether to laugh, cry or scream for help.

Finally, not far off through the foliage, I spotted the candlelight that marked the shaman's hut. We moved directly toward it and soon reached the hut, our boots and feet drenched in a baptism-by-bog.

Don Antonio was there to welcome us. He wore his black ritual *cushma*, a jaguar tooth necklace, and his eyes already had the faraway look of one in touch with the spirit realm. He invited us to sit on the logs that formed a ceremony circle in front of the hut. In the middle of the circle was a splendid table altar, his holy *mesa*. Lit candles formed a numinous ring around the table's edge, interspersed with boughs of healing plants. The candles represented our prayers and intentions for healing. In tonight's ceremony we would ask the spirits of the higher realms to heal us of things for which we had found no cures in the human realm.

"The spirits are already present around us," he said softly. His statement immediately deepened the mood of our group. It often seems that our plight on earth is to suffer the bondage of self—in troubles manifesting as physical, emotional, or spiritual afflictions—until death, the great *purge* (purging), takes us into the beyond. We three had come far, at great expense and through much hardship, to reach this place in our lives, to attend this healing ceremony, to pray to unseen forces beyond our known reality for divine healing. Our allies in tonight's journey into the spirit realm sat in the center of the mesa, two hand-carved balsa figurines, a jaguar and anaconda—el tigre and el serpiente—and between them a dried piece of brown gnarled serpentine vine—ayahuasca. Don Antonio's shamanic healing tools—the tobacco, ayahuasca brew, bowls of perfume and camphor water (for protection, don Antonio explained)—also sat on the table. "Tonight," don Antonio began, "we will call on three friends and allies, three fearsome entities—the jaguar, the anaconda, and ayahuasca—for their great healing powers."

After briefly instructing Kay and Marcie regarding the ayahuasca experience and the formalities of the healing ceremony, he offered prayers and requests to the spirits of the heavens on our, and his behalf. As ayahuasca ceremonies are performed in complete darkness, he extinguished the candles, welcoming the spirits closer, then poured us each our dose of medicine. We drank it in turn, managed to hold it down, and settled back to await its effects. We occupied ourselves by wiping away the rivulets of sweat pouring down our faces, and waving our arms to chase away the ever-present swarms of mosquitoes that were eating us alive.

What an ordeal these jungle night ceremonies can be! Yet the outer jungle discomforts soon give way to internal phenomena of another order—dizziness, purging, visions and altered states—as the Medicine takes effect. Then one finds oneself in a completely expanded and fluid dimension where normal limits on reality do not hold. This is the place where healings occur.

As I sat there feeling these multidimensional effects, two luminous apparitions, a man and a woman, walked out of the velvety darkness of the jungle and stepped into our circle. Their bodies were almost like living X-rays, not quite skeletal, not flesh and blood, but glowing, three-dimensional entities distinctly human in size and shape. Oddly, they wore Western medical garb and comported themselves almost matter-of-factly, like ordinary physicians. Their faces were devoid of all expression, as if they were above human emotion. I knew that they were not humans, but spirit doctors, the healing nature spirits we had ritually invoked at the beginning of the ceremony.

Nothing in my previous ayahuasca journeys had prepared me for this extraordinary encounter. They stood

> There is nothing like the jungle's intense heat, pesky mosquitoes and non-stop tickling sweat to wear you down. The jungle is the medicine, to merely show up the jungle guarantees a confrontation. And performing intense physical labor there forces a deeper level of surrender.

in the ceremonial circle and I watched them, heart pounding. I looked for don Antonio but he was no longer beside us. Then I looked around, straining my eyes in the darkness. He stood in the clearing amidst a swarm of bright yellowish orange dots. Face turned skyward, he waved his arms like a maestro in beautiful rhythmic gestures, conducting a ballet of fireflies and clouds.

The shaman was in his element, in deep communion with the spirits and full of ecstatic power, seeming both surrendered and very much in control. I saw that I was on my own. I could feel my heartbeat in my throat. My body was in a state of hyper-vigilance beyond the typical physiological effects of the Medicine.

It was time for a reality check. Focusing intently, I scanned my surroundings as best as I could in the dark to compare these two spirit apparitions with what I knew to be tangible realities. I saw: Kay and Marcie on their benches, retching on the ground, oblivious to our two luminous guests; the *mesa* in front of me; the hut; and the two spirit doctors. All seemed equal, reality and spirit were indistinguishable to my present perceptions. This fact, both frightening and fascinating, was wreaking havoc with my sense of reality. I felt no fear of the spirit entities, who seemed benignly intent on their own purpose.

They went up to Kay, to whose healing this ceremony was primarily dedicated, and for whom we had invoked these spirits. I assumed they would work on Kay's left polio-stricken leg. Instead, to my puzzlement, they went behind her and stood looking intently at her back. "No...what are they doing?" I protested silently. "Can't they see that her leg is the problem?" I wondered again if this was a mere drug-induced hallucination.

I didn't have the confidence or presence of mind to speak to these spirit doctors and ask them what they were doing. Silent, I watched the event unfold. The male spirit now produced out of nowhere a glowing white globe of energy about the size of a bowling ball. He and the female spirit together held this ball of white light directly against Kay's spine at the base of her neck, then began to move it very slowly down her spine. After what seemed like an hour, they finally reached Kay's sacrum with the glowing ball and held it there for some time. Then, in an instant, they vanished.

Now I looked over and saw Marcie, lying on the ground in fetal position, moaning, clutching her head and her stomach, so ill she could not sit up. The Medicine does that sometimes. Don Antonio now came and knelt beside her and began working with her. He was still attending to her when Kay and I finally stumbled back to our rooms many hours later, and he continued attending to her through the night and into the morning.

I was disappointed by the spirit doctors' failure to treat Kay's stricken leg, and by Marcie's prolonged ordeal with the Medicine. I had hoped they would both have a strongly positive experience. But this apparently had not occurred.

Getting to the Source of the Problem

In the morning I crawled from under my mosquito net, still weak from the previous night's ceremony. Seeing Kay refilling her canteen at the water jug, I went and joined her, to rinse the putrid taste from my mouth and check in on her and see how she was feeling.

Shaman's Sacred Medicine, Ayahuasco Ready to Brew.

"Well," she asked me hopefully, "did you see me get a healing last night?" I swished some water around in my mouth, trying to find a diplomatic answer, since I believed she hadn't received the healing she so desired. If I was disappointed, I knew she would be also. I felt responsible for her experience, and guilty that I had enthusiastically recounted to Kay, days earlier, several extraordinary ayahuasca healing stories. I felt I had given her false hope.

"Well, umm, I don't know, Kay," I began. "I'll just tell you what I saw." I then told her how two spirit doctors had come to her out of the jungle, pressed a bright ball of light against her spine for some time, running it from her neck down to her sacrum, and after leaving it there a while, had suddenly vanished. I didn't mention their glaring omission... they had ignored her leg. I was surprised when Kay lit up at my report with a huge smile. She noticed my puzzled look.

"Don't you get it, Connie?" she said. "Do you remember the etiology of polio? The virus attacks the motor neurons of the spinal cord. The polio-damaged motor-neurons in my spine that were still functioning are now failing me. That's what post-polio syndrome is." She was quite excited. "Those spirit doctors went right to the source of the problem. It sounds like they were recharging my failing spinal motor – neurons with that glowing ball of energy."

This struck me as utterly remarkable. I had paid little attention to polio as a healthcare professional...it had essentially been eradicated in the United States before I reached pharmacy school. I now realized the misunderstanding had been mine. I was expecting them to treat the branches, while they had gone straight to the root of the problem. Had they merely treated Kay's leg as I had expected them to do, they would have ignored the real problem, the damaged motor-neurons in the spine which were responsible for her post-polio disintegration.

When I asked her what she had experienced, she made the following report. "I saw a golden ball of light moving toward my body and stop still in front of me. I gazed at its inviting glow and saw my life bathed in a new light. As I continued staring at the golden light, I saw pieces of my life rearrange themselves. I realized that I was working too hard in a job that was not my true calling. When I was thinking about my job, the light grew dimmer. When I thought about my life continuing as it is, into the future, the light was nearly extinguished. When I thought about my real passion for making Ecuadorian pottery, the golden light grew bright and intense, and it made me feel warm, loved, connected and ecstatically happy. I feel physically and emotionally energized right now, even though I feel like I should rest."

This contradiction between my perception of what had happened, and Kay's experience, showed me both my own limitations and the mysterious power of the Medicine. I would try to keep in mind after this that there was often far more going on than I was aware of.

We all spent the day recuperating, quietly reflecting, taking naps to recharge and catch up on the sleep we'd missed during the all-night ceremony. Yet despite the intense nature of ayahuasca, it does not wear the body down. Overall, ayahuasca is profoundly healing and rejuvenating. Not only do I feel a greater sense of energy and aliveness over time, I also feel calmer and more grounded because of it as well. That is one reason it is called the Medicine. Late that afternoon don Antonio came into my room off the *maloca* and announced an ayahuasca healing ceremony to be held the next evening for Marcie. When he left I moaned and rolled over on my cot, wondering if I could really go through this again so soon. Still recuperating, I felt physically spent, emotionally drained, and my mind was in shreds.

> I experienced the familiar pre-Medicine tension, a mixture of anticipation, excitement, anxiety, fear of the unknown, and a peculiar heightening of the senses, almost like a shadow cast by the Medicine's approach.

"Well, you can be a shamana," I reminded myself, "or go back to pharmacy." Neither option seemed particularly appealing at the moment. It took what little energy I had left to crawl from under my mosquito netting and grab some dinner. After that I went straight back to bed again. I would need all my strength for tomorrow evening's ceremony.

The Doctors Return for Marcie's Healing

At 9 p.m., the next evening, after another day's fast, we were again seated on the logs of the ceremonial circle outside the shaman's hut, as prepared as we could be for the long night ahead. The smell of the burning *copal,* an aromatic jungle tree resin, on the mesa helped us to turn our focus inward to our intentions for the night. Don Antonio finished his preparations and blessed each of us with songs and tobacco smoke, covering Marcie in a blue swirling cloud. Marcie, the focus of tonight's ceremony, had no physical maladies or complaints. I wondered what she might need besides a general healing and a spiritual blessing.

After the ritual blessing, don Antonio offered us each a dose of the Medicine and we settled in to wait. The sky was clear tonight and the light of the full moon radiated through the jungle canopy, pouring down through the clearing over the ceremonial area. This would make it easier to navigate back and forth when the *purga* began. And begin it did…soon we were taking turns vomiting into the bushes. After this subsided, my mind cleared and my senses sharpened.

Forty-five minutes into the ceremony, I saw a far-off glow in the jungle, steadily approaching. As it drew nearer I made out the two spirit doctors. They had come again. They walked straight to Marcie and began a formal, even clinical examination. They first lifted her tee shirt and took turns palpating her stomach. Each carefully pressed and felt all around her abdominal area, as any western physician might do. Marcie seemed oblivious to their presence. Don Antonio was sitting on his log, looking elsewhere, absorbed in his own experience, seeming unaware of what I was seeing.

Tonight I was determined to speak with the spirit doctors, to interact with and learn from them. So I asked them if they were teaching me how to palpate patients. When they didn't respond, I reached over to Marcie and put my hands directly on top of theirs, thinking to learn their technique.

"No," the female spirit doctor clearly said. "You don't do anything. We do all the work. You just host the vision." Having been given my place, there was nothing to do but sit back and watch them work. Next they lowered Marcie's pants and took turns palpating her pelvic area, from left to right, slowly, intently, with great care. Then I noticed them focusing on Marcie's left pelvic area. After spending a good deal of time there, they stopped to converse in undertones. The female spirit doctor seemed quite concerned. She pressed deeply several times on one particular spot on Marcie's left pelvic side. Each time Marcie would clutch her abdomen, groan, and then vomit. But she still seemed unaware of the two entities working on her.

Then, to my utter surprise, the female spirit doctor looked up at me and said, "She has ovarian problems." "Are you sure?" I asked. "She hasn't complained or said anything about it." "We are sure," she replied. "What should I do about it?" I was feeling very troubled and at a loss. "*You* don't do anything about it," the spirit doctor said, reminding me of who has the real power here. "We will take care of her. We are going to perform surgery."

Riveted, I sat on my log and watched fascinated while the spirit doctors performed some sort of operation on Marcie's ovaries. They both bent over her, focused intently on her pelvic area. One of them held Marcie's clothing out of the way while the other moved both hands over Marcie's ovaries. I was unable to distinguish exactly what was being done, but it seemed effortless and was over soon. When they had finished the procedure, Marcie's vomiting episodes had subsided. Then, in silence, the spirit doctors walked off into the jungle whence they came.

Again, once they had disappeared I immediately began doubting what I'd seen. I looked over at Kay and don Antonio for confirmation, but they were both busy retching by the side of the hut. Marcie, her "surgery" finished, lay exhausted on the ground. I still didn't know what to think or believe. I decided to talk to don Antonio in the morning about my "vision".

Confirmation of the Vision

In the early morning hours, exhausted by the Medicine and the night's events, I climbed into the hammock inside the hut and fell into a deep sleep. When I woke the next morning, Kay, Marcie and don Antonio were gathered out front around the mesa for a ceremonial closing circle, a kind of group debriefing. Kay would do the translating for us. Don Antonio had made everyone a tall glass of *limón* water, with jungle lime, a post-ayahuasca morning tonic. Don Antonio nodded to me as I joined in, and then toasted the group.

"*Salud*, to your health," he raised his glass and sipped the tart green limewater. He began with a heartfelt acknowledgement, and then got to the point. "Marcie, I'll start with you. First, I want to thank you for the sacrifices of time and energy you made to come here and participate in this healing ceremony. Now I must tell you something. I'm afraid that you have ovarian problems."

Marcie's eyes showed fearful concern. I was dumbstruck. Don Antonio's words seemed to corroborate my vision of the previous night. I had spoken to no one, had told no one what I had seen, and believed that only I knew what had transpired during last night's healing ceremony. Had don Antonio also seen the spirit doctors? Had we entered the same healing realm together last night? Could I, as his apprentice, now access the spirit realms where this healing work was done?

"What does that mean?" asked Marcie. "What should I do?" "Don't worry," said don Antonio, gently patting her shoulder. "The spirit doctors performed spiritual surgery on you last night during the ceremony."

My god! I thought. *They're real!* Apparently I wasn't the only one who saw the spirit doctors last night, who heard their diagnosis and witnessed the "surgery". This was the confirmation I needed. Now I could finally believe my own eyes. The spirit realm was real.

Meanwhile, Marcie looked relieved, even radiant. The color returned to her face and she said, "That's interesting… you see, I had ovarian surgery as an adolescent. When my mother was pregnant with me she took the hormone DES, diethylstilbesterol, and it screwed up my ovaries. It didn't occur to me to tell you about it, since it happened so long ago. I thought I was done with all that.

"I was so sick last night," she continued. "Sick to death of myself. I've always felt ashamed that I couldn't have children, that I'm no good for any man. I've run away from every meaningful relationship I've ever had. But I feel like I've purged all the shame from my body somehow. I don't feel defective right now. I feel lovable."

Being a pharmacist, I knew the daughters of women who took the hormone diethylstilbesterol during their pregnancies suffered many reproductive problems as a result. Marcie's story further corroborated my experience with the spirit doctors, and the accuracy of their diagnoses. And it implied that a deeper spiritual healing, which Western medicine did not offer, was still needed some thirty years later.

"This is the start of a healing process for both of you," replied don Antonio, looking at Marcie, and then at Kay. "But it's up to you to make this a turning point. This is not a magical ceremony that removes a lifetime of physical distress. Even when spirit heals, you must still do your part afterwards, and make necessary life adjustments and changes. Otherwise you may simply reproduce further illness later on. This is how it is. You must follow the rest of the prescription, or you may lose what you have gained here."

Now he looked at Kay. "Spirit showed you that you must stop working full-time at your job," he said. "It is robbing you of vital energy you need to heal. Use the extra time you have to do what you really love, something that makes you feel good. Spirit has given you much positive energy with the healings and ceremonies. Now you must generate your own *energia positiva* for your ongoing healing."

Kay's eyes lit up as she quickly answered him. "Making pottery is the passion of my life. But I haven't had the time or energy to do it for years. I'm afraid that if I don't work, I won't have enough money to take care of myself because of my deteriorating health."

"My dear lady," don Antonio replied firmly, "if you don't stop working so hard, you won't have a life worth saving. You are killing yourself slowly. But it's your life!"

I could see that Kay took his words

> During my apprenticeship to a powerful Amazon rainforest shaman, and in the course of my own peculiar ordeal, I learned deeper spiritual truths of healing which my previous medical training failed to provide.

seriously. She knew in her heart that he was right. And she now promised to act on his words when she got home. Now don Antonio turned his attention to Marcie, who nervously awaited his "prescription".

"Marcie, you must find yourself a good man and settle down. I can see in your heart how unsettled and out of balance you have been. Your sexuality is in chaos." Don Antonio sipped his lime drink and waited.

"You're right," said Marcie. "My relationships have always been confused and fleeting. I never realized how much it had to do with my DES condition."

"Our physical health reflects our spiritual and emotional health," don Antonio said. "Mind, body and emotions are interconnected. A shaman never treats the body as separate from the whole being. What you have experienced here is a start. You have a deep wound. Find a healing relationship. Listen to your spirit."

I took a sip of lime drink and stared deeply into the green liquid. A mysterious medicinal world in microcosm seemed to swirl, with bits of lime, in my glass. Now I told don Antonio of my ayahuasca experiences with the spirit doctors, how I had spoken with them and watched them perform spiritual surgery on Marcie's ovaries. I asked him to explain what it all meant, and what part he played in the healing ceremony.

"So who were the spirit doctors I saw?" I asked. "They were the spirits of the nature who help shamans. The patient drinks the ayahuasca in order to open up to the actions of these nature spirit doctors, whom they do not see. I can invoke and work with the spirit doctors because I have become one with the Medicine. Now you see them, because through your apprenticeship with the spirit and power of ayahuasca, you are also becoming one with the Medicine.

Shaman don Antonio Preparing Plants for Sacred Medicine Brew

This is what it means to be a shaman."

As don Antonio drank up the last of the lime water, he wiped his mouth with the back of his hand. He looked up at me and added, "This is the difference between your Western medicine and my spirited medicine. Your medicine has no magic in it."

The Dream of the Nature Spirit Doctors

Around 8:30 PM I climbed through the mosquito netting into my bed and tucked myself in. I lay there, thinking about the spirit doctors, fascinated by their healing abilities, and amazed at their remarkable participation in the ceremonies. I felt that we were developing a working relationship.

Yet I was puzzled as to who or what these entities actually were. *"Who are these spirit doctors?"*

I kept thinking. And with this last question lingering in my mind, I drifted off to sleep.

In the middle of the night, the spirit doctors appeared to me in a dream as a mass of swirling energy.

"You called for us?" they asked, almost like genie's summoned from a lamp. "Yes," I answered.

"I'm curious. Exactly who and what are you? How can I explain you to others?"

"We are the shear unbridled healing forces of nature that you, as a shamana, are learning to harness and call upon," they answered.

I first took this in relation to myself, and wondered if I was due a bit of credit for Kay and Marcie's healings. But they quickly spoke in answer to this unspoken thought.

"It is we, the generative forces of nature, who do the healing. Not you." And with that, they slipped away.

And so did I, into the depths of a sound sleep.

Amazon Reflections

It was time for me to go home. Don Antonio and I shared the first leg of the return journey, a long boat ride through the primal jungle towards civilization. He was going with me as far as Iquitos.

I planned to check in on Marcie and Kay in a few weeks, to see what effects their healings might be having over time.

After a while, I became aware of the hum of the boat's engine vibrating through the hull, and through my own body, lulling me into a pleasant trance. I sat quietly, looking out into the jungle— a mass of vegetation—simply feeling what was happening. I noticed my body swelling with the sound, as in previous ceremonies, and realized I was like an antennae picking up vibratory frequencies from the mass of vegetation that surrounded me, resonating to the primal sounds, the music and vibration of the rainforest.

In a kind of rapture, I looked up at don Antonio, caught his eye, and motioned to our surroundings. "This jungle is in my body and in my blood," I said to him.

He gave a nod, surveying the lush panorama.

"Yes, I know," he said. "Me, too."

Epilogue

I am now emerging from nearly a decade's apprenticeship to the spirits of the Amazon jungle, one of them being the rainforest shaman don Antonio. Pleased with my progress, and having recently released me from the rigorous *dietas* and *disciplinas* of my early apprenticeship, don Antonio he says he has found in me—an ordinary middle-aged Western woman, and his only non-indigenous apprentice—someone to carry on his lineage of healing knowledge. He refers to me as "the blue-eyed, white shamana who has become the spirit of the jungle."

Who would have thunk?

I went to the Amazon in search of my own healing, and I became a shaman's apprentice to find the magic that was missing in my own healing tradition. There I was cooked in a cauldron of shamanic medicine rituals, *disciplinas* and unusual life-experiences, and blown apart by the magnitude and mystery of spirit. In the end, this intense apprenticeship forced me to "let go." At some point, it became clearly more useful to open my mind, disregard my prejudices, and discover what works rather than continue stubbornly to cling to the superiority of my Western medical model beliefs and presumptions. Letting go into the mystery of the healing power of deep nature has been a most liberating and humbling experience.

Conclusion

During my apprenticeship to a powerful Amazon rainforest shaman, and in the course of my own peculiar ordeal, I learned deeper spiritual truths of healing which my previous medical training failed to provide. I realized that the wealth of vital healing wisdom which the shamanic tradition offers could be combined with the technological wizardry of modern Western medicine to create a new paradigm of healing and health that encompasses the physical, mental, and spiritual domains.

As a pharmacist, I know that the conventional view of medicinal plants is one in which the plant is ingested for its pharmacologically active principles that change the physiology of our bodies to affect a cure. This is like functioning by the letter of the law of healing. But there is also the spirit of the law of healing by which all shamans who use the spirited plant medicine of ayahuasca function.

I have come to believe that both the letter and the spirit are needed for a truly holistic, or spirited medicine, to be achieved. What we need to evolve to in our Western medicine for our deepest healing is *spirited medicine by spirited healers*.

References

Dossey, L. (2001). *Being Green: On the relationship between people and plants*. Alternative Therapies, 7 (3), 1-28.

Grauds, C. (2004). *Jungle Medicine*. Minneapolis, MN: The Center for Spirited Medicine Press.

Mighty Amazon River: The Giver of Life

Assessing a Quest to Heal HIV with Vegetalista Shamanism

Robert Tindall

During the years that my wife, Dr. Susana Bustos, and I have spent studying and training in the Peruvian *vegetalismo*, a mixed-race healing tradition that combines indigenous shamanism with Western elements such as Catholicism, we have come to appreciate the paradoxes that indigenous medicine comes wrapped in for Westerners. Among them is the distinction between curing and healing of disease, concepts which, as in Venn diagrams, overlap yet remain experientially distinct. The thrust of modern Western medicine is to "cure," from Latin *cura* "to care, concern, trouble," by either managing disease within, or excising it from, the body, and disease is usually considered cured when symptoms abate. In indigenous styles of medicine, which give equal importance to curing as the West, healing, from Old English *hælan*

Rolf meditating by river at Mayantuyacu.

"to make whole, sound and well," may also involve searching out the hidden origin of the disease in the body/mind. In this healing quest, a cure may be found, and may not. The valence of the disease, however, will change. In such cases, it is the entire self that is engaged in unraveling a disease's enigma, and the body is the laboratory wherein the cure can be found. As a consequence, such healing is often idiosyncratic, because each body's laboratory is unique.

Paradoxically for Western medicine, if disease is cured shamanically, the medications used (which in *vegetalismo* is a complex synergy of plants, the shaman's *icaros* – or sacred songs – and the ecology of the healing locale itself), will often elude scientific researchers in search of a "silver bullet" molecule. The medicine may be frustratingly non-exportable – its efficacy may vanish as soon as it is separated from the culture that gave rise to the healing in the first place.

Robert Tindall, M.A. is a writer, classical guitarist, long-time practitioner of Zen Buddhism, and an inveterate traveler, whose work explores the crossing of frontiers into other cultures, time depths, and states of consciousness. He is the author of two books on shamanism, *The Jaguar that Roams the Mind* and *The Shamanic Odyssey: Homer, Tolkien, and the Visionary Experience*, along with numerous articles on themes such as pilgrimage along the Camino to Santiago, the medieval quest, and the indigenous prophetic and healing traditions of the Americas. Visit his blog at: www.roamingthemind.com.

In my view, the plant medicines used in the Amazon, among which the visionary plant *ayahuasca* is only one, facilitate healing, but do not necessarily do the ultimate trick of curing. Whether it is worthwhile to cure a disease without healing the conditions that gave rise to it is not much considered by Western medicine, but if a disease is bringing an urgent life message to the patient, it may be folly to suppress its teaching. This, of course, is a paradox for many Westerners, who prefer the freedom, as Robert Bly once put it, to stagger from Burger King to Burger King over taking full responsibility for their spiritual, psychological and physical conditions.

Unlike hamburgers and pharmaceuticals, Amazonian medicines are more akin to allies to be won in a battle of the soul. In this way, a patient seeking healing in the *vegetalista* tradition has much in common with the Native American on a vision quest or the Buddhist monk withdrawing into the forest to practice meditation.

During our recent stay at an Amazonian healing center outside of Pucallpa, Peru, I often caught sight of the figure of Rolf, seated in meditation and swathed in veils of steam arising from the geothermally-heated water flowing below him.

With the support of his partner, with whom he runs a school of Ayurvedic studies, Rolf has done the unthinkable. He had set aside the medications Western medicine now prescribes to suppress symptoms of HIV and is seeking healing under the guidance of the *curandero,* or traditional healer, Juan. Despite the iron wall of opposition from his physicians, Rolf is committed to the proposition that HIV can be cured in the body using traditional medicine.

Not that Rolf is a reckless character, or is disregarding his body's needs. Quite the opposite, he is a quiet, gentle man who worked as a banker for many years and is now grateful to the HIV virus. "My idea was: I'm staying in the bank until I'm 65 and then I retire," he confessed, "without too many other exciting events happening in my life. Ultimately, I didn't want to be here on this planet. The HIV basically taught me different."

His calling, peculiar as it is, he chalks up to the fact that, "Some people immediately go to the doctor and take whatever the doctor is prescribing them, but for me that is the unnatural way. Some people might question things like drinking ayahuasca, they would think it was way too weird."

In my eyes, Rolf came to represent a now rarely practiced, but time-honored, approach to healing: that of the vision quest, where the "goal is to get back inside nature to hear her original medical voice." Even today, healers in the Amazon, rather than maintaining an objective distance from their object of study, use their own body as their research laboratory to "diagnose and cure illness through subjective links between themselves and nature. They present their own bodies, and they heal by the actual health emanating from their being. Training is literally death, rebirth, empowerment" (Grossinger 2005).

Such training is often a calling, not a rational decision, involving as it may reckoning with serious disease within oneself. To heal, whether under the guidance of a mature shaman or not, is an initiation in the healing path itself. I was moved, therefore, to interview Rolf, not only to document what is his process of healing HIV, but also to give a snapshot of what such a healing apprenticeship within the *vegetalista* tradition of Amazonian shamanism looks like.

Rolf's treatment is not his first immersion in *vegetalismo*. A year previous, he had worked with another *curandero* in the area of Iquitos, who stated outright that he could cure HIV, and initiated Rolf into the synergy of diet, purge, and work with the psychoactive brew ayahuasca, which constitutes jungle medicine.

Rolf now sees such statements, possibly meant to lure in the ayahuasca tourist dollar, as "dangerous, because you give someone hope, and if that hope doesn't get fulfilled, the disappointment is bigger. That is exactly what happened. It was a very strict diet, with meditations, but I came back and the test results were worse."

The diet, one of the lesser known elements of Amazonian healing, required withdrawal into isolation and virtual fasting while drinking medicines prepared from the plants sarsaparilla, uña de gato (cat's claw), and purging with the bark of the ojé tree and the emetic huancahui (also known as yawar panga). His final nine days were spent in bed. "I couldn't leave my room, everything was brought to me. I couldn't talk to anyone."

Yet, despite the absence of a cure, there were other important healing outcomes. Rolf's energy was restored to a post-HIV level, and he found his medications functioned better. He was visibly healthier, his skin clean and eyes clear, to such a degree his friends were initially pleasantly shocked by the visible change in his aspect. All of this Rolf attributed to the strictness of his diet. Beyond his feeling of internal integration, his perspective had also changed. Being cured of HIV was no longer tantamount – healing the conditions that had allowed HIV in his body was. Although he had come to recognize the limitations of the *curandero* he was working with, Rolf was convinced that Amazonian shamanism was his path.

"Love was missing," said Rolf, reflecting on the *curandero*'s conduct toward his patients and his lack of veneration for the plants. Under the guidance of his current *curandero,* Juan, Rolf has begun

> In indigenous styles of medicine, which give equal importance to curing as the West, healing, from Old English hælan "to make whole, sound and well," may also involve searching out the hidden origin of the disease in the body/mind.

apprenticing in the *vegetalista's* communion with plants. "Before, I didn't relate with the plants, but now when I drink my tamamuri, I light a mapacho cigarette and blow smoke on them first.[1] There's some sacredness going on, which gives me a deeper sense of connecting to my heart."

Previously, Rolf also felt disconnected from his own healing process. "It was a very passive time. I had my little cabin, I drank my drink everyday. I stayed alone and had my diet of two fish and bananas with no salt. This time I'm much more active."

Not only is Rolf, at Juan's recommendation, not living in isolation, but he is engaging in active work with the visionary plant ayahuasca, which for Rolf is now key: "During those ten weeks of strict diet I did not attend any ayahuasca ceremonies. In the few ayahuasca sessions I had with the previous *curandero*, there were very few visions and much more purging going on."

Due to the catalytic and pedagogical nature of visionary plants, working with ayahuasca, in tandem with other healing plants, is allowing Rolf to take on the role of "a healer for myself, and possibly to learn how to help other people in their own healing process. This may be part of my healing."

"There is no evidence that Juan can cure HIV," he said, "and I had to ask myself, why am I not just taking the Western medications and, like many people, being happy with it? They have a few side effects, but you can have a natural life span. I realized that I need a method that can bring me to a deeper healing, not just of the virus but also of what my being, my soul, my whole existence means."

Rather than treat HIV as an enemy to be vanquished, Rolf has made it his ally: "The virus is guiding me toward, 'This is where you need to bring healing to yourself.' And I still don't know if I will be delivered of the virus." He paused, and then added, "That's almost beside the point."

Cooking Ayahuasca.

In Rolf's work with ayahuasca, a word which translates from Quechua, the language of the original Incans, as "the vine of the spirits," one can see the delicate balance between visionary experience and healing work in the Amazonian tradition. Whereas some healers rightly emphasize purging in treatment of serious disease, it can be at the cost of developing insight into the etiology of the disease on the part of the patient – an insight that traditionally was reserved for the shaman alone.

On the other hand, the Western fascination with visions can divorce them from the reality that Amazonian healing works on the level of the body. Much of Rolf's struggle during ayahuasca sessions has been with fear of an overwhelming, dark, otherness, as the plants in his body have found their alignment with his condition and begun flushing him out.

Orchestrating such a delicate balance of forces is the responsibility the shaman, who uses icaros, or healing songs, to activate the healing power of the plants used in treatment. Without his icaros, the plants such as tamamuri, came renaco, and chiri sanango that Rolf are taking would lack the vitality to be effective in his treatment. The vitalizing agent is the indigenous communion with what are conceived of as the spirits of the plants. When asked by a researcher if there had been any scientific studies of the plants he uses for healing, Juan answered, "All the plants that we are taking, I have already processed through my body. If it's passed through my body, it's good to share. The laboratory is my body, yes?"

Due to Juan's focus on healing, visions occur more as benchmarks at his center for traditional medicine than as the menu of the day.

When I asked Rolf about the visionary contents of his ayahuasca ceremonies, he related an experience in that otherworldly landscape of spirits integral to the practice of *vegetalismo* that seems particularly illustrative of the plant's catalytic power. When the body is prepared properly, then the visionary experience *is* an act of healing.[2]

Moving beyond the sense of terrible otherness he had confronted repeatedly, he entered more deeply into his core self. "I felt very safe, and I could observe everything. Things were done to me, but I wasn't taken over. Initially, I felt soothing vibrations in the body, really feeling my entire body vibrating. At some point I could see, feel, how my body turned into a grid, and how that grid was very gently expanding, and showing me how this grid was part of a bigger grid."

---

1   South American black tobacco, which is 18 times stronger in nicotine content, is used extensively as a medicinal plant in the Amazon, both for cleansing and as "the director of other plants." A shaman blows tobacco smoke over remedies in order to potentiate its healing powers.

2   It's good to remember that ancient and indigenous cultures do not separate the act of seeing from experiencing. For example, seeing "in Greek as well as Latin – when the verb occurs in an emotionally charged context – always means more than just 'to observe' or 'to witness' something; it means 'to experience,' 'to be involved in a meaningful event'" (Luck 2001). Seeing into something, therefore, is a participatory and potentially investigative act.

Anthropologist David Lewis-Williams, best known for his work in reinterpreting the Paleolithic cave art of Europe, has come up with a rough-hewn model to explain the stages of visionary experience, based both in cognitive science and anthropological work, including Reichel-Dolmatoff's among the Tukano Indians of Colombia.

Following the stages of what Lewis-Williams (2002) calls the "intensified trajectory" of human consciousness, Rolf passed first through the initial stage of entoptic phenomenon – associated with "geometric visual percepts," such as "dots, grids, zigzags, nested catenary curves, and meandering lines"[3] and entered the second stage of construal, where the interpretive faculty of the mind struggles with the significance of the imagery:

"Everything is part of this grid," he continued. "I have a feeling that in future sessions they might show me this grid is something far more than I see and feel my body to be. At other times, when I've seen that grid, I've also seen liquids running through it."

Finally, entering the third stage of the intensified trajectory, which Lewis-Williams mistakes for "hallucinations," Rolf moved beyond the ordinary constraints of the human mind. This stage is often entered as a spiritual landscape at the end of the entoptic tunnel.[4] Such visions are considered to have significant diagnostic and problem-solving potential in Amazonian medicine: "This all happened when I was lying down, and then I sat up and observed myself. I was thinking, 'this body is new', everything felt completely different. Any limitations I impose on myself are limitations of the mind. Also that the virus doesn't belong here, the virus is about accident, it got there because of low self-worth and having desires for sensations. I saw because the grid is so loose, anything can be taken out, and anything else can be put in. It's like a membrane, through which things can be easily exchanged, rather than having the virus locked in the body. The most amazing thing was my mind wasn't chattering, like, "Yeah, don't think you can get rid of the virus…" It's the mind that can destroy many things, if you have those fearful, worrying thoughts. There was a feeling of total peace, calmness, centeredness, including the thought, 'Even if I have the virus, I can live my life from this place of peace.'"

"So it would be better to have the virus and this calmness and insight than to not have the virus and be frantic?" I asked.

"That's the ultimate healing. All diseases come from the mind, and here my mind felt empty. It really felt empty. Every step was peaceful, with total awareness of what I do. I was also very tired, because I had to sit there for three or four hours."

Unlike the common image of hallucinations imposing themselves upon a passive recipient, healing work in visionary states requires a far more active, inquiring state of alertness than is usually maintained even in ordinary, waking consciousness:

"You have to stop that chattering mind, because many things your mind can't explain anyways. Juan told me about learning from the plants – you don't sit there like a schoolboy. Instead, you have to find the way that they communicate with you. It's good to learn about not seeing things as your mind sees them, because at times the mind comes from a place of fear. That last ceremony, I didn't feel limited. I did some yoga postures, and I thought, 'I can do any posture. It's my mind that's limiting me.' Some postures there might be a physical limitation, but if you open your mind to them, there's no reason you cannot achieve them. I became really clear how the mind is the culprit."

Rolf is now midway through his healing process, and will soon begin drinking the barks of the chulla chaqui caspi and ayahuma trees. The ayahuma, in particular, is known among the Ashaninca as a very powerful, ancient healer, who is connected with the spirit of the water and the animals of the water. When I asked Rolf to describe the action of the healing plants upon his system, he said, "I don't know if you can put it into words, because it's an energetic cleansing. I still envision that the DNA has to be rewritten, a reprogramming has to take place."

If Rolf is right, Amazonian medicine has been way ahead of the biotech companies for thousands of years. The proof of the curative efficacy of Juan's treatment will come in mid-October, after Rolf has returned to his home in Amsterdam and waited a month to be tested for HIV. It won't be too surprising if he is cured; we have already documented one *curandero*'s successful removal of a brain tumor that Western medicine had been powerless to achieve (Tindall, 2008). But Rolf is no longer staking everything on a cure, tempered as he is from his previous disappointment. "It

> Whether it is worthwhile to cure a disease without healing the conditions that gave rise to it is not much considered by Western medicine, but if a disease is bringing an urgent life message to the patient, it may be folly to suppress its teaching.

might take another twenty years," he said, "but I'm not only here for my own healing, that would be too selfish. It might be the healing happens through helping others."

And what if, in October, Rolf finds he has not only experienced healing but is also cured of HIV? Will he be ignored by the medical establishment? Or will there be a sudden influx to the Peruvian Amazon by researchers from pharma-

---

[3] Such visionary patterns occur in Amazonian Shipibo art, which originate in what their shamans claim are the energetic signatures of each living thing – and which are necessary to access in a work of deep healing.
[4] Think of Alice falling down the rabbit hole to Wonderland.

ceutical companies and entrepreneurs in the holistic health field, who will throw around money or invite Juan to travel abroad with his cures?

An ethnobotanist Mark Plotkin discovered when he documented another Amazonian healer successfully curing severe Type 2 diabetes (Plotkin, 2000), such medicines are not easily removed from their matrix: the jungle and the shaman's intimate communication with the plants (Tindall, 2007). Without the potentiating power of the icaros and *vegetalismo*'s communion with the innate intelligence of healing plants, researchers will scrutinize Juan's medicines in vain for that "silver bullet" molecule they can patent, reduce to a white powder and make a fortune on. One must ask, if Juan chooses to travel out of the jungle and share his medicinal techniques, would it turn out as culturally dislocated as the vanquished warrior shaman Geronimo selling souvenirs of himself at the World Fair?

Without comprehending the *vegetalismo* tradition from within, which requires a long arduous apprenticeship such as Rolf is taking his first steps in, there will be little bridging of this rich medicinal practice into the West.

Postscript

Tests after Rolf's return from the healing center show that he was not cured of HIV. In fact, his CD4 levels are lower and his viral load levels higher than they were after his initial treatment, and he is dealing with infections that indicate his immune system was overtaxed during his months in the jungle. Rolf is now recuperating on mild doses of antibiotics.

The events and interviews documented in this article occurred during our visit to the healing center when Juan was in residence, and at the time of our departure, Rolf's treatment appeared to be well underway. Around the same time, however, Juan also left for Canada, leaving Rolf's care in charge of his youthful apprentice.

Under the new dietary regime established by Juan, salty foods, even sugary desserts, began appearing upon the table. When questioned, Rolf was assured that the *dieta antigua,* eschewing salt, spices,

Peruvian ayahuasca.

and fruit, much less processed sugar, was no longer necessary. Rolf gave in, because he needed some salt to keep up his strength, but with some reservations, since it had been the dietary component of his previous treatment that had been so restorative to his health. Shortly after Rolf's partner Coen, a practitioner of ayurvedic medicine, arrived, something more ominous appeared. Rolf developed an infection in his leg.

The days that followed Coen relates with gallow's humor: the shaman's apprentice, lacking adequate direction to treat Rolf's leg injury, which was oozing puss and displaying holes the size of gunshot wounds, kept switching from one medicinal plant to another. Rolf kept hobbling down the steep slope to participate in ayahuasca sessions every few days, supported on the arm of Coen.

Both men knew that one takes one's life into one's hands upon catching that boat upriver in the Amazon, and that shamanism often works on the brink of paradox, yet the treatment, to which Rolf remained unswervingly committed, was now felt as a purgatory. Observing the signs that Rolf's immune system was weakened, Coen lived in fear that toxemia might carry Rolf off in a day. Coen confessed, "I prayed harder than I've ever prayed in my life."

Rolf's condition, as is often the case in the jungle, was not viewed as cause for alarm upon Juan's return. As Coen paced the floor, the *curandero* lingered in the compound below for a day before making his appearance in Rolf's cabin. Juan's mere presence restored calm, however, as he proceeded to apply a Western medicinal salve to the open wounds. He assured Rolf the infection was actually a sign of the disease leaving the body. The salve was effective in bringing down the swelling, and Coen thought, with some irony, it would have been effective much sooner if Juan had been in active communication with his apprentice.

Juan invited Rolf to stay for another month. Even at that stage, Juan may have been incorrect in his evaluation of the progress of Rolf's treatment, however, if Rolf's most recent tests are an indicator of its efficacy.

As veteran observers of the practice of curanderismo, we had already become alarmed from a distance. In our previous experience, we had observed that the therapeutic container was critical to allowing the catalyzing work of the plants to succeed. For example, in documenting the healing of Carolina, a patient with a brain tumor some years earlier, we had observed that, "Healing comes from re-embedding the patient into a living cosmology, a hierarchy of being that supports and gives meaning to their process of living and dying" (Tindall 2007). In the secure container provided by the jungle setting and the *curandero*'s attentions, we had watched as Carolina radically opened herself, allowing the healing power of nature, which is the basis of the *curandero*'s art, to permeate her.

A tough city girl from Santiago, Chile, Carolina found herself, in the midst of her treatment, spontaneously hugging the trees in the jungle. As I had speculated at the time, "Her embracing of the trees in the forest probably did as much to heal her as any of the plants she drank or any of the rituals conducted by the *curandero*. I dare say it fulfilled one of the deepest needs of our souls: to live in a reciprocal universe, a benevolent order in which, when we call out, we are resoundingly heard. This, I now believe, is the true basis of shamanism" (Tindall 2007).

This was the delicate container we were apprehensive hadn't been established for Rolf. Upon Rolf and Coen's departure from Peru, Juan himself recognized that Rolf's healing process was not yet complete. Although Rolf wished for the plants to continue their work in his body, his condition was such he went in for testing sooner rather than later. Since the dire results came back, Rolf has managed to take the outcome philosophically and with a sense of humor.

Although a cure has eluded Rolf, in our conversation over Skype, as he dabbed at the puss flowing from his eye, he told me he is still grateful for the experience: "Healing has taken place. I feel more peaceful, balanced. What I have learned is to find that silent place within me, where now by just focusing on my breath I can access this place. I have a bigger need to spend time in silence, quiet."

He also added, "I can imagine more benefits emerging once my body is back to regular health. I have no severe health issues, but many little ones, including feeling depressed. I expect another shift once these complaints are gone – right now I'm just busy with my body."

Rolf is also asking, however, "If Juan communicates with the plants, how could it not have been clear my treatment wasn't working? I made my decisions from hope, my drive to get rid of the virus. I am very confused how the Maestro couldn't have known."

Rolf and his partner are keeping in mind that their effort was a pioneering one. Unlike the many reports of successful cures of cancer using indigenous medicine, there are none of cures for HIV: "The virus may be stronger than the healers think – it's cleverer than a cancer. If it were easy, many more people would be going to the Amazon."

When and where the circumstances will arise to effectively address the treatment of HIV through *vegetalismo* again is anyone's guess. Nor is the game over with for Rolf, for whom an analysis of the outcome of his treatment based in the effective cause alone may be too limited. Significant long term benefits may still be in the offing. As

> Since the HIV, my life has become more colorful and intense. Not always pleasant, but certainly more intense and I'm saying "Yes" to life much more than I used to.

was observed above, the practice of shamanism often involves death, rebirth and empowerment.

Certainly, Rolf's faith in the healing potential of plant-based shamanic practices remains unshaken, as well as his commitment to his work: "More than ever I know my work is in the healing profession." Perhaps Rolf is right. Perhaps serious disease, when all is said and done, is our final wake up call, even a merciful avatar: "I always thought if I hadn't gotten HIV, I would've gotten something else, something to kick my ass," said Rolf. "It was needed for me to wake up. And since the HIV, my life has become more colorful and intense. Not always pleasant, but certainly more intense and I'm saying "Yes" to life much more than I used to."

References

Dobkin de Rios, M., & Rumrill, Roger. (2008). *A Hallucinogenic Tea, Laced with Controversy.* Westport, CT: Praeger Publishers, p. 76.

Grossinger, R. (2005). *Planet Medicine: Origins.* (Vol. 1). Berkeley: North Atlantic Books, p. 97.

Luck, G. (2001) *"The Road to Eleusis."* American Journal of Philology 122:1, 135-138.

Lewis-Williams, D. (2002) *The Mind in the Cave: Consciousness and the Origins of Art.* London: Thames and Hudson, 125.

Plotkin, M. (2000) *Medicine Quest.* New York: Viking. Xi-xvi, 203-206.

Tindall, R. (2008). *The Jaguar that Roams the Mind.* Vermont: Park Street Press, 183-199.

Tindall, R. (2007). *Mark Plotkin, the Shaman's Apprentice, on Indigenous Healing and Western Medicine.* Retrieved July 10, 2009, from http://www.mariri.net/rainforest-blog/?p=14.

Picture of the AIDS quilt.

Walking in the Shaman's Shoes

A Transformational Walk with the Family Soul

Francesca Mason Boring

Imagine ancient healing circles, campfires burning while wisdom teachings were given from one generation to the next. The charcoaled embers of those fires remain in the soil on every continent. The stories which were told at the fire may be embedded in our genetic memory. The legends of magic and trauma may be stored in our cellular memory. It may also be that each of us is surrounded by a 'knowing field' which holds the accumulative traumas and secrets of those from whom we descend.

The shaman often had the gift of 'knowing'. The healer was able to see ancestral influences and invoke the conversation which could put wandering souls to rest. The mystery of shamanic technology even brings proven and repeatable results. Yet modern psychiatric and medical models' "best practice" often conflict with the way of the shaman. Providing evidence that one could engage the dead in a therapeutic conversation is not a prerequisite for most Ph.D.s.

First, I acknowledge that the word *shaman* does not have its roots in Native American indigenous culture, the context in which I live—instead, it comes from Siberia. The terms *medicine person, shaman, healer* and *seer* have been used interchangeably in our common vernacular; academic disciplines focused on these iconic labels to catalog and debate their cultural criteria and existence.

There seems to be a modern need to reference and investigate shamans, and descriptions of shamanic states of consciousness explored by aboriginal (including Native American) traditions and spiritual practices are varied and complex. This need reflects an emergent quest for *something*. That *something* can be found in what might be called *neoshamanism*.

The discussion evokes more questions than answers. Let us start by exploring the *shamanic state of consciousness*, a term coined by anthropologist Michael Harner to refer to the particular state that a shaman must attain to be able to communicate with the spirits (1990). According to health, mind and body therapist Jeanne Achterberg (1987), the shamanic state of consciousness (SSC) is the very essence of shamanism and critical to the premise that the shaman is the past and present master of the imagination as healer.

As we start to explore the shaman's world, we find that rigid rules don't apply, and semantics become tricky. In his *Encyclopedia of Native American Healing*, William S. Lyon (1996) noted, "Some scholars object to the use of this term, opting to define shamanic abilities/activities as the products of several different levels/states of consciousness. For example, some shamans remember their trance possessions, while others do not" (p. 249).

Perhaps the quest for Shamanism is

Francesca Mason Boring, lecturer, facilitator/trainer of Systems Constellation, enrolled Shoshone, is the author of Connecting to *Our Ancestral Past: Healing through Family Constellations, Ceremony, and Ritual* (North Atlantic Books, 2012), *Feather Medicine, Walking in Shoshone Dreamtime: A Family System Constellation* (Llumina Press, 2004), *Coyote Dance* (Llumina Press, 2005), and *Botschaften aus dem indigenen Feld* (Carl-Auer, 2009). Fran advises and writes for The Knowing Field (London, England). Instrumental in the development of Nature and Environmental Constellations, Constellation as Ceremony and Community Constellations, Francesca is inspired by the work of Bert Hellinger and her own indigenous teachers and elders. See www.allmyrelationsconstellations.com

not a yearning for a single particular academic history or cultural atmosphere, but a holistic search for a Spirit Way. Those who look for shamanism may really be searching for what already exists within their *own* family ancestry and field: the echo of a *universal indigenous* spiritual tradition.

Back to Your Roots: The Universal Indigenous

Many people in the United States and Canada have family histories that draw on spiritual roots, traditions and ancestral blood in other lands. But modern people have a nagging sense of isolation and disconnection from their ancestors and extended family; and modern psychology, at least humanistic psychology, has been misconstrued to indicate that self-actualization is the desired spiritual life path, the aboriginal "Red Road" of living in harmony with nature, the Creator and all living beings. Urbanites, academics and displaced teens may be seeking their own connection to their ancestors and the natural world. Frustrated clerics, cynics and seekers might be in need of a legitimate vision quest.

As a Shoshone and bicultural woman, I have a sense that many of the links that modern people yearn for in the quest for a shaman are available in the therapeutic discipline of *Family Constellation*, when it is facilitated in a phenomenological way. The phenomenological approach in constellation work utilizes that world view which the shaman integrated with ease. It involves a way of seeing solutions using information beyond our normal objective reality. This phenomenological way of working does not involve client assessment, treatment plan and intervention. Rather, it involves waiting, listening, and allowing an organic healing movement which comes from a field beyond the cognitive mind.

Family Constellation is an orphan with many parents. Some wrestle to assign the "designer" of the method. Is this the work of Virginia Satir? Is this the work that was introduced by Bert Hellinger, a German therapist, philosopher who, with the support of many others, moved the work into international circles? Perhaps 'Family, Human & Natural Systems Constellation' and 'Constellation as Ceremony' are smooth stones that they found at the river that has been seen and recognized as a normal part of the landscape in many cultures, places and times.

Family Constellation is a therapeutic method that has gained popularity throughout Europe and many other parts of the world. It is a method by which facilitators and individuals unravel those barriers in life that people carry as a result of historical or trans-generational trauma.

The basic process is simple. According to Family Constellation pioneer Bertold Ulsamer (2003),

> the person doing the constellation chooses a representative for each important member of his or her family, including a representative for him – or herself. Without any prior plan, and without speaking or explaining, the client then places the representatives in spatial relationship to one another, showing them which direction to face, but nothing more. When all the representatives have been placed, the client is again seated and remains a spectator from this point on, observing the actions and words of the course leader and the representatives. The course leader asks the representatives to pay attention to the impact of their positions on their feelings, thoughts or sensory awareness. After a short while, the course leader asks each representative for a report of his or her experience. Tensions in the family are revealed through the reports of representatives. The leader then searches for a resolution for this individual family, with continual feedback from the representatives as things change in the constellation. These resolutions seem to reflect certain orders, or patterns, which Bert Hellinger has documented over many years with this work (p. 19).

In the Knowing Field

In constellation therapy, participants often have a stunning ability to "know" things about the family system that reveal the core of an individual's fears or symptoms. Often that core trauma had actually occurred in generations prior to the client's birth.

In Family Constellation, participants and the facilitator are often able to "know" many specific things that help unravel unhealthy entanglements within a family system. If several generations ago, a number of ancestors had frozen to death, in a constellation, those who stood as representatives of that traumatized family (and in some instances participants who were supporting the healing of a family) might feel unusually cold.

Some representatives in the constellation might report a fear of freezing

> The shaman often had the gift of 'knowing'. The healer was able to see ancestral influences and invoke the conversation which could put wandering souls to rest. The mystery of shamanic technology even brings proven and repeatable results.

while they stand as a representative of someone in the family system. This can occur even if no one in the group knows the other representatives or their family history. In some cases, individuals who came with an issue may not even know their *own* family history in detail, and only later discover the traumatic event.

This history of family groups facing freezing temperatures and even mass deaths from cold was not an unusual occurrence in the past, particularly where forced migrations put people in danger. These forced migrations often resonated with a collective field of trauma; they impacted whole extended family groups or communities. People were being displaced from what was familiar, so there was the grief of leaving. Those descended from such a collective trauma may have anxieties in their lives that they cannot explain. Inexplicably, they may have an avoidance of travel, or a visceral dislike of colder landscapes; they may experience intense anxiety when preparing to leave their house. Often the echoes of these systemic traumas have been with people ever since they can remember, even before they had any life experience that could account for such a level of discomfort.

This *knowing*, or *knowing field*, previously attributed to shamans and traditional healers, seems to be available to facilitators of Family Constellation, as well as representatives of family members when they stand in to help clarify painful family dynamics. The field extends even to the participants who are seated in the workshop but not actively standing in the constellation.

The knowing demonstrates itself in many ways. Some experience knowing dreams in relation to the constellations that are about to happen. Some experience a smell that may specify a moment in the family history. For instance, someone may smell fresh-baked bread; it may be that in the family, several generations ago there lived a family of bakers who were impacted by an epidemic and suffered multiple deaths of family, loss of home and business all at once. Such a dramatic level of loss may leave a psychic footprint on subsequent generations. In one constellation regarding difficulty with relationships, several people in the circle smelled and tasted alcohol. Alcoholism had not been mentioned as a factor in the family history, but as indicated by the knowing field, it had a definite impact on the ability to trust.

Family Constellation can resolve longstanding issues that competent Western psychotherapy has not been able to impact. Utilizing the healing support of others in the group, the facilitator and the Circle formation create a healing ceremony. But the emotions evoked can be extremely powerful. Family Constellation practitioner Daan van Kampenhout (2001) analyzes this intensity:

> In Family Constellations, the representatives often take on the suffering of others in a direct way. For example, if someone was never able to express grief, the representative standing in his place may shed tears and suffer the pain of mourning in his place. Every inner shift a representative makes is a step taken for someone else; the representative is doing it for the other person. Because a representative does not usually personally know the individual he represents, there is little danger of taking on the suffering out of entanglements. Besides that, the representatives are chosen by somebody else to do the job; they cannot voluntarily choose to represent a specific person. A representative takes on suffering during the constellation and afterwards, steps back into his own life, giving back the responsibility to the one he represented. Although the form of the constellation obviously differs from those of shamanic healing rituals, when suffering is taken on for others in order to help them, both constellations and old shamanic rituals make use of the same spiritual principles (p. 45).

The working model of psychotherapy that focuses on identifying pathology is very different than that of Native traditional healing. In many Native traditions, illness and distress are more often identified as teachers, something that will help us learn along the Path. Distress or lack of ease may result from someone who had died not being at peace, or the living not being willing to release the deceased to complete their journey. In a view of illness that differs greatly from the Western perspective, one can find healing without necessarily having a problem. As French psychotherapist Patrick Obissier (2003) notes, "The concept of a 'problem' is naturally subjective. What poses a problem to one person does not necessarily poise a problem to another. Whether something is a problem depends on cultural and ancestral predisposition" (p. 26).

Deep resonance for constellation work came easily when I read the title of one of Bert Hellinger's many books: *Acknowledging What Is*. A common Shoshone expression is "It is just so." This is just what is; this is just what is true. Not a judgment, not a diagnosis—just a statement of truth.

That all people have within their ancient roots some indigenous field allows an opening to wisdom arising within our individual family fields. Citizens of the U.S., Canada, and Australia (countries of immigrants and descendents of immigrants), still have within their knowing "fields" the motherlands that once held their ancestors blood and bones. A person may, on the surface, have no history, no roots, and no remembrance of traditions. However, within the family field, our ancestry, our genetic memory, and within our blood, there is a remembrance of old songs and ceremonies and a different way of knowing. The ancestries that refugees and transplanted peoples deny or dismiss still contain within their fields truths, teachings and secrets which can restore strength and release our sense of isolation.

Hellinger's Movements of the Soul, or Spirit Mind

Among the pioneers of Family Constellation therapy, Bert Hellinger's work greatly expands and hones that of earlier proponents of a similar kind of constellation work: examination of relationship through special representation, observation of dynamics in family systems, structural theory regarding family dynamics.

> The shamanic state of consciousness (SSC) is the very essence of shamanism and critical to the premise that the shaman is the past and present master of the imagination as healer.

Hellinger was willing to bow to something that he called *movement of the soul*. This was a phenomenon that produced an organic movement among participants, which seemed consistently to support healing in a family system. He observed a connection between family members that was so supreme that he spoke of a *family soul*. Perhaps Hellinger's willingness to include this unpredictable movement was due to a number of years working with the Zulu people in Africa (Hellinger, 2006).

In addition to the movements of the soul (also sometimes referred to as the *spirit mind*), Hellinger began a discussion about group conscience. Deep group loyalty is actually what many human beings have used as their barometer for good and evil; this group consensus and support actually serves as a collective conscience. Many of the horrible (and heroic) acts of humanity have been supported by some form of this group conscience. The genocide of Native Americans in the United States, slavery, the torture of prisoners in Abu Ghraib—all were approved within a group.

When it experiences a shift, this collective conscience carries severe implications for both families and individuals. At one level, the soul knows that an inhumane act has been perpetrated; however, the mind and the group conscience can be supported to such a degree that an individual uses the collective ideology as rationalization.

Sometimes, even generations later, at the level of the soul, descendents of those perpetrators attempt to make amends by unconsciously standing with the victims. Perhaps in limiting their own opportunities, perhaps in having difficulty experiencing joy, perhaps through illness, one attempts to bring back a balance, to rectify the wrongs that were done to another in good conscience under the family name. Through constellation work, the spirits of victims who are not at rest can find peace. The descendents of the perpetrators can finally step away from the family guilt and acknowledge their own human bond with both victims and perpetrators of family traumas.

Learning from the Ancestors

Untitled ledger drawing of dance.

Before coming to constellation work, I was nurtured in a place of trans-generational knowing dreams. Since the age of 17, I have had dreams of ancestors. Originally, they were my ancestors preparing me for deaths of those around me. Certainly, in modern Western suburbia, this was not considered normal. A referral to psychotherapy by school administrators inspired my mother, who was from a Shoshone reservation on the Nevada/Idaho border, to send me to my maternal grandmother, who was a "dreamer."

Now, some 40 years later, this *knowing* dreaming is part of my waking hours as well. It is not preceded by any chant or rattle; it is just like breathing. Now, there are times when the ancestors of others come to share some frustration or pain they had no possibility to resolve in their life. Often their only wish is that their anguish not be visited on their descendents.

When I was introduced to constellation work, I felt that the knowing field was very much the same as the place of dreams and vision I had learned so much from in my earlier life. The knowing field of Family Constellations felt very familiar to me, though sometimes shrouded with psychological verbiage and a Western worldview that wanted all the perimeters of knowing to be defined and contained.

Family Constellation, originally heavily influenced by the German nuclear family and urban dynamics, examined the inter-relationships of mother, father, grandparents and children. In Native American communities, there is a waking, walking memory that we are all connected to. What I have seen, having facilitated constellations in Germany, Switzerland, Holland, Singapore, Canada and the United States, is that at the level of the soul, we all remember how extended our family truly is. In this state, many learn to remember what it was like when we were deeply connected to the land, the animals and the trees.

Under the Tribal Tent

We all originated in the *tent*. We were

> Those who look for shamanism may really be searching for what already exists within their own family ancestry and field: the echo of a universal indigenous spiritual tradition.

all originally tribal. Deep in our DNA, our family field, our indigenous knowing, we remember these fierce loyalties, the certainty and reliability of bonds. Now (so distant from that place and time for some), many modern people feel adrift, and are in fact in a kind of spiritual forgetfulness. "What was that? What do I remember? What is that which I no longer consciously remember? Did I ever *know*?"

In Family Constellations, often people are able to experience in a holographic way what it is that they have always known at the level of the soul. In a constellation, people *re-member* the connection between themselves and their parents, siblings and partners. They become strengthened by the gifts of their ancestors and learn to separate themselves from the traumas and limitations of their predecessors. (In constellation work, many facilitators use the term *re-member* to refer to the dual experience in which forgotten or excluded members of a family are brought back into the family system through remembering in a more accurate way the isolation of their trauma and the impact of their trans-generational pain on a family or descendent.)

Expanded Constellations

As Family Constellation has moved into other arenas and cultures, the work has expanded to include a systemic examination of organizational stresses and difficult dynamics in corporate systems. Organizational Constellations focuses on increasing profit, productivity and flow in a business.

Another addition to the constellation field has been the growth of Nature and Environmental Constellation, and the inclusion of nature as a resource even in some family constellations. The participation of and focus on nature in constellation work is contingent upon the facilitator being comfortable with those fields. For many who are coming from a psychotherapeutic background, or who are synthesizing constellation in a purely constructivist, structural way, the introduction of nature into a family constellation is superfluous. For other facilitators, it is a natural resource.

Melding Western and Indigenous Wisdom

Much of my work in Family Constellation is influenced by Bert Hellinger's *orders of love* and his introduction of the movements of the soul. Much of my work is also influenced by Native traditions and my own learning through knowing dreams of the past 40 years, as well as the shared experience of that knowing from my grandmothers and other Native Elders who instructed me (with and without my solicitation).

Family Constellation can gently integrate the indigenous knowing fields into Western practices. We are challenged to look at the limits of our disciplines, and see where the knowing field may have the capacity to fill in the gaps. Metaphorically: 'Constellations' may provide a sort of reintroduction of chicken soup as good medicine rather than an 'old wives tale.'

Kete Women and Children in front of Birch Bark Tent.

The wisdom traditions throughout the world have many common elements associated with shamanism or aboriginal healing methodologies that are almost universal. One such early technology is smudging. Throughout Asia, Western and Eastern Europe, the Americas, Australia and Africa, people have burned incense or herbs to honor or appease the dead and to reaffirm life and commit to living in a way that honors the ancestors. The African medicine man or shaman may burn Impepho, among a long list of plants and herbs. Some Australian aboriginal peoples may burn a combination of aromatic plants including eucalyptus and gum tree leaves. North American Native Americans and Canadian First Nations people burn white sage, sweet grass, cedar and other regional plants or herbs, depending upon their environment. Europe not long ago had its own history of burning incense made of local pitch or herbs. China, Japan, India and many East Asian cultures have a history of burning joss sticks to honor and appease the dead.

Smudging has been a universal indigenous technology, worldwide. Modern medicine, psychology and aspects of Western academia have made a concerted effort to discredit this universal tool. Fortunately, many spiritual psychologists and holistic health practitioners have begun to make room for a wider variety of belief systems and practices than their own individual immediate familial cultural tradition.

Perhaps in this universal technique lies the balm of some human knowing. It is one of those things that we can concede we may not be able to completely fathom in a cognitive way. This tool of the shaman may be used by facilitators to prepare a room or a group, or used in closing a workshop when constellation work is done in a phenomenological way, and particularly when the ethnicity of the group would indicate such a practice when working with resolving issues between the living and the dead.

Using Shamanic Elements in Constellation Work

Elements previously relegated to the field of shamanism are easily integrated when Family and other Systems Constellation are facilitated and experienced in a phenomenological manner. Aspects that have historically been identified with shamanic or spirit-way traditions present in constellation work include:

- Incorporating the ancestors as resources
- The participation of the natural world in healing
- Transcending linear time during, before and after a constellation
- Synchronicity before, during and after a constellation workshop supporting a movement
- Field magnetics, or pulling people together with systemic dynamics in common. These field magnetics are reminiscent of the understanding of destiny. In constellation, the

pattern of attraction of individuals with similar family fates is often seen. "Those two were meant to be together."
- Consciousness that everything is connected
- Trusting the knowing that comes from the ancestral field
- Helping the dead who are not at peace find rest
- Helping the dead who are not aware of their own death to find their place with the dead
- Helping the living bereaved to let go of the dead

These are not concepts subscribed to by all facilitators. Some state firmly that there is no magic in constellation work; it is about linear concepts regarding systemic structures that have overriding therapeutic impact on participants. Others are clear to state that synchronicity before, during and after a constellation are illusion, and nothing exceeds the impact of the experience of the constellation itself.

As with many disciplines, the facilitator's worldview impacts both what is seen and perceived. An observation of particular structures that benefit family and human systems (such as organizational systems) is very helpful in constellation work. And there are facilitators of constellation who are able to combine awareness of systems with an easy integration of intuitive (sometimes seemingly extra-rational) knowing.

Meanwhile, multiple disciplines have found ease with this omnipresent human knowing. John Veltheim (1999) utilizes an innate healing wisdom in a multidimensional healing methodology called *Body Talk*. Combining kinesiology and a series of protocols, the method Body Talk is applied to introduce balance to the body, mind, spirit and emotions, enlisting the innate wisdom of the body.

The body's morphogenetic and morphic fields are also investigated and discussed extensively by biologist Rupert Sheldrake (2003):

> Morphogenetic fields are part of a larger class of fields, called *morphic fields*, all of which contain inherent memory given by morphic resonance… Morphic fields also underlie our perceptions, thoughts and other mental processes. The morphic fields of mental activities are called *mental fields*. Through mental fields, the extended mind reaches out into the environment through attention and intention, and connects with other members of social groups. These fields help explain telepathy, the sense of being stared at, clairvoyance, and psychokinesis. They may also help in the understanding of premonitions and precognitions through intentions projecting them into the future (p. 279).

Making a Place for Magic

As quickly as much of the world wakes to the universality of the knowing field and the spirit way, the *seeing* of the shaman, there is a push-back to squeeze the world back into a small box. We may be at an interesting juncture. Will the pathologies of psychotherapy and the Cartesian medical model rule the day, or will we really be able to open to what we begin to *know* works in healing? Will our institutions be fluid enough to incorporate deep, holistic healing, the healing of the shaman that nurtures body, mind and spirit, and hears the needs and interplay of the living and the dead?

Be it ritual, integral knowing, Family Constellation, releasing the dead and the pain of generations long past, appropriate medical or psychological intervention, or an intuited combination of several methodologies, how do we openly invite healing—and address the resistance of the modern status quo that rejects the efficacy of magic?

What will we be allowed to know? As parapsychology researcher and author Dean Radin (2006) states, "…consensus opinions advance through authoritative persuasion… Use of rhetorical tactics like ridicule [are] especially powerful persuaders in science, as few researchers are willing to risk their credibility and admit interest in 'what everyone knows' is merely superstitious nonsense" (p. 278-9). Modern man is challenged when faced with 'mystery.' One may feel most comfortable when faced with a miracle, to busy the mind searching for the 'sleight of hand'.

The Constellation Vision Quest

When I experienced the knowing field in Family Constellation and identified it as an indigenous field, very soon I began to equate it to the *vision quest*, the consummate spiritual activity of many Native American people. Again, the term has become a modern expression that sometimes carries traditional Native American implications, and at others simply describes any exercise in the search for one's soul and true meaning. New-age books and workshops are rife with the term, and some resources even support the concept legitimately.

In nature, there are many teachers. I remember my own elders often dating tribal stories back to "when the animals spoke." There was a time when the horse people, the coyote people, the mouse people… everyone spoke. Almost 40 years ago, when I asked my maternal grandmother (who lived to be more than 100), "When did the animals stop speaking?" she replied casually, "They did not stop speaking. The people stopped listening."

> Almost 40 years ago, when I asked my maternal grandmother (who lived to be more than 100), "When did the animals stop speaking?" she replied casually, "They did not stop speaking. The people stopped listening."

Facilitating Family Constellation

in the knowing field, it would have been irresponsible and disrespectful not to include the resources and healing influences from my own family field: the field of knowing dreams, the ancestral field that included relatives who had spoken with the animals with ease.

There is a dusty concept of animism and shamanism that misses the core of the experience. Historical Western interpretation has at times envisioned aboriginal people in an altered state, sometimes drug induced, disconnected, and having as the result of sleep deprivation or chemical disorientation a "vision" of an animal teacher. What this misses is the reciprocity of this experience. The participant is not "visited" by an animal or nature teacher solely because of their desire for spiritual enlightenment. The teacher (some being or element of the natural word) willingly and intentionally extends him/her/itself to the student.

Native and shamanistic traditions have a long history of seeing the world in an interconnected way. In Family Constellation, working as a facilitator with the knowing field, and having met others who were drawn to learning from the natural world, it was a natural progression that in many groups I would begin to include a Nature Constellation, which in many respects echoes the experiences found in a vision quest.

Authors Larry P. Alitken and Edwin W. Haller (1990) discuss the connection that we have with all of nature—flowers, deer, the earth, all living and non-living things and the Creator. They speak of the Native American tradition of experiencing, viscerally and spiritually, other beings in a living, breathing way. In their book *Two Cultures Meet: Pathways for American Indians to Medicine,* they introduce in a gentle and pragmatic way, the benefit in being able to walk in the path of being connected, aware and respectful of all life.

Creating Connections: Nature Constellation in Action

Much of Western psychology and

> As a human being, I am only part of life. I am here on the earth for a short time. I am here with all my relations: The two legged, the four legged, the six legged, the eight legged, all those who swim, crawl and fly.

medicine is about the self. Symptoms and pathology are "isolated." In the work of Bert Hellinger and the subsequent emerging phenomenological approach to constellation work, the focus is interrelatedness. This acknowledges the connectedness of human to family, human to human in organizations, and nature to human and nature to nature. The relationship of the living to the dead is

New life emerges.

also woven deep into the fiber of many Native American and aboriginal traditions.

In some constellations, the individual knew of no person in their family who could stabilize them or support them in going forward in a positive direction in life. In these situations, Hellinger would sometimes place individual representatives for "the greater soul," "life" or "destiny."

Taking Family Constellation therapy into aboriginal communities, it was a natural step to place representatives for Nature, Mother Earth, a Tree, the Wind or Water. Each of these entities has its own traditional field of supporting healing and can often bring great peace to a person seeking something tactile to hold on to as a resource before and after the session.

In one type of Nature Constellation, the representative can stand within the field as an animal that invites them to stand as their representative. Instructing this type of constellation is crucial; it must be by invitation. The representative does not say, "I want to stand for a bear" and proceed to do so. Nor does the facilitator assign the roles. This vision quest requires a deep listening, waiting and seeking to discover which animal or nature being is inviting one to stand as its representative.

This constellation has deep implications. One person who was deeply stressed and exhausted was invited to stand as a representative for a deciduous tree. The individual sensed, while standing as a representative for the tree, the changing of the seasons. There was a deep sense of relief when there was the shared experience of winter. In that space, the individual described experiencing greater rest, quiet and peace in a span of a few minutes than she had gained in the past three years. In keeping with the tradition of a vision quest, many participants begin to report years later that they have continued to find teachings from a single Nature Constellation.

There are profound implications for us and for nature through constellation. The shaman steps into the animal world, and the spirit world can be heard again in the knowing field of Family and Nature Constellations. The soul can again journey to understand the interconnectedness and knowing that we have distanced ourselves from to win the mantle of being modern.

Vast Spaces

Challenges exist. Those traditions that worked with interconnectedness and vision quests had the container of communal teaching about community and responsibility. The vision quest was part of life and could inform a person how better to live with others. To attempt to integrate this concept into a Western model stretches a number of boundaries. Healing as something nurtured by a knowing field or the soul and not exclusively under the directive of a doctor or psychotherapist is not a modern Western concept. More individuals are being called to include this other venue in their soul's journey in one form or another.

Family Constellation may be used by practitioners in many disciplines, though it is my belief that phenomenological ways of working may not be for everyone, facilitator or client. Family Constellation is not a panacea. I often tell people at the beginning of workshops that Family Constellation is not a substitute for necessary medical care. It is not a substitute for serious psychotherapy. It is not a substitute for good nutrition. It is not a substitute for prayer, and it is not a substitute for good common sense.

The shaman, medicine person or traditional healer was often understood (within those communities that long held such practices) to be assigned by the Creator to their duties, or supported by the spirit world. This licensure might be defined as grandiosity by Western thought. Our modern approach is to give license, based upon studies, and other human beings regulate that license.

In many wisdom traditions, one does not always have permission to work with an individual. Anecdotally, I have heard that the best medicine men referred at least half of their patients to other practitioners. Although many shamanic traditions had apprenticeships, the ability to work effectively in a knowing field was not something that could be assigned externally. Certainly, it was also something that could be taken away.

Humility:
The Essential Ingredient

Perhaps the greatest factor in walking in the shoes of the shaman, whether as a facilitator or a participant in Family, Human, Nature, or Community Constellation, is humility as an essential ingredient.

I may be afforded an opportunity to know something that facilitates healing, but I am only a human being. As a human being, I am only part of life. I am here on the earth for a short time. I am here with all my relations: The two legged, the four legged, the six legged, the eight legged—all those who swim, crawl and fly.

Grateful that we have met on this path for a short while, I wish you a good walk, and leave you with the Great Spirit Prayer. The author is 'Anonymous.' The prayer is often said or read in many healing ceremonies and gatherings:

Oh, Great Spirit,
whose voice I hear in the wind,
Whose breath gives life to all the world.

Hear me;
I need your strength and wisdom.

Let me walk in beauty, and make my eyes ever behold the red and purple sunset.

Make my hands respect the things you have made and my ears sharp to hear your voice.

Make me wise so that I may understand the things you have taught my people.

Help me to remain calm and strong in the face of all that comes towards me.

Let me learn the lessons you have hidden in every leaf and rock.

Help me seek pure thoughts and act with the intention of helping others.

Help me find compassion without empathy overwhelming me.

I seek strength, not to be greater than my brother, but to fight my greatest enemy,

Myself.

Make me always ready to come to you with clean hands and straight eyes.

So when life fades, as the fading sunset, my spirit may come to you without shame.

References

Achterberg, Jeanne (1987). *"The Shaman: Master Healer in the Imaginary Realm"* In Shamanism: an Expanded View of Reality", Edited by Shirley Nicholson. 103-124, Wheaton, IL: Theosophical Publishing House.

Alitken, Larry P., & Haller, Edwin W. (1990). *Two cultures meet: Pathways for American Indians to medicine.* Garrett Park, MD: University of Minnesota Garrett Park Press.

Harner, Michael. (1990) *The way of the shaman,* San Francisco, Harper San Francisco.

Hellinger, Bert. (2006) *No waves without the ocean: Experiences and thoughts,* (transl. Jutta ten Herkel and Sally Tombleson). Heidelberg, Germany: Carl-Aur-Systeme, Verlag,

Lyon, William S. (1996). *Encyclopedia of Native American Healing.* New York, London: W.W. Norton & Company.

Obissier, Patrick. (2003). *Biogeneology: Decoding the psychic roots of illness; freedom from the ancestral origins of disease.* Gap, France: Le Souffle d'Or; Inner Traditions International; (English transl. 2006). Rochester, VT: Healing Arts Press.

Radin, Dean. (2006). *Entangled minds: Extrasensory experiences in a quantum reality.* New York, NY: Paraview.

Sheldrake, Rupert. (2003). *The sense of being stared at, and other unexplained powers of the human mind.* New York, NY: Three Rivers Press, Crown Publishing Group, Random House.

Ulsamer, Bertold. (2003). *The art and practice of family constellations: Leading family constellations as developed by Bert Hellinger* (transl. Colleen Beaumont). Heidelberg, Germany: Carl Auer-Systeme Verlag.

van Kampenhout, Daan. (2001). *Images of the soul: The workings of the soul in shamanic rituals and family constellation.* Heidelberg, Germany: Carl Auer-Systeme Verlag.

Veltheim, John. (1999). *The body talk system: The missing link to optimum health.* Sarasota, FL: Pa Rama, Inc.

The Contemporary Artist as Shaman

Denita M. Benyshek

The Healing Path.

Standing in the dark, I sense a large room around me, seemingly empty. I walk forward. A soft, white glow appears in the distance. I walk towards the light. Gradually the glow acquires the form of a white mare, muscular, with a broad breast, and ears nearly touching the high ceiling. I stretch up towards her gracefully curving neck. My hands reach her shoulder. Desire lifts me up and onto her strong back. She walks slowly forward, majestically.

We enter a long, hallway with harsh fluorescent lights, linoleum floors, and sterile white walls. Other hallways lead off right and left, but the mare continues forward, carrying me through and out of the institution.

We move through a large medieval cloister. Tall, elegant columns frame the courtyard, forming narrow arcades around a central fountain. Moonlight illuminates pale stone and gently splashing water, casting deep shadows into mysterious corners. My mare walks on, incessantly forward. Riding bareback, I feel the fluid movement of her muscles and the potential of her strength. I know she belongs to me – and I to her.

We travel north, parallel to, but not upon, a narrow asphalt highway. All other constructs of humanity are absent. The surrounding trees are sparse and short. We are in the tundra of Alaska.

As a young artist, I did not make the traditional pilgrimage to New York City. Instead, I went the opposite direction. I wanted to create without influence from contemporary art or the coastal art scenes. For 15 years, I taught visual arts, modern dance, and performance art in the Native villages of the Alaskan bush. Amidst that vast silence, far from metropolitan distractions, I traveled into the frontier of my soul. There I heard my unique artist's voice. Illuminated by the slow flowing rose, coral, and gold of the midnight sun, my work became my own.

I look through the scope between the mare's pert ears. Gentle hills dissolve into hazy distance. The mare and I converse telepathically, a light chat, becoming acquainted as friends. Then, full body conviction seizes me: I must keep her with me.

How?

At this fenceless time in my life, I don't have a home. My peripatetic existence is without stall or pasture. I fly village to village with few possessions. When I occasionally return to Seattle, I

Denita Benyshek, a professional visionary artist and cross-disciplinary scholar, explores the relationship between shamanism and artistic creativity through visions, dreams, artwork, and autobiographical stories. Using the definition of shaman constructed by anthropologist Ruth-Inge Heinze, Benyshek demonstrates how artists shamanically journey to other realms, undergo destruction and rebirth, unite opposites, and receive inspiration from nonordinary states of mind, transcendent consciousness, and sacred spirits. Painter Paul Cezanne, choreographer Martha Graham, sculptor Constantin Brancusi, and Mande blacksmiths provide examples of shamanic creative processes. Additional studies may find that shamanic artists contribute to individual, societal, and planetary healing.

sleep in my black Ford van and shower in friends' apartments, making sporadic income from fashion modeling and scene painting for theatres, dance companies, and films.

My mare cannot graze on the runways of bush planes or fashion shows. She cannot sleep in my van or travel in my suitcase. Resolving to find a home for both of us, I awaken from what Jungians, inspired by American Indian and African cultures, call a "big dream" (e.g., Whitmont, 1969, p. 225). Big dreams are revealed either through repetition or extraordinary vividness and power. Often, the dream serves as a conduit for communication with a power animal. The messages may be literal and urge immediate enactment of the dream. Precognitive dreams, wisdom-becoming and awareness-awakening, may presage the future.

The Institution

A decade later, I completed a Masters of Fine Arts degree. In my final thesis, I described numinous personal experiences that arose during the act of painting. I used words such as enlightenment and epiphany. The painting department "head" vehemently crossed out all spiritual references with a thick, red pen. Few words of meaning survived the attack. He ordered a complete rewrite.

After the head strode away, I was defiant, "No, I won't rewrite. This censored thesis, with every red marker scar, perfectly represents my experience at this school." I gave the slashed thesis to the department secretary, instructed her to place it in my file, and walked away down the long institutional hallway of harsh fluorescent light, linoleum floors, and sterile white walls. Other hallways led off right and left, but I continued forward.

In the sanctuary of my studio, I drew a prayer to my mare protector, asking her for the strength to hold onto my genuine self.

In the privacy of my journal, I wrote:
I am White Horse in the home of my heart.

The White Horse

I entered a seminar on shamanism and sat upon a rigid chair amidst other seated students. With pen and notebook ready, I expected a didactic presentation.

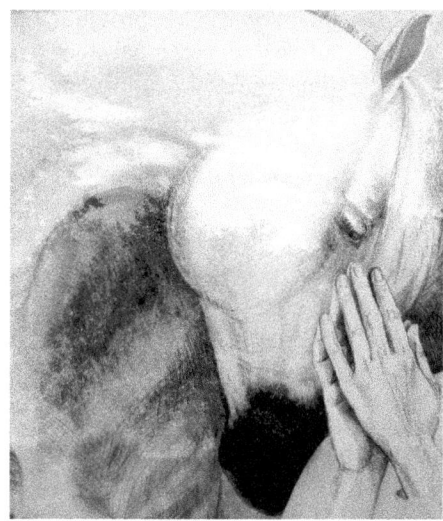
Praying to the White Mare.

Instead, Dr. Heinze instructed us to lie down and close our eyes. Upon trance-inducing drum beats, Dr. Heinze led us into visionary journeys. She encouraged us to "ride the drum."

During the fourth session of drumming, my white mare returned.

Without saddle, bridle, reins, or clothing, I ride. A nude man loosely embraces me, riding behind me. Along a wide, sandy beach, naked to joy, we are ecstatically galloping, galloping, galloping.
Free.
We rode where the ocean meets and strokes the earth.

But, galloping over the beach sands of time, we were not the only riders of the white horse. In Siberia, the shaman's drum is oft conceived as a galloping white horse. Ethnologist Dioszegi (1968) learned from the Karagasy that "while shamanizing, they call the drum white horse or reindeer bull. The denominations of each part also prove that the drum represents an animal, more specifically, an animal for riding" (p. 260).

Carried on throbbing drum hoof beats, I walk through the perpetually revolving door. The glass shatters and falls. I kneel, carefully, laboriously, stacking and restacking the bricks of future plans. The towers repeatedly collapse. I stand naked on the wide green prairie of my youth. Picking handfuls of long-bladed grass, I put the prairie inside me, filling myself with grass. I would move the prairie into me. I would become the prairie.

Four brief drum sessions led me beyond the charted bounds of consensual reality into a land of living images, rapidly back along the path of stolen dreams, opening the gate of lost hope, and carrying me into golden sunlight. There, wind-blown grass bowed towards the distant horizon and then reached towards a sky of robin's egg blue.

Such visionary realms were already familiar to me, often entered and traversed during artistic acts of creativity. I wondered: do shamans and artists embark on comparable journeys, following analogous paths down into darkness, heading back into the past, climbing up to momentous view points, and arriving at like destinations? If these routes were charted on one map, to what extent would the journeys be the same, indicating the existence of an artist-shaman?

Contemporary Artists and Shamanism

Art historians and art critics sometimes refer to contemporary artists as shamans. Rushing (1986) noted how "shamanic intent" influenced the painting of Jackson Pollock (p. 283). Such statements romanticize artists, waving a magic wand of words, without offering comprehensive support for assertions regarding shamanism. Similarly, Weiss (1995) equated Kandinsky's creative process with shamanizing. However, she did not provide support for her assertion. Levy (1993) and Tucker (1992) relied

> In the privacy of my journal, I wrote: I am White Horse in the home of my heart.

heavily on the classic book by Eliade (1951/1964), *Shamanism: Archaic Techniques of Ecstasy.*

Several problems arise from use of Eliade (1951/1964) as primary reference. First, Eliade has been criticized for cross-cultural overgeneralization of certain culture-specific myths (Kirk, 1973, 1974.). Second, Eliade did not perform his own field work, instead using field reports from graduate students (Heinze, June, 2005) and also synthesizing the

Calling from the Mirror.

research of others (Kehoe, 2000) Third, the original publication of Eliade's *Shamanism* occurred 58 years ago and does not reflect recent thought regarding shamanism.

Furthermore, the art historians did not utilize data regarding the creative process to explain how shamanic practices are like artistic creativity. And finally, art historians cannot speak from the perspective of artists who share personal experiences from decades of creative work.

Who is a Shaman?

For Heinze (1997), a shaman performs community service in response to psychological, social, or spiritual needs, mediates between different states of consciousness, and creates connection to "higher powers" in a culturally meaningful and understood form. Are these actions also performed by contemporary artists?

Shamanic Journey

Through trance states and altered states of consciousness, shamans take journeys to other realms to gain knowledge, increase power, and help individuals and societies (Harner, 1986). "The pre-eminently shamanic technique is the passage from one cosmic region to another," commented Eliade (1951/1964, p. 259). Noel (1997) identified an imaginal reality of subjective experience where shamans work, further explained by Winkelman (2000) as operating through a "focus on internal visual imagery [that] provides an internal experiential focus, a figure-ground cognitive reversal that enhances the primacy of the internal imagetic reality to the degree that it provides an alternate experience to the external world" (pp. 85-85). The travel of artists through levels of consciousness is the equivalent of shamanic flights to other worlds.

Riding upon the horse of color, Cezanne entered a lower realm:

A painting is an abyss in which the eye is lost. All these tones circulate in the blood. One is revivified, born into the real world, one finds oneself, one becomes the painting. To love a painting, one must first have drunk deeply of it in long draughts. Lose consciousness. Descend with the painter into the dim tangled roots of things, and rise again from them in colors, be steeped in the light of them. (Knafo, 2002)

Cezanne descended into the abyss of the underworld, not to view the picturesque beauty of buds, leaves, or branches, but in search of tangled roots. He saw what is beneath appearances. In the ecstasy of seeing, the boundary dissolves between Cezanne and the painting.

As Cezanne returned to consensual reality, he reintegrated. Then, the "dim tangled roots" changed in light. Painting functions as a mother through which Cezanne is reborn. Likewise, after suffering, the shamanic initiate is reborn into a new identity.

A similar process of loss, destruction, and rebirth is found in the repertoire of choreographer Martha Graham. Graham knew that to create, the artist must be destroyed. Moreover, the medium of dance must also be destroyed. Beiswanger (1980) described how Graham choreographed:

Companion to this act of 'destruction' was the effort to lay bare the impulses from which the affirmative stuff of art spring....Furthermore, the desire to draw from deep wells was largely inhibited in the American character itself, so far as conscious art-making was concerned. (pp. 144-145)

Graham's creative process broke up "the surface of dance (the conventional idioms, the accepted evasions, the brittle shell)....so that the underlying structure could be disclosed" (Beiswanger, p. 145) – like a skeleton, "an emotional core....a soul...bared" (Beiswanger, p. 146) upon which new dances were created. Thus, an art medium may also be reborn into a new identity. Similarly, initiation into shamanism often includes the transformative process of deconstruction or dismemberment, followed by reconstruction and rebirth (Grim, 1987; Vitebsky, 1995).

Accessing the Inaccessible

Artists may access spirit realms through creative processes. When the seer receives spiritual insight, divine presence is often felt as white or golden light. Such experiences have been described as illumination or enlightenment by artists. Matisse contrasted representational painters with enlightened artists:

Most painters require direct contact with objects in order to feel that they exist, and can only reproduce them under strictly physical conditions. They look for an exterior light to illuminate them internally. Whereas the artist or the poet possesses an interior light which transforms objects to make a new world of them – sensitive, organized, a living world which is in itself an infallible sign of the Divinity, a reflection of Divinity.

That is how you can explain the role of the reality created by art as

> The travel of artists through levels of consciousness is the equivalent of shamanic flights to other worlds.

opposed to objective reality – by its non-material essence. (in Flam, 1994, p. 61)

How does essence enter an artist? The recipient is filled with divine guidance and arousal, causing enlivening and exalting emotion. As its Latin root suggests, inspiration is the act of taking spirit in. In Mongolia, the same word indicates artistic inspiration and spirit possession. "Shamanism is wholly the world of inspiration…it is the expression of human world and inspiration world… inspiration is the agent of the secret world" (Batbayar, personal communication, March 21, 2011).

The "belief in the inspired source of creativity…is, today, a tenet not held by many," noted Funk (2000, p. 55). However, Funk's personal encounters with numerous reports of numinous experience and nonordinary states of inspiration led him to question the rational and environmental theories regarding creativity. Funk argued in favor of considering the "non-ordinary states of mind that, to varying degrees, can be ascribed to transpersonal sources of inspiration" (p. 55).

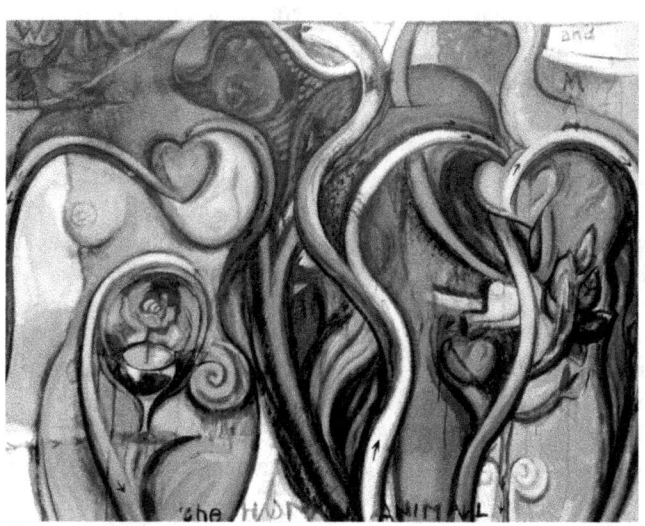
Woman and Man: The Human Animal.

While transcendence may be experienced at any developmental level or age, Funk believed "transpersonal experiences are more likely to occur to those at higher developmental levels since one's ego boundaries become ever more permeable and open to the numinous…." (p. 58). He commented," in the transpersonal view, people we label geniuses have the ability, some of the time at least, to access this transcendent consciousness" (p. 58). During mystical communion with the infinite, with spirit or the divine, the artist perceives "cosmic patterns existing beyond Newtonian space and time" (p. 59).

Shamans are renowned for presumptive paranormal abilities, including precognition, telepathy, clairvoyance, levitation, divination, changing weather, seeing souls of the dead and hearing their conversations (Kalweit, 1992; Krippner, 2000; Rogo, 1990). Funk (2000) mentioned that "creators reported insights in dreams, sometimes of a paranormal nature; that is, they seemed to exhibit some degree of extrasensory knowledge (ESP)" (p. 63). One incident of creative ESP or merging of different levels of reality and consciousness began in a dream:

I paint upon a canvas pinned to a wall. I stand near the painting, working intently, swimming in creative flow. I feel the weight of gravity. Light pours down upon the wall, from somewhere behind me, from up high. On the canvas, I work on the upper left corner which is white but thick with oil paint. I add black lines that curve this way and that. I observe the dream and think, "This is not like a dream. This is like reality."

I float a green glaze over the white and black, making a transparent tint. I stand so close to the painting, without stepping back. I never view the entire work.

Five months later, at the Ucross Foundation, the director gave me a private studio with a high bank of clerestory windows illuminating the opposite wall. I pinned rectangles of canvas onto this wall. After completing all preconceived paintings, I decided to paint spontaneously.

I stood near the painting. I drew the torsos of a woman and a man. The transparent figures, including their hearts and the rivers of blood veins, physically interconnect. I felt the weight of gravity. I painted two spirals, indicating the woman's ovaries and fallopian tubes, merging in the wine glass of her womb.

Light poured down upon the wall,

> I observe the dream and think, "This is not like a dream. This is like reality."

from behind me, from up high.

Two more spirals represented the generative power of the man. I worked on the upper left corner which was white but thick with oil paint, painting about creativity. I added black lines that curved this way and that. Black lines and luminous, jewel-like colors suggested stained glass. I floated a transparent green glaze over the white and black corner.

Suddenly, as though lightening struck me, I remembered the dream, the dream which was now waking reality. My knees weakened. Life presented a choice: sit down or fall down. I sat.

Confused, my concept of time fell apart, dismembered, and irreparable. Past, present, and future no longer fit on a linear continuum. How could I dream about the studio at the art foundation before my physical arrival, before my grant application was considered? How did I see the painting before the act of "spontaneous" creativity? I thought I was making a stream of choices in the moment, yet the painting obviously already existed somewhere, with all choices made. If the painting already existed, who was the artist, me or some entity speaking through me? How could I orient myself in nonlinear time and nonlocal space? Did I exist in three realms, past, present, and future, at the same time? Could I travel, like a shaman, not only up and down to different realms, but also backwards and forwards in time? Is time a level of consciousness? How did I access this?

Such questions, according to Krippner (2006, personal communication) are "only a problem if one thinks in linear terms. Most indigenous shamans come from societies with different time models." Certainly, my dream pushed me towards a different understanding of time and space.

May (1975) recognized the power of artists as "frontier scouts who go out ahead of the rest of us to explore the future" (pp. 146-147). Time is generally considered the fourth dimension of space. Is the fourth dimension of time explored during liminal acts such as painting, dreaming, and shamanizing?

Shamans transcend conventional Western concepts of space and time (Kraus, 1972). Likewise, during the creative journey, artists readily exit what Bourdieu (1990) referred to as "homogenous, continuous space" (p. 84).

In a 6' tall watercolor, *The Healing Path* (see right), I painted a child with golden curls. Later, my golden son is born (see below). As a toddler, he was adamantly against a haircut. I thought, "It's his hair. It's his choice." His hair grew until the blond curls reached down his back. He did not care what others thought, proudly declaring "I'm a boy!"

In a previous essay, I included a photograph of my son at age three with his long, golden curls. Several pages later, I inserted a detail from *The Healing Path*. During the final edit, I recognized the golden child in both images. Only then did I realize that the spirit of painting knew my son – *fifteen years before his birth*. Once again, painting had provided access to another realm.

Hatterer (1965) commented on artistic access of "dreamlike or depersonalized states… during the creative act. Such states represent the artist's extreme degree of flexibility in ascending and descending to different levels of consciousness" (p. 29).

Higher Powers

McNaughton (1988) studied sub-Saharan Mande, or Bamana, blacksmiths. *Nyama,* a free floating, ubiquitous, natural, and mystical force, is believed to fuel and empower all blacksmith activities.

The Healing Path.

This power is a prerequisite to all action and a by-product of every act. In massive concentrations, *nyama* can be dangerous, even deadly; however, blacksmith shamanic practices harness this power.

The challenge of working iron demands great *nyama*. Each hammer blow directs and implants additional *nyama* into the metal. In the crafted object, great power reservoirs are constructed and contained through skill and lengthy production. *Nyama* is carried by utilitarian objects such as lamps, tools such as spear blades, and ritual objects such as sacred staffs. Mande blacksmiths qualify as archetypal artists who, as defined by d'Azavedo (1973), maintain the bridge linking sacred and secular. By capturing *nyama* spirit in the understood form of iron objects, the blacksmiths occupy the common ground between shamanism and artistic creativity.

Understood Form

Constantin Brancusi was born in a Romanian village. As a young man, he walked to Paris. While urban sophisticates scorned folk art, Brancusi nurtured and sustained his relationship with peasant life through wood carving.

Folk art provided Brancusi with animist infused design and content. His sculptures embodied the spirit world in abstract form. Brancusi spoke of portraying a fish, not through illustrative depiction, but by expressing "the flesh of its spirit" (Shanes, u.d.) The artist believed "what is real is not the external form but the essence of things" (Wood, 1999, pp. 341-342).

In the *Endless Column* (see opposite page), one part of an ensemble of monuments comprising a war memorial, Brancusi refers to a folk legend about a pillar that holds up heaven. The column is approached through *Kiss Gate (see opposite page).*

The title refers to an earlier sculpture, *The Kiss*. In this work, Brancusi used two concentric ovals to indicate the eyes of lovers, merged in gaze. This ultimate act of seeing, where boundaries dissolve, became a central motif of the monument. The sculptor created a liminal zone where visitors enter another realm.

The gate joined male and female, in a loving monument to peace, a passage way via the ecstasy of sexuality, and a means of transcendence. Such liminal zones are also typically respected and mastered by shamans.

Hansen (2005) wrote of "liminal persons, phenomena, and events [that] tend to blur boundaries, upset classification schemes, and foster ambivalence and ambiguity. Such conditions are dangerous, but they can also be a source of supernatural power" (p. 3).

Hans Janos Benyshek van Wyk Age 3

Nurturing connection with the ineffable, Brancusi clothed spirit in art. Thus, the sculptor satisfies the requirement that shamans connect to higher powers in an understood form.

Healing the Split

By attempting to heal splits, unite opposites, and re-member society, shamans and artists provide community service. Venezuelan artist Javier Tellez collaborated with the "human cannonball", David Smith. To transcend the division between Mexico and the United States, Tellez shot Smith from a cannon. Tellez soared over the barricade separating the two countries (Spagat, 2005). Granted status as a Korean Living National Treasure, shaman Kim Kum-hwa performed trance rituals in Los Angeles to create community harmony after riots (Looseleaf, 2002).

Wilber (1979) asserted "The ultimate metaphysical secret… is that there are no boundaries in the universe" (p. 31). Instead of being enclosed by boundaries, the shaman relates to a holistic, ever-expanding web of continuous relationships.

Artist Jaune Quick-to-See-Smith, a Native American, perceived her role as "a harbinger, a mediator, and a bridge builder. My art, my life experience and my tribal ties are totally enmeshed. I go from one community with messages to the other, and I try to enlighten people" (Server, Binstock, Connors, Everett, & Hartigan, 1996). Many artists attempt to heal splits in society and within individuals, reuniting what was separated, assembling a whole out of parts.

The Medium of Access

Regressive forces, according to Knafo (2002), "allow artists to frequent levels

The Endless Column.

of consciousness not usually accessible to most adults." From the Freudian box of psychopathology, the term "regression" bears a pejorative connotation. In Freudian theory, regression is a return to an earlier life stage, functioning as a defense mechanism and indicating mental pathology (Corsini, 2002). This definition implies backward movement and the presence of immature behaviors. Following Freud backwards, Kris believed creativity occurred during a return to an earlier developmental level (Corsini), during "regression in service of the ego" (p. 821).

Because creativity facilitated my developmental growth and psychological health, the term regression seems inappropriate to me. Perhaps, more accurately, the creative process is ego in service of regression. Ego serves by constructing an adequately strong, and flexible, container to "hold" the creative process. As Kremer (personal communication, July 9, 2011) noted, "This type of regression is far from a defense mechanism, it is a process of creating wholeness out of the depths of past experiences."

In contrast to the pathological concept of regression, Krippner (2000) offered an alternate concept, stating shamans "engage in activities that enable them to access information not ordinarily attainable by members of the social group that has granted them shamanic status." Consider the meaning of access. As a noun, access is a means of approaching, entering, communicating with, making use of, or exiting. As a verb, access obtains, reaches, or retrieves. Access allows multidirectional movement and relatedness through communication.

According to McNiff (1986), "artists typically have more direct and visceral contact with a realm that is available to every person" (p. 17). How is this realm formed into apprehensible form?

Consider the definition of medium. Medium means midway or between. As an intervening substance through which transmission occurs, art is a medium. Likewise, the artist is a medium, a person who communicates with other worlds, dimensions, or realms. Heinze (1982) studied shamans and mediums, concluding that both:

> … are individuals who mediate between different states of consciousness for those who seek immediate, personal experience of spiritual powers. Mediums and shamans fulfill spiritual and psychological needs which cannot be satisfied otherwise. Both have com-

Kiss Gate.

mand over a wide range of alternate states of consciousness which they use for the benefit of others. (p. 38)

Art for Cultural Healing

The shaman is recognized by the following actions: mediation between different states of consciousness, connection to higher powers, communication through understood forms, and service to community (Heinze, 1997). As demonstrated within this essay, all of these activities may be performed by artists. Why is this endeavor important?

The myth of progress built a house-of-cards foundation for our society. During the past century, the flaws in this *weltanschaung* became increasingly obvious, with increased crime, environmental degradation, and horrific wars (Hoppal, 1996). In response, a growing number of people became interested in shamanism. Heinze (1991) recognized the validity of the twentieth century shaman who emerges "whenever an environment develops needs… it is the individual shaman who translates the sacred into the secular in a language s/he creates along the way." (p. 17).

If the shaman-artist can alleviate suffering, nurture empathy, strengthen societal bonds, and raise awareness of the sacred, then additional studies will contribute to individual, societal, and planetary healing. Our survival may depend, in part, on the work of the shaman-artist.

References

d'Azevedo, W. L. (1973). Sources of Gola Artistry. In W. L. d'Azevedo (Ed.), *The traditional artist in African societies*: Indiana University Press.

Beiswanger, G. (1980). Martha Graham: A perspective. In B. Morgan (Ed.), *Martha Graham: Sixteen dances in photographs* (pp. 143-148). New York, NY: Dobbs Ferry. Original publication 1941.

Bourdieu, P. (1990). *The logic of practice* (R. Nice, Trans.). Palo Alto, CA: Stanford University Press.

Corsini, R. (2002). *Dictionary of Psychology*. New York, NY: Brunner-Routledge. Emily Dickinson. Retrieved January 10, 2009 from: www.gutenberg.org.

Dioszegi, V. (1968). *Tracing Shamans in Siberia*. Oosterhout, The Netherlands: Anthropological Publications.

Flam, J. (1994). *Matisse on art*. Berkeley, CA: University of California Press.

Funk, J. (2000). Inspired creativity. In M. E. Miller & S. R. Cook-Greuter (Eds.), *Creativity, spirituality, and transcendence: Paths to integrity and wisdom in the mature self*, 55-72. Stamford, CT: Ablex Publishing.

Grim, J. A. (1987). *The shaman: Patterns of religious healing among the Ojibway Indians* (Vol. 165, The civilization of the American Indian series: Religion and spirituality). Norman, OK: University of Oklahoma Press.

Halifax, J. (1983). *Shaman: The wounded healer*. New York, NY: Crossroad Publishing.

Hansen, G. P. (2005). *Ghosts and liminality: A brief introduction*. Retrieved January 12, 2009, from http://www.tricksterbook.com

Harner, M. (1986). *The way of the shaman: A guide to power and healing*. San Francisco, CA: Harper & Row.

Hatterer, L.J. (1965). *The artist in society: Problems and treatment of the creative personality*. Brattleboro, VT: The Book Press.

Heinze, R. I. (1982). Shamans or mediums: Towards a definition of different states of consciousness. *Phoenix Journal of Transpersonal Psychology*, 6, 25-44.

Heinze, R. I. (1991). *Shamans of the twentieth century*. New York, NY: Irvington Publishers.

Heinze, R. (1993). Phoenix rising. In R. Heinze (Ed.) *Proceedings of the Tenth International Conference on Shamanism and Alternative Healing*, San Rafael, CA: Independent Scholars of Asia.

Heinze, R. (1997). *Trance and healing in Southeast Asia today* (2nd ed.). Berkeley, CA: Independent Scholars of Asia.

Heinze, R.I. (June, 2005). *Psychology of shamanism*. Symposium conducted at the Residential Conference of Saybrook Graduate School, San Francisco, CA.

Hoppal, M. (1996). Shamanism in a postmodern age. *Folklore, Estonian Folklore Archives*, 22. Institute of the Estonian Language. Retrieved May 30, 2005, from http://www.folklore.ee/Folklore/

Kalweit, H. (1992). *Shamans, healers, and medicine men*. Boston: Shambhala. (Original Publication 1987)

Kehoe, A. (2000). *Shamans and religion: An anthropological exploration in critical thinking*. London: Waveland Press.

Kirk, G.S. (1973). *Myth: Its meaning and functions*

Uncertainty Rides.

in ancient and other cultures. Berkeley, CA: University of California Press.

Kirk, G.S. (1974). *The nature of Greek myths*. Harmondsworth: Penguin Books.

Knafo. (2002). Revisiting Ernst Kris's concept of regression in the service of the ego in art. *Psychoanalytic Psychology*, 19, 24-49.

Kraus, R. F. (1972). A psychoanalytic interpretation of shamanism. *Psychoanalytic Review*, 59, 19-32.

Krippner, S. (2000). The epistemology and technologies of shamanic states of consciousness. Retrieved January 5, 2011 from http://www.stanleykrippner.com/papers/shamanic_epistemology.html.

Krippner, S. (2002). *Conflicting perspectives on shamans and shamanism: Points and counterpoints*. Paper presented at the American Psychological Association Conference, Chicago, IL.

La Barre, W. (1979). Shamanic origins of religion and medicine. *Journal of Psychedelic Drugs*, 2, 7-11.

Levy, M. (1993). *Technicians of ecstasy: Shamanism and the modern artist*. Norfolk, CT: Bramble Books.

Looseleaf, V. (2002). Performing arts invoking the spirit of peace: Through dance and costumes, a South Korean shaman seeks community harmony 10 years after the L.A. riots. *Los Angeles Times*, April 2, F49.

May, R. (1975). *The courage to create*. New York, NY: W.W. Norton & Company.

McNaughton, P. R. (1988). *The Mande blacksmiths: Knowledge, power, and art in West Africa*: Indiana University Press.

McNiff, S. (1986). *Educating the creative arts therapist: A profile of the profession*. London: Charles C. Thomas.

Noel, D.C. (1997). *The soul of shamanism: Western fantasies, imaginal realities*. New York, NY: Continuum.

Ripinsky-Naxon, M. (1993). *The nature of shamanism: Substance and function of a religious metaphor*. Albany, NY: State University of New York Press.

Rogo, D. S. (1990). Shamanism, ESP, and the paranormal. In S. Nicholson (Ed.), *Shamanism*, 133-137. Wheaton, IL: Theosophical Publishing House.

Rushing, W.J. (1986). Ritual and myth: Native American culture and Abstract Expressionism, in *The spiritual in art: Abstract Painting, 1890-1985*. Los Angeles, CA: Los Angeles County Museum of Art, 273-295.

Server, J. D., Binstock, J., Connors, A., Everett, G., & Hartigan, L. (1996). *American kaleidoscope: Themes and identities*. Retrieved November 24, 2008, from http://americanart2.si.edu/collections/exhibits/kscope.html

Shanes, E. (1989). *Constantin Brancusi: Interior images*. Retrieved November 9, 2005, from http://www.abbeville.com/Products/Product0896599299.htm.

Spagat, E. (2005). Human cannonball fired across U.S. border. *ABC News International*. Retrieved June 23, 2006 from http://abcnews.go.com/International.

Tucker, M. (1992). *Dreaming with open eyes: The shamanic spirit in 20th century art and culture*. San Francisco, CA: Aquarian/Harper.

Vicol, E. R. (2009). Kiss Gate by Constantin Brâncuși. Târgu Jiu, Romania: Retrieved March 3, 2009 from http://public-photo.net.

Vicol, E. R. (2009). The Endless Column by Constantin Brâncuși. Târgu Jiu, Romania: Retrieved March 3, 2009 from http://public-photo.net.

Weiss, P. (1995). *Kandinsky and old Russia: The artist as ethnographer and shaman*. New Haven, CT: Yale University Press.

Whitmont, E. C. (1969). *The symbolic quest: Basic concepts of analytical psychology*. New York, NY: Putnam for C.G. Jung Foundation for Analytical Psychology.

Wilbur, K. (1979). *No boundaries*. Boulder, CO: Shambhala Publications, Inc.

Winkelman, M. (2000). *Shamanism: The neural ecology of consciousness and healing*. Westport, CT: Bergin & Garvey.

The Indigenous Spiritual Healing Tradition in Calabria, Italy

Stanley Krippner, Michael Bova, Ashwin Budden, and Roberto Galante

In April 1995, before it became the Center for Alternative and Complimentary Medicine, the Office of Alternative Medicine (OAM) of the United States National Institutes of Health held a conference on research methodology. The objective of the conference was to evaluate the need for research in the field of complementary and alternative medicine (CAM), which they designed several working groups to address with consensus statements on a variety of essential topics. Given that most of the world's population uses and spends 60 billion dollars a year on complementary and alternative medicine, the OAM recognized the demand for its study. Americans spend approximately 17 billion dollars per year on CAM practices, many of which can be classified as traditional medicine, or ethnomedicine (Freeman, 2004; Traditional, 2003).

The OAM panel accepted a dual charge: To establish a definition of the field of complementary and alternative medicine for the purposes of identification and research, and to identify factors critical to a thorough and unbiased description of CAM systems; one that would support both quantitative and qualitative research. The panel defined CAM as follows:

Complementary and alternative medicine (CAM) is a broad domain of healing resources that encompasses all health systems, modalities, and practices and their accompanying theories and beliefs, other than those intrinsic to the politically dominant health system of a particular society or culture in a given historical period. CAM includes all such practices and ideas self-defined by their users as preventing or treating illness or promoting health and well being. Boundaries within CAM and between the CAM domain and the domain of the dominant system are not always sharp or fixed (O'Conner et al., 1997).

The panel's second goal was to establish a list of parameters for obtaining thorough descriptions of CAM systems. The list consisted of 13 categories first conceptualized by Hufford (1995):

This investigation was supported by the Chair for the Study of Consciousness, Saybrook Graduate School and Research Center, San Francisco, California. An earlier version was presented at the Annual Conference for the Study of Shamanism and Alternative Modes of Healing, San Rafael, California, September 2004, and was published in the proceedings of that conference. The authors express their appreciation to Jeffrey Kirkwood for his assistance in preparing the current version of this report.

Stanley Krippner, Ph.D., is professor of psychology at Saybrook University in Oakland, CA. He holds faculty appointments at the Universidade Holistica Internacional (Brasilia) and the Instituto de Medicina y Tecnologia Avanzada de la Conducta (Ciudad Juarez, Mexico). In 2002 he received the Award for Distinguished Contributions to Professional Hypnosis from Division 30, and APA's Award for Distinguished Contributions to the International Advancement of Psychology. He is a Fellow in the Association for Psychological Science, the Society for the Scientific Study of Religion and the Society for the Scientific Study of Sexuality.

Michael Bova is director of a psychiatric residential program with Northeast Community Center for Mental Health/Mental Retardation in Philadelphia, a Certified Recovery Educator with the Copeland Center for Wellness and Recovery, a Registered Art Therapist and on the Board of Directors of Consciousness Research and Training Project, Inc. Mike co-edited *Healing Tales: The Narrative Arts in Spiritual Traditions and Healing Stories: The Use of Narrative in Counseling and Psychotherapy.* In New York City, Mike was an art therapist at Bellevue Hospital Center, Department of Psychiatry, and research assistant to Stanley Krippner, Ph.D. at the Maimonides Medical Center's Dream Laboratory.

Ashwin Budden is a Senior Monitoring, Evaluation Officer and Global Health Scientist with PATH, an international nonprofit organization. He strives to empower cultural and community-level knowledge and action for health systems strengthening. Ashwin leverages evidence-based technologies to reduce health disparities and poverty in resource-limited settings. He was a Postdoctoral Research Scientist/Project Coordinator with Swiss Tropical and Public Health Institute.

Roberto Galante is an independent documentary filmmaker who uses his media to raise social consciousness. He directed and produced, *Una devozione a passo di danza/A Devotion with a Dance Step,* a documentary of the spiritual practices of Calabria's ROM and a recent project giving opportunity to the impoverished children of Mozambique. Roberto, originally from Matera, Italy, currently lives in Rome and Florence.

1. **Lexicon:** What are the specialized terms in the system?
2. **Taxonomy:** What classes of health and sickness does the system recognize and address?
3. **Epistemology:** How was the body of knowledge derived?
4. **Theories:** What are the key mechanisms understood to be?
5. **Goals for Interventions:** What are the primary goals of the system?
6. **Outcome Measures:** What constitutes a successful intervention?
7. **Social Organization:** Who uses and who practices the system?
8. **Specific Activities:** What do the practitioners do? What do they use?
9. **Responsibilities:** What are the responsibilities of the practitioners, patients, families, and community members?
10. **Scope:** How extensive are the system's applications?
11. **Analysis of Benefits and Barriers:** What are the risks and costs of the system?
12. **Views of Suffering and Death:** How does the system view suffering and death?
13. **Comparison and Interaction with Dominant System:** What does this system provide that the dominant system does not? How does this system interact with the dominant system?

A 14th category was provided for researchers, listing critical procedures for formal investigations of CAM systems. As this article is a descriptive account of Calabrian healers and healing practices, and not a formal assessment of their efficacy, we omit consideration of this final guideline.

A Brief History of Calabria

Calabria is renowned for its Mediterranean climate and history of conquest and settlement, reaching back to antiquity. This narrow strip of land in Southern Italy is 250 kilometers long, with no point beyond 40 kilometers from the coast. It is located between the Tyrrhenian and Ionian Seas, forming the "toe" of Italy's "boot." Human presence in the area dates back to the Paleolithic Age (as determined by the graffito in Cosenza), and artifacts of *Homo erectus* from about 700,000 years B.C.E. have been recovered in coastal areas. Researchers have discovered remnants of the Copper Age and Bronze Age, often in caves, as well as from the Iron Age (e.g., tombs in Cassano Ionio). When the Neolithic replaced the Paleolithic age, hunters converted to farming and founded the first villages roughly 3500 B.C.E. (Douglas, 1915/2001).

Calabria prehistory ended with colonization about 2000 B.C.E. The term "Italy" was derived from King Italo of the Enotrians or Arcadians, the first colonizers, and the name eventually spread to the entire peninsula. Beginning about 720 B.C.E., various city-states from Greece established rich and colorful colonies meriting the name *Magna Graecia* (i.e., "Greater Greece," a name that conveyed the comparatively small size of the mother country). *Magna Graecia* was well reputed for the health of its people, which was the result of proper territorial management and ecological balance. In those days, Calabria was known for its fertile farmlands, as well as its precious minerals and silks. Bronze tablets, unearthed in 1732, described how the Greek colonists were obliged to replace wind-swept or dead trees, and initiate land reclamation works.

Roman occupation brought with it a disregard for traditional ways of life, tilled fields instead of pastures, and a diminishing population. Malaria casualties took farmers away from their plots, and the uncultivated land produced marshes that compounded the spread of malaria (Danubio, Piro, & Tagarelli, 1999). In time, Italy became the center of the Roman Empire, which began its conquest of Calabria in about 275 B.C.E., defeating most of the Calabrian tribes within a few years. Many of these tribes supported Hannibal during the Second Punic War, but when Hannibal withdrew from Italy, he murdered his Calabrian allies to protect himself against facing them in battle should they defect to Rome. When the threat of Hannibal and Carthage ended, the Roman conquest of Calabria was completed in 211 B.C.E. The mass deforestation initiated by the Romans marked the first serious environmental challenge to the area. Such deforestation practices expanded marshy areas

Galante holding an ex voto.

> The goal of interventions, whether by prayer or the administration of herbal remedies, is to restore the vital force of the person who has fallen ill.... An intervention is considered successful if the vital force has been restored completely or partially. Restoration of this force allows someone to return to work, participate in family life, or rejoin community activities.

ideal for mosquitoes, and consequently malaria.

Goths and Visigoths invaded the area, sacked towns, and destroyed much of Calabria's Greek and Roman legacy. After the fall of Rome in the 4th century C.E., Byzantines dominated the area and named it "Calabria" in the 7th century C.E. Eastern Orthodox monks came with the Byzantine rulers, establishing monasteries and building shrines in the secluded mountains. Their rule lasted until the 11th century C.E. and was followed by the Normans, who arrived about 1050 C.E., creating the Kingdom of the South. The Swabians conquered the Normans in 1194 and cultivated one of the most civilized nations in that part of the world, the so-called "Kingdom of the Sun," in which people of different religious persuasions (e.g., Islamic, Greek Orthodox) lived as peaceful neighbors. This kingdom was followed by others, specifically Anjou in 1266 and Aragon in 1435, whose rulers created a system of feudalism in Spain, which conquered the area in 1503. Austrian domination began in 1707, followed by Bourbon rule in 1734. Under the title, "The Kingdom of the Two Sicilies," the Bourbons exploited local natural resources, especially what was left of the forests.

Even though they had lived in Italy for 12 centuries, probably longer than in any other place in Europe, Jews suffered persecution at the hands of the Catholic Church. The move dated back to 1290 when a Dominican friar accused the Jews of Apulia of putting a Christian child to death in mockery of the crucifixion of Jesus Christ. Calabrian Jews put up strong resistance to maltreatment, but organized Jewry virtually disappeared from southern Italy for several centuries after being expelled from Calabria in 1541. Frederick II and his immediate line protected the Jews of Sicily from the Crusaders and fanatical church authorities. However, Spain controlled Sicily during the years when Ferdinand and Isabella began the expulsion movement. Half of the Jewish population converted to Catholicism to prevent the loss of their property. Jewish communities slowly regained equality and emancipation only to be persecuted again during the Fascist era in the 20th century.

Another instance of gross intolerance occurred under Spanish rule in 1571, whereby the Waldenses were massacred for their allegiance to the Protestant movement in Europe. During the era of Islamic expansion, there were periodic forays by Muslims. Bourbon rule was interrupted by French domination from 1805 to 1816, and then resumed until Garibaldi unified Italy in the middle of the 19th century.

Reggio Calabria, View of the south zone of the city taken from the Rotonda Square, near the Saint Paul's Sanctuary.

In the meantime, disastrous agricultural practices had transformed the pristine coastlands into marshy and malarial swamps. Much of the population withdrew inland to avoid both malaria and pirate raids, primarily by the Saracens and the Turks from 1100 to 1800. Chapels and churches constructed by Roman Catholic monks helped preserve Calabria's culture. However, a major earthquake in 1783 destroyed many of those buildings and cultural artifacts.

In the early 19th century Secret societies abounded, working to help Garibaldi unify what is now Italy. The efforts of Garibaldi and supporting subversive groups were confirmed by a plebiscite on October 21, 1860 (Crawford, 1901).

The term "traditional southern Italy" refers to the provinces of Calabria, Abruzzi, Basilicata, Campagna, Molise, Puglia, and Sicily before World War II. After the war and the downfall of Fascism, Italy underwent a dramatic transformation that erased many folk traditions or modified them beyond recognition. This process was not as noticeable in Calabria as it was elsewhere due to both internal and external isolation (Orlando, 1998). This is one reason why folk healing traditions have survived over the millennia.

Calabria represents what Keates (1915/2001) has called a "savage Europe" that existed alongside its more "civilized" equivalent, a place where the Renaissance and the Enlightenment were unknown. It has always been among the regions of Europe most resistant to the Europeanizing process (p. 7) and, later, to industrialization. Without the production base that accompanies industrialization, many of the local agrarian-based customs remained, including folk health practices.

Keates (2001) continued, "Lonely, intractable, often impenetrably strange, sheltering the oddest of paradoxes, the weirdest of survivals and the darkest of secrets, Calabria endures, sullenly defiant of our modern manias for system, connection, and universal openness" (p. 8). However, it was not so much that Calabria waged an open or even covert revolution against Rome and its more contemporary rulers; its remoteness was responsible for neglect by the forces of modernization.

Our Observations of Contemporary Calabria

We encountered a somewhat different Calabria, as we stayed in the populated areas of the Locride (the topographical area that is claimed to have been influenced by the Greek city of Locroi Epizhyroi). Young adults and families with children are leaving their ancestral mountain villages for the coastal towns and cities to seek job opportunities and a modern lifestyle. The Calabria that was once resistant to change now ensures that all of its children learn foreign languages in school, and many of the children we met spoke or understood at least basic English. Computers are part of many households, and thus the world beyond their historical isolation is at their fingertips. Indeed, we suspect that the "savage culture" described by Keates (2001) is misleading, perhaps held over from colonialist attitudes.

Calabrian institutions and culture have been deeply influenced by Roman Catholic traditions. For example, the 12th century Calabrian abbot Joachim of Fiore first introduced the distinction between the Holy Spirit and Divine entity into Catholic theology (McGinn, 1985) and several folk healers in the area continue to evoke the Holy Spirit. The alleged conversation between St. Peter and Jesus Christ in the olive grove is salient evidence for the commingling influences of native belief and Catholicism, in which Christian figures are substituted for folk characters.

St. Peter: It takes too much time to collect all these small olives. Let's make them the size of melons.

Jesus Christ: Very well. But something awkward is bound to happen when you suggest improvements.

After the olives were enlarged one of them fell on top of St. Peter's head, ruining his new hat, provoking laughter on the part of Jesus Christ.

This story is typical of "folk Catholicism," practiced in mountainous and rural areas; a syncretic mixture of some pre-Christian elements with a dose of Roman Catholicism, still relatively resistant to much of the official church doctrine. The church traditionally allied with the elite political and economic classes, causing it to be viewed as a conspirator in the cultural and economic oppression of Calabrian peasants. Italy has been rife with anti-clericalism, in part because priests disapprove of such folk activities as non-religious festivals, birth control, and premarital sex. Nevertheless, Calabrian folk healing has a Roman Catholic veneer (Ramage & Clay, 1987).

Folk Healing Practices in Calabria

In 1898, A.D. White wrote that medical science has frequently been blocked by belief in "supernatural agencies," but that folk traditions have gradually given way to Western biomedical science. However, there are exceptions in remote locations such as the mountains of Calabria. One can find, in this area and even in some nearby urban settings, a mosaic of rituals and remedies that fall into the category of Calabrian "popular medicine" (or "folk medicine"). It survived, at least in part, because biomedical practitioners were rare and costly. However, in 1866 the government began to fund physicians, sending one to every small town in the newly unified nation. As a result, many popular medical practices have disappeared; those that have survived can be described using the OAM framework (O'Conner et al., 1997). We have used the "ethnographic present" in these descriptions; some of them do not reflect contemporary beliefs and practices while others survive, primarily in isolated areas. Knowledge about folk medicine circulated without written texts, and therefore contains regional variations. Nevertheless, this account reflects Calabria as a whole, with a particular emphasis on the regions we visited.

> Calabrians believe that the world is inhabited by a variety of local spirits as well as by angels, demons, and saints. These beings can be invoked to aid survival, but may also be hazardous. Appeasing them with prayer and magic is not seen as sorcery or witchcraft, but as common sense, or protection.

The Office of Alternative Medicine (OAM) Framework

1. **Lexicon**: *What are the specialized terms in the system?*

The key term in Calabrian popular medicine is *malocchio*, the "evil eye," an illness brought about either unintentionally or by malice (Simorto, 1990). In the former instance, it can result from simple envy or jealousy. In the latter instance, it can be evoked by *attaccatura* (attachment), *fascino* or *legatura* (binding), or *fattura* (fixing). The perpetrator of *malocchio* dominates the victim's body by one of these three mechanisms, producing such maladies as "dryness," which might take the form of barrenness, the inability to have or bear children. Especially vulnerable to *malocchio* are "wet youth" (because "wetness" represents fertility, and therefore opposes "dryness"), new brides, pregnant women, and even livestock, if they are the objects of envy for someone who knows how to cast the "evil eye."

It is believed that hunchbacks know how to cast *malocchio*. Priests also possess this ability and may practice it upon losing their moral bearings. One practitioner of *malocchio* confessed, "Every good thing I ever had was gained at the expense of a neighbor."

Another term dates back to ancient times. Pliny the Elder wrote about women who could transform themselves into birds of prey, flying by night, looking for babies to slaughter. The Inquisitors, who prosecuted women suspected of practicing witchcraft, promulgated belief in this folkloric witch, and these women still appear in local folktales, referred to as *streghe*. These women have the power to give people *malocchio*, and are in turn highly feared. There are a few male *streghe*, though either gender can transform themselves into animals rather than birds.

There are a number of traditional folk terms for special conditions. *Il mal caduco*, or the "falling sickness," is dreaded but can be prevented by charms. *Il male di San Donato* or epilepsy is felt to be due to supernatural causes, and can be controlled if the afflicted person carries iron nails or keys, or pictures of lunar crescents and frogs, practices that date back to pagan times.

2. **Taxonomy:** *What classes of health and sickness does the system recognize and address?*

In Calabrian popular medicine, folk healing, sorcery, witchcraft, magical spells, and religious causation overlap. Not only did we derive this information from our review of the literature, but from conversations with local inhabitants, and personal observation. Indeed these were the three sources from which all of our data was obtained.

3. **Epistemology:** *How was the body of knowledge derived?*

Popular medicine in Calabria can be miraculous, medical, or magical. Miraculous healing defies natural law; its effects are attributed to divine intervention, often mediated through the panoply of Roman Catholic saints who have appeared over the centuries. Knowledge of magical practices has been disseminated throughout the rural population rather than being limited to a secret group of practitioners. Our conversations with local informants suggested that self-medication is common, both for oneself and one's family.

Folk practices in Calabria, and elsewhere, are derived from local economies as well as from local modes of subsistence and production. Folk medicine relies on herbal and animal substances, some of which date back to Greek colonization. They are believed to work because of the intrinsic power of the substance; no special rituals are required to summon these qualities.

On the other hand, magical medicine is a collection of rituals, spells, elixirs, and potions that resemble cookbook recipes. Their purported effectiveness results from an established and sequential methodology that activates their latent properties. Both benevolent and malevolent practitioners employ magic, but in Calabria it is also the province of ordinary people. For the inhabitants of Calabria, until fairly recently, life was a precarious enterprise, full of dangers at every turn. Magic was one of many protective strategies people relied upon to ensure the survival of themselves and their family. Calabrian magical practices are a pastiche of Egyptian, Greek, and Roman influences, and even contain a Roman Catholic component; some of them (such as *malocchio*) survive in Calabria today.

4. **Theories:** *What are the key mechanisms?*

The Calabrian universe is an interconnected whole; tweaking one part of the fabric is likely to bring about changes in another part. For example, peasants often plant according to the phases of the moon. Calabrians believe that the world is inhabited by a variety of local spirits as well as by angels, demons, and saints. These beings can be invoked to aid survival, but may also be hazardous. Appeasing them with prayer and magic is not seen as sorcery or witchcraft, but as common sense, or protection. These practices are not limited to a small group of esoteric practitioners but are widely practiced. Recipes for protective formulae are typically passed on to younger family members on Christmas Eve or St. John's Eve (January 23rd), after which time the previous practitioner stops using the procedure.

Before the arrival of Western biomedicine, a number of causal mechanisms were advanced for common ailments. For example, malaria was attributed to sorcery, the evil eye, evil spirits, eating putrefied vegetables, consuming too many blackberries, or drinking stagnant water (Danubio, Piro, & Tagarelli, 1999).

The use of wire netting, beginning in 1899, was thought to be an effective mode for preventing malaria. Calabrians, even physicians, initially suspected that quinine was addictive (Douglas, 1915/2001). Such practices are no longer used, and we found no evidence for their presence in contemporary Calabria.

Although some illnesses, such as *malocchio*, are still treated by magical procedures, Calabrians now rely on the modern medical model to explain the success of most herbal and animal substances. However, God, Jesus Christ, the Holy Spirit, Mary, and the saints are given credit for ostensibly miraculous recoveries. Intercessory prayer by the afflicted person, a friend, or family member initiates these healings.

Undergirding all of these conditions and practices is the notion of a "vital force," resident to all Calabrian and southern Italian belief systems. They claim that this force can be strengthened or restored in miraculous healings. It resides in medicinal plants and foods, and is available through magical rituals. It can also occur naturally; for example they believe that the vital force is transferred from a mother to her child during nursing (Binde, 1999).

5. **Goals for Interventions:** *What are the primary goals of the system?*

Ride Hans (left), a frequent visitor to Il Scoglio tells Bova about his extraordinary spiritual experiences with Fratel Cosimo.

The goal of interventions, whether by prayer or the administration of herbal remedies, is to restore the vital force of the person who has fallen ill.

6. **Outcome Measures:** *What constitutes a successful intervention?*

An intervention is considered successful if the vital force has been restored completely or partially. Restoration of this force allows someone to return to work, participate in family life, or rejoin community activities.

7. **Social Organization:** *Who uses and who practices the system?*

Calabrian popular medicine is not a unified set of beliefs and practices. It has deep roots in the past, but is not a systematized extension of an ancient religion. Rather, it is an integral part of a rural peasant economic and social way of life, highly syncretized with folk Catholicism.

In addition, there are some practitioners of popular medicine, usually female, who have extensive knowledge of herbs and are able to treat minor illnesses (with the exceptions of tuberculosis and malaria). Their knowledge is frequently combined with popular magic and Roman Catholicism. These female folk healers are referred to as *maghe* while male practitioners are called *maghi*. The "fixers," or practitioners of magic, are referred to as *fattuchhiere*. Many of these practitioners are felt to have inherited their gifts from their ancestors. Genetics aside, it is a common practice for mothers to pass on herbal recipes and other folkloric knowledge to their daughters.

Some of the *maghe, maghi,* and *fattucchiere* work in altered states of consciousness. This may involve "merging" with their patient's condition. Practitioners may involve spirits, especially if they dabble in sorcery. While in an altered state, a folk healer may be asked to find lost objects, stolen livestock, or determine if a client has been "bewitched." However, there is a considerable overlap of folk healing, sorcery, witchcraft, and religious ritual.

8. Specific Activities: *What do the practitioners do? What do they use?*

Popular medicine is extremely dependent on herbal preparations. Its advocates hold that "only death can not be cured by plants." Especially popular are plants with an "anti-thermic" or diuretic effect, such as "embittering plants" (e.g., bitter pomegranate roots, male fern, wild olive, oak and willow bark, lupine seeds, sea onions, ergot of rye, sabina, mustard, and Cajenna (Cayenne) pepper (De Giacomo, 1899). Popular medicine also utilizes animal parts; they believe that "nearly every animal has been discovered to possess some medicinal property" (Douglas, 1915/2001, p. 71).

Informants Giuseppina (far left) and daughter Rosa share their knowledge of traditional remedies with (clockwise) Bova, Giuseppina's husband Pasquale, Krippner and Galante.

The most popular herbal and animal medicinal substances include chamomile tea (prescribed for cases of anxiety), swallows' hearts, tortoise blood (believed to strengthen people's spines) puppy dogs' hearts (thought to be especially effective for scrofula), undigested fish taken from the stomachs of larger fish (used for "sea fever," sicknesses felt to be due to exposure to the sea), chamois blood (given to shepherds' children to enable them to function at high altitudes), and snake blood (thought to enhance glandular functioning) (Douglas, 1915/2001, pp. 70-71).

Over the years, the treatment of malaria by popular medicine has included a variety of practices. They ranged from applying witchcraft to overturn a sorcerer's spell to such practices as drinking wine infused with the embers dug out of a fire on St. Lorenzo's night, using herbal preparations (e.g., juice from bergamot oranges), eating a preparation of viper's head and wormwood, and tying a variety of supposed curative agents (e.g., toads, lizards, nuts) to the area around a patients' spleen. Historically, there were regional differences in popular practices; in the city of Reggio, Calabria, it was common to have sick people swallow three living bedbugs wrapped in tissue paper. In Cassano allo Ionio and Bisignano, folk practitioners had their patients eat cobwebs, drink their own urine, swallow pulverized insects, or ingest a preparation made from wine and baked rabbit's blood. People living in other areas took great stock in drinking their own saliva or masticating chunks of tobacco. Prayers were also used to counter malaria. In Consenza, for example, Madonna della Febbre (i.e., "Mary of the Fever") was frequently petitioned (Genovese, 1924).

Treatment of *malocchio* runs a wide gamut. People who accidentally feel resentment or jealousy can prevent the other person from succumbing to *malocchio* by immediately blessing him or her. Another remedy is to apply a mixture of water, salt, oil, wheat seeds, and molten lead to a victim. Vulnerable people can take preventative measures by wearing amulets, such as horns made of red coral, phallic symbols (e.g., keys, roosters, snakes, daggers, fish), a *mano fica* (a fist), or a *mano cornuta* (a horned hand). Some of the amulets thought to be most effective, are made from silver or tin, and contain cimaruta, the top of the rye plant. Some large amulets are shaped as trees with various other symbols (e.g., horns, suns, moons, fish, keys, Sacred Hearts) at the tips of each branch.

The use of amulets can be attributed to Roman times, in which women often wore *bullae* (small bags filled with phallic-shaped objects) around their necks. These evolved into *brevi*, small bags filled with rue and lavender, semi-precious stones, ashes taken from sacred fires, flowers grown near churches, or images of saints. Especially valuable components of *brevi* are stones filled with iron-rich clay that rattle when shaken. Special *brevi* are filled with *pietre della gravidanza* (pregnancy stones), *pietre del sangre* (red-spotted jasper that will stop a wound from bleeding), and, for protection against sorcery and witchcraft, *brevi* filled with *pietre stellar* (star stones – polyporic pebbles dotted with tiny star-like spots that are sometimes carved into crosses and carried with the image of a saint) or *legno stregonia* (holly twigs carved into crosses).

Rue is a popular medicinal herb, especially for the treatment of colic, digestive problems, skin eruptions, and even sorcery or witchcraft.

9. Responsibilities: *What are the responsibilities of the practitioners, patients, families, and community members?*

Even though a sizable proportion of the community may practice popular medicine, there is a responsibility to perform it in a skilled manner. Family and community solidarity is an important value, and this balance must not be put at risk by an intervention.

10. Scope: *How extensive are the system's applications?*

a.) Calabrian popular medicine is still practiced by people living in rural areas, in the mountains, and by Calabrian Romani. However, it generally focuses on health problems that are transitory. During our stay in the small town of Roccella Ionica, we conducted interviews with several of its inhabitants, inquiring about the "home remedies" they employ. The resulting list provided us with contemporary examples of popular Calabrian medicine. If someone is the victim of *malocchio,* friends and family members can address the condition with prayer. Specialists are needed for more specific treatment. Not much can be done to prevent *malocchio,* but its diagnosis can be made with a special preparation: Start with a cup of water. Add five pinches of salt, and five grains of incense. Add pieces of five palm leaves that have been blessed by a priest, five leafs from an olive tree, and a few embers obtained by burning twigs from an ash tree. Drop five pinches of salt into this concoction; if the salt turns black, the person in question is the victim of the "evil eye." An alternative is to let three drops of olive oil fall into a cup of water; if the drops separate, the person in question has *malocchio*. In both cases, the liquid solution must be thrown away at a crossroads.

b.) To treat small cuts in the skin, boil water, add salt, wait until the water is tepid, and then apply it to the skin. If possible, soak the afflicted body part in the salty water for half an hour. Another treatment is to substitute the section dividers from the reed plant for the salt. If the cut occurred far from one's home while working or playing, urine can be applied immediately.

c.) To treat a recurring cough, put sugar into a foot-warmer or a similar receptacle. Ask the person with cough to breathe the fumes, and place a blanket over his or her head so that the fumes do not escape. Another remedy is to drink *vino cotto* (wine that has not yet fermented). *Vino cotto* is commonly used in cooking.

d.) For stomachaches, dry the stems of several cherries, boil them in water, and drink the brew once it cools down.

e.) For the treatment of bronchitis, saturate waxed paper with olive oil, warm it by placing it near a fire, then apply the paper to one's chest. Another treatment is to boil linen seeds and place them on one's chest.

f.) For second-degree burns, mix olive oil and plaster; apply it to the burned area of the skin. Later, once the burned area scabs, substitute strono leafs for the olive oil and apply.

g.) For treating high blood pressure, olive leaves can be crushed and mixed with water, then imbibed.

h.) In the case of a headache, sliced potatoes can be applied to one's head and held in place by a headband. If the headband is soaked in vinegar beforehand, the treatment is thought to be even more effective. Linen seeds can be substituted for potatoes.

i.) Chamomile tea is frequently used to calm someone having an anxiety attack.

j.) If a baby is constipated, the tip of an oregano stick coated with human hair or parsley can be carefully inserted into his or her anus.

k.) In the case of recurring dandruff, use soap made from pig fat, soda, olive oil, and lemon skin.

l.) If a mother cannot nurse a baby, and if a substitute is not available, almond milk is better than cow's milk for the baby's milk bottle. If the baby develops an intestinal disorder, a solution of water and leaves from a ruta plant is an effective remedy.

m.) When washing clothes, add embers from an ash tree to the water, even if the clothes are washed in the river. This serves as a disinfectant.

We were told that these remedies are passed down from person to person, usually from mother to daughter, as most home practitioners are women. One informant remarked, "Everybody knows about these treatments."

11. Analysis of Benefits and Barriers: *What are the risks and costs of the system?*

Prior to Italy's introduction of free

> Prior to Italy's introduction of free public medicine in the 1970s, folk medicine was the treatment of choice for those who could not afford Western biomedicine, or who lived in areas where physicians were rarely seen. Since that time Western biomedicine has become the keystone of healthcare, though Calabrese maintain their cultural affinity for folk medicine, prayer, and the enactment of religious rituals for health and betterment.

public medicine in the 1970s, folk medicine was the treatment of choice for those who could not afford Western biomedicine, or who lived in areas where physicians were rarely seen. Since that time Western biomedicine has become the keystone of healthcare, though Calabrese maintain their cultural affinity for folk medicine, prayer, and the enactment of religious rituals for health and betterment. Older adults still possess knowledge of folk remedies, and seem to be willing to use both traditional and Western modalities.

Of course, with respect to *malocchio* and witchcraft, there are social risks and costs. As with many societies, people are often reluctant to address such issues in the open, even though these spiritistic orientations may be commonly and deeply believed. Suspicion of witchcraft or giving evil eye can carry the price of social stigmatization or even ostracism. Given increasingly modern and "rational" attitudes toward these matters, dabbling in these arts may subject one to epithets like crazy, superstitious, or backward. Nevertheless, belief in *malocchio* and witchcraft is still a powerful undercurrent, even in the cities. Some will turn to the latter to solve various social and health related problems, but most tend to keep a respectful distance.

12. Views of Suffering and Death: *How does the system view suffering and death?*

An omnipresent "vital force" is felt to be a substance that can be lost or gained. Losses lead to illness, weakness, or death. Gains can be evoked from external sources that reinvigorate the body. When death occurs, there is a "transcendence" in which a new body is created, manifesting itself in a different type of "vital force."

From the perspective of folk magic, suffering often results from sorcery or witchcraft. From the Roman Catholic perspective, suffering is part of the human condition, often representing God's "test" of one's faith.

13. Comparison and Interaction with Dominant System: *What does this system provide that the dominant system does not provide? How does this system interact with the dominant system?*

There are several "dominant systems" in Calabria. There is Western biomedicine, the Roman Catholic Church, and

Romani, many costumed, dance tarantella in the town square anticipating the passing procession and sacred statues of Saints Cosmo and Damian.

such familial organizations as Mafia and Camorra (known in Calabria as 'ndrangheta). The latter organizations originated to protect households against greedy landlords.

The Feast Day of Cosmo and Damian

We visited the town of Riace on September 25 to participate in a three-day feast honoring the saints Cosmo and Damian (*Cosimo* and *Damiano* in Italian). It was also our intention to document a gathering of Romani[1] who participate in the festivities. The two holy physicians lived in the region of

---

1 The Romani, Rom or Roma, are an ethnicity of Indian origin, living mostly in Europe and the Americas. This is the proper name in Southern Italy vs. the more well known, yet derogatory term, Gypsy. The Romani find this term offensive.

Cilicia, Turkey in the 4th century C.E., and some of their followers, most of them Byzantine monks, arrived in Calabria around 1000 C.E. According to legend, however, Cosmo and Damian themselves once sailed to an area near present-day Riace, coming ashore and instructing a local shepherd to build a church. Another tells of how the physicians converted to Christianity, much to the consternation of the Romans who depended upon their healing ministrations. The physicians were urged to drop a few seeds before the statues of the Roman deities, promising them that this would save them from the wrath of temple authorities. Cosmo and Damian refused and, as a result, were secretly beheaded in a distant field. According to the legend, their faith was so strong that they picked up their heads with their hands, and walked several meters singing Christian hymns before they expired. Thanks to stories of this nature, and subsequent claims of miraculous healings, they were canonized by the Vatican.

The central ritual of the feast is the journey of the statues of the physician saints, along with a procession of devotees, from Riace's Church of San Nicola di Bari to a smaller church (the Sanctuary of Cosmo and Damian approximately a quarter of a mile away). The Church of San Nicola di Bari, where the statues of the doctor saints Cosmo and Damian are housed, is ornately festooned with vibrantly-colored paper called *paratu*, on the church's walls, arches, and ceiling. Parishioners and devotees enter the church and approach the statues for blessings. Some brought their children who they lifted to touch the base adjoining the effigies. Others came with *ex voto*, special devotional replicas of body parts, made from wax or bread. These devotions represent the parts of the body either healed by the saints, or about which those believers had prayed to them.

A vendor told us that people requesting a healing often purchased a replica of the ailing body part. The wax effigy would be placed at the feet of the statue as an offering. When we asked if there were any wax *ex voto* of phalluses, the salesman explained that they were only made for witchcraft, primarily in coastal cities in the Locride, and that he did not have any. He did not remember seeing them, though in his youth, he knew of witchcraft practices. The lack of contact with witchcraft or magical practices was typical in the area, although a member of our group's family also recalled hearing about this practice. Someone in our group commented that perhaps there were no phalluses, because curing sexual dysfunctions is beyond the purview of the saints. In any event, the man selling the *ex voto* lamented that too few people were buying them and that it would likely be his last year selling them at this feast.

The statues remain in the Church of San Nicola di Bari[2] all year, except when they are transported to the Sanctuary of Cosmo and Damian for the duration of the feast. During the closing ceremony they are returned to the church. While attending a service at the church, several people placed *ex voto* offerings at the base of the statues, and children were positioned at their feet, or touched them, presumably for blessings or good luck.

A hand-carried caravan later took the statues through the town to their ordained sanctuary, a smaller church built and named in honor of the saints. The procession of the statues through Riace involved dynamic participation by several thousand parishioners, devotees of the cult of the saints from other towns, and Rom who played a visibly-distinct and traditionally separate role in the feast. Parish priests, followed by church members and volunteers, carried the caravan and led the procession, which was accompanied by a choir, brass band, and police. People attending the feast, but not formal participants in the ceremony, surrounded the procession. The route between the church and the sanctuary was lined with booths selling *ex voto* and other religious items.

Romani primarily convened near the sanctuary of the saints. Since most of the Rom were already assembled closer to the destination point, they preceded the assembled procession. One of our photographs clearly shows a group of Roma at the very head of the procession, followed by a line of police that separated them from the other members of the procession (priests, a choral group, non-Romani community members, and visitors joining the procession).

Scattered throughout the procession were clan leaders with large wooden staffs, or *paranze* (singular is *paranza*). The *paranza* was used in a popular martial art of southern Italy, especially in Sicily and Calabria, first seen in the Middle Ages. The ancient name for the stick is *paranza*, but has evolved to become a sign of command, called *capo bastone*, which can be roughly translated as "chief cane" or "chief stick." This name was transmitted to local Mafia groups in which the holder of the stick is the *capo*, or mafia boss (English, 1993). In the setting of this feast, however, each man holding a *paranza* was simply the head of his Rom clan.

One of the Rom explained that his clan was from Gioia Tauro, a city on the western coast of Calabria. He mentioned that there would normally be many more Roma from his group, but that many of his compatriots stayed behind to mourn the death of a clan elder. Those that did come to Riace were festively engaged in the feast. Some were dressed in colorful costumes, and many danced tarantellas and played tarantella music on traditional instruments.

Three instruments that we identified were the *tamburrello* (a type of tambourine), the *organetto* (a traditional accordion), and the *zampogna* (an instrument very much like a bagpipe, with five pipes of uneven length and a double reed).

The tarantella has Greek origins, apparently being related to the orgiastic rituals of Dionysus, the god of wine. Tarantella was also a type of trance performance used by women as an idiom of psychosocial distress. A common folk belief about the tarantella is that it was induced by the bite of the spider *Lycosa tarantual*. More recently, it has evolved into a folkloric dance. The musicians are known to adapt to the dancers, adjusting the tempo as it seemed appropriate. Most the performers are women, who dance ecstatically until, exhausted, they collapse (supposedly cured). This behavior could be interpreted as a socially-approved outlet for women whose self-expression and emotional expression is often muted by local customs. The dance

Bova (left foreground), Krippner (right foreground), Galante (right background), and anonymous woman in front of ex votos. These will be offered to Saints Cosmo and Damian through reverence and with dedications to their statues.

is also popular among Romani, whether or not it is attributed to a spider bite (English, 2000). Customs related to this dance must have changed throughout the course of history, as we saw as many men dancing as women.

One of the authors (RG) returned to the Riace feast the following year to further document the role and customs of Rom at the Riace feast. He interviewed church and community leaders as well as Roma participants and filmed the feast procession. Special attention was paid to the Rom and Sinti (two divisions of the Romani) dancing the tarantella.

In Galante's short film, *A Devotion*

---

2 The Church of San Nicola di Bari is also known as Riace's Matrix church or the Mother church. The route between the church and the sanctuary was lined with booths selling ex votos and other religious items.

with a Dance Step / Una devozione a passo di danza (Galante, 2007) he summarized, "the remnants of two ancient cultures, one farming and one gypsy, once again meet in the sacred space of devotion. The spirituality of the Roma people is simple, immediate and very intense in the expression of the various languages among which dance and music are the most important. Through dance they express the desire to unite with the divinity, with their own bodies, their feelings, their own beings... Dance in front of Saints Cosimo and Damiano is to symbolize their union with the divinity. Their language is symbolic, made up of gestures where the body language prevails over the verbalism of the prayers..."

Don Pino Strangio, a priest and church leader in the province, described some features of Rom and Sinti devotion including their offering their children to Cosimo and Damiano by raising them as an offering to the statues of the saints. The children are dressed with the color used to represent the Saints; blue is the color representing devotion to Saint Damiano who was a chemist, and green is the devotional color for Saint Cosimo who was a doctor. Those who get dressed in their colors want either to release themselves from a vow or ask Cosimo and Damiano for a blessing (Galante, 2007).

Another feature of the Rom spirituality is expressed through offer of locks of hair, especially for grace and the blessing for marriage or engagement (Galante, 2007). One Romani's (Rom's) invocation revealed the emotional tensions and hope for her home's safety that she brought to her prayer to the feast, "Oh St. Cosimo that I be able to pay you a visit every year... first of all let my daughter walk...secondly, I ask that you grant me a great favour, you who have already granted me a great one... Oh St. Cosimo, it is a year that I do not place a pan on the burner (a custom of the Rom when there is a death in the family)...To whomever is responsible for the misfortune of my son, that within the year they may pay the same price...Remember what they did to my house...that they never enjoy grandchildren, that they never enjoy children, that they never enjoy any of their family...(Galante, 2007)."

Procession of Saints Cosmo and Damian.

Jacopo Arrigotti, an Italian musicologist, describes Riace's feast of Saints Cosimo and Damiano as a rite divided into three phases: waiting for the procession, outgoing procession, returning procession. Three main social groups take part at the rite: 1) the local community, under the guide of the Church; 2) pilgrims coming from the mountains of the hinterland; 3) Roma communities, coming from all Calabrian provinces. The unique symbol of the saints is then the pivot for at least three main ritual structures, which are expressed in a variety of performative activities. Singing is a priority in pilgrms' ritual. The pilgrimage ends in the main church, in front of the statues. Music-based performances are the very final act of the pilgrimage.

> The procession of the statues through Riace involved dynamic participation by several thousand parishioners, devotees of the cult of the saints from other towns, and Romani who played a visibly-distinct and traditionally separate role in the feast. Parish priests, followed by church members and volunteers, carried the caravan and led the procession, which was accompanied by a choir, brass band, and police.

The Roma community is characterized by tarantella dancing. Secular dancing is viewed as a vehicle for social meanings, but also as sacred dance in front of the saints, which involves altered states of consciousness (Arrigotti, 2007).

As well, members of the local community of ethnic Italian Calabrese take on an ancient tradition using altered states of consciousness. Members of this group use prayer and dream incubation (in Italian, *l'incubazio*) to commune and communicate with the saints for healing in the Matrix church the night before their statues are removed for the procession to the chapel where they will stay for three days. This follows a tradition—

in ancient Rome, at the temple dedicated to Castor and Pollux, the spot where physicians swore their ethical oath to Aesculapius, the sick often slept on the floor of the sanctuary. The divinity would appear to them in a dream, either granting them a cure or indicating a healing path. With the affirmation of Christianity, in place of the pagan temple, a basilica was erected, dedicated to the thaumaturgic Saints Cosma and Damiano; in turn, the ancient cult and its rites became somehow Christianized. (informant, Galante, 2007).

The doctor saints Cosmo and Damian are considered to be protectors of the Romani community. Hence, the Romani maintain profound reverence for them, and passionately participate in the feast. On a wall of the sanctuary is a beautiful fresco of Zefferino, who is the only Roma beatified by the Vatican. This permanent image of a holy Rom added fervor to their activities in the celebration.

On the day of the procession to the sanctuary, two members of our group had video cameras. We separated several times, but always found each other. Going off the main road we went up the side of a hill where several Romani were waiting. We followed an elderly woman who spoke of a "short cut" to a local cemetery. One member of our group spoke in Italian to this Rom woman, noting that she crossed herself whenever our colleague mentioned the saints. Despite the merchant's earlier lamentation about poor sales that year, we observed numerous *ex voto* being placed at the feet of the statues of the saints both while in the church and during the procession. The *ex votos* were removed after just minutes to accommodate more of them.

As the statues in the procession approached their destination, rambling past the multitude of *ex voto* booths on their way to the Sanctuary of Cosmo and Damian, the crowd appeared to be in a frenzy of excitation. Many Rom played and danced tarantella in the piazza area in front of the sanctuary-church. We worked our way into the crowded church while the statues were still in front of the piazza.

At last the statues entered the church backwards, allowing Cosmo and Damian to face the processional crowd that accompanied them to the sanctuary. The crowd pulsed with elation in a courtship of the sacred and the profane, whereby tarantella music and dance welcomed the statues of the saints to the sanctuary. *Ex votos* continued to be placed on the statues and were taken off just as quickly. People continued to lift children up to the statues while several priests received confessions in as much "privacy" as a filled sanctuary can offer.

While this is an ancient rite of a Calabrese village, there was certainly an international flavor to the day. We met several African priests who were part of the Church of Nicola di Bari, and who took part in the procession. There

> As the statues in the procession approached their destination, rambling past the multitude of ex voto booths on their way to the Sanctuary of Cosmo and Damian, the crowd appeared to be in a frenzy of excitation. Many Romani played and danced tarantella in the piazza area in front of the sanctuary-church.

were also a number of African vendors selling wares along the procession route, as well as many Afghans, some of whom we met, living in the town sanctuary.

In his book, *Old Calabria*, generally regarded as one of the finest travel books in the English language, Norman Douglas (1915/2001) comments that "A foreigner is at an unfortunate disadvantage; if he asks questions, he will only get answers dictated by suspicion or a deliberate desire to mislead" (p. 72). At the same time, Douglas felt that Calabrians were the "ideal prey for the quack physician; they will believe anything so long as it is strange and complicated" (p. 73). Insofar as the clergy are concerned, Douglas added, "they can keep people at a consistently low level of intelligence" (p. 73), and that "the intense realism of their religion is what still keeps it alive for the poor in spirit" (p. 74). Nevertheless, Douglas felt that the land itself had healing properties. He wrote, "A landscape so luminous, so resolutely scornful of accessories hints at brave and simple forms of expression; it brings us to the ground where we belong; it medicines to the disease of introspection" (p. 333).

Our experiences in Calabria, these many decades since Douglas' writing, indicate that the same quaint picture of the land and its people cannot be painted. Not only did we find that Calabrians were both embracing and adaptive to the influx of modernization and social change, but they were extremely hospitable and keen to inform us about the more obscured aspects of their surviving traditions, and as well, many were informed about issues of their country and world.

The Shrine of Madonna dello Scoglio

During our 2003 sojourn through southern Italy, we paid two visits to the Madonna dello Scoglio shrine at Santa Domenica di Placanica in the hilly coastal region of Eastern Calabria. We had heard of Fratel Cosimo, who leads a grass-roots spiritual community in the area, and who has gained an international reputation as a devout visionary. During our visits, we attended two evening worship sessions and were able to meet Cosimo and interview several members of his volunteer staff and congregation.

Cosimo Fragomeni was born in 1950. From an early age he was a dedicated Roman Catholic. As a boy, he was frail and suffered frequent bouts of illness. Nevertheless, his faith endured as he continued a pious life, punctuated with hermitic periods in the nearby hills. At the age of 18, Cosimo reported four visions in which the Virgin Mary, standing on a rock or *scoglio*, appeared to him. During the first of these visions, in 1968, the Madonna instructed him to build a shrine at its current location "to bring people closer to God."

Fratel Cosimo is thought by local informants to be spiritual heir of San (Saint) Pio[3] as Fratel Cosimo's Marian visions started in 1968, only months before Padre Pio died. Several informants showed their affinity with Saint Pio to members of our group when we were invited into their homes. One elderly woman wore a gold pendant of Saint Pio, another elderly woman had a needlework portrait (approximately 4' by 4') of Saint Pio which she proudly hung over her bed. A woman in her 30's had an altar in her house devoted to Saint Pio. Shortly thereafter, Cosimo began building this shrine, which he named Madonna dello Scoglio (Madonna of the Rock), using funds from local donations. Cosimo also began to lead prayer and devotional sessions for pilgrims who placed their faith in his visionary experiences and messages. Cosimo had little formal education and no seminary training or even Bible study; however, he was admitted to the lay order of the Franciscan brothers and was given the title of "Fratel."

In the following years, the shrine grounds and facilities have been expanded to accommodate increasing numbers of pilgrims. A foundation has been established to channel donations into projects to expand the shrine. Most saliently we noticed the simplicity of the shrine's angular construction (made from concrete and sheet metal), and the spartan nature of the pews, which were plastic chairs arranged into linear rows, with gravel aisles. The focal point of the shrine is the Madonna dello Scoglio itself; a life-sized white marble statue of Mary set within a rock that is roughly 12 feet (about 3.6 meters) high. Here, supplicants come to pray and touch the sacred rock through the metal fencing in which it is immured.

A small chapel with a slender spire sits just to the side of the shrine. A highlight of this chapel is a stunning painting of the Madonna that follows Fratel Cosimo's description. Apparently, the artist had painted the body of the Madonna according to the suggestions given him by Fratel Cosimo

Interior of church San Nicola di Bari covered with paratu, a decorative paper, during the feast of Saints Cosmo and Damian. The saints' statues are continually approached, revered, and petitioned during the two day feast.

and was about to begin with the face, but he found himself unable to paint it. He claimed that he was blocked from further work. He put the painting aside, but when he re-embarked with a new canvas he still could not depict the face. Discouraged after a third attempt, he consulted Fratel Cosimo who replied, "Don't worry, the Madonna will think of it." The following morning Cosimo came back and found the painting completed. However, the artist denied having worked on it during the previous evening, concluding that it was Heaven's work. In any event, the resulting painting is regarded as an object of special devotion.

We were told that Fratel Cosimo and a community of about 60 volunteers preside over bi-weekly devotional services that attract anywhere from several hundred to over one thousand pilgrims. Special Masses are held from June to October, and we were informed that nearly 50,000 people attended a special Mass in May 2003. During the winter months, services at the shrine begin at 3:00 PM, and during the summer at 4:30 PM. The average service lasts about four hours and involves singing, praying, recitation of the rosary, testimonies, and concludes with a sermon and prayer from Cosimo.

During the early part of the service, Cosimo holds private meetings with 100 individuals, 90 of whom scheduled an appointment by phone, and an additional 10 individuals chosen by lottery at the shrine. An ecclesiastical visitor attended during one of our visits, who we were told came for another religious ceremony in the neighborhood. By chance, we found out that the honored ecclesiastical guest was staying at our hotel, which gave us an opportunity to tell him about Fratel Cosimo. They had a personal meeting the day before the service, after which the guest expressed his conviction that Fratel Cosimo did indeed lead a mystical life, which is why he came to the following day's service. Fratel Cosimo's superiors in the Roman Catholic Church have forbidden him from conducting formal "healing" sessions, but he is allowed to pray with afflicted individuals.

Indeed, Fratel Cosimo does not claim to be a "healer," nor is healing the focus of his work. Rather, the core of his message, as relayed to us by several members of his congregation, is that one must "open one's heart to Christ," which is best done through prayer. Of central importance is the belief that spiritual growth is more important than physical healing; if physical healing follows it is a sign of the deeper "miracle" in one's heart. Regardless, many people come to Madonna dello Scoglio to seek help for physical ailments and relief from emotional distress.

Suffering seems to be a prominent theme in Cosimo's sermons as he contends that it is an important part of spiritual growth. He points out the suffering of Jesus and the sorrow of Mary, both of which brought light to the world. He asks his followers to make changes in their hearts through the endurance of their own suffering. Often, he alludes to his own trials in God's work, such as spending time with distressed pilgrims. We noticed that Cosimo often shed tears

---

3 Saint Pio, was a priest popularly known as Padre Pio from Campagna, another region of southern Italy who was acclaimed for his spiritual gifts that included stigmata, healings, prophecy, and bilocation. He died in 1968 and was canonized in 2002 by the Vatican.

as he led the congregation in prayer and recited the rosary.

Another feature of this community is its un-dogmatic approach to belief and practice, a factor that attracted criticism from Roman Catholic officials. Fratel Cosimo's "doctrine" does attend to the conventional roles of Mary, Jesus, God the Father, and the Holy Spirit. However, as described by a member of the community, Mary is seen as an intermediary "who takes you by the hand to God." Another depiction of Mary was as the "temple of God." Congregants pointed out that Cosimo is not dogmatic in his approach. Rather, he emphasizes prayer as the primary vehicle for opening oneself to God beyond ritual prescriptions. Although the ritual activities at Madonna dello Scoglio are in accord with Roman Catholic practice, they are much less formal.

Some of our informants expressed their attraction to Cosimo and to his brand of simplicity. Their enthusiasm bespoke a kind of "getting down to the basics" devotion, something they found liberating. For example, we chatted with a couple from Switzerland, "Hans" and "Bertha," who frequently visited Madonna dello Scoglio. Hans expressed his enthusiasm for worshipping at the shrine because in his daily life as a corporate executive, he could not discuss his spiritual feelings and beliefs with his colleagues. For him, coming to the shine was like "breaking out of the cage of mundane everyday life." Moreover, his wife professed that she was a "tried and true Protestant," yet, for her, Fratel Cosimo's message transcended the division between denominations despite a Catholic bias. As a result, she now prefers to simply refer to herself as "a Christian."

Following Cosimo's sermons, congregants typically lined up in procession, often with their children, to receive his blessings. At these times we noticed that many congregants, mainly women, would beckon aloud for his attention, excitedly calling his name, and sometimes waving their hands or scarves, eager to make eye contact with him or receive some gesture of acknowledgment.

Occasionally, we witnessed individuals collapse on the ground, mildly convulsing. According to René Laurentin (1988), the French theologian well known for his expertise of visionary and supernatural phenomenon, these collapses are probably a sign of the Holy Spirit's work in those people, some of whom attest to experiences of deep liberation. The phenomenon differs from mere hysterical collapse, which can also occur. It was apparent that the majority of congregants adored Fratel Cosimo and that many of them were deeply moved by his physical presence and proximity as well as by his public messages. Cosimo, however, eschewed any sense of celebrity, instead projecting pronounced meekness and piety, one of sincerity of purpose in his dedication to the Divine.

This type of relationship is suggestive of Cosimo's public role as a charismatic leader. Charles Lindholm (1992) has described charisma simply as "a certain quality of an individual personality by virtue of which he or she is considered extraordinary and treated as endowed with special power or at least specifically exceptional powers or qualities" (p. 289). The notion of charisma also embodies a sense of intensified emotion and excitement; the extreme case evidenced in the euphoric episodes we witnessed. Cosimo did not engage in any ecstatic or overtly manipulative behavior that we noticed; however, he was certainly viewed by congregants as a truly exemplary person, blessed with divine powers.

In this regard, Cosimo does not resemble the stereotypical charismatic leader. Rather, his charismatic properties emanate, arguably from his embodiment of central Catholic values and imagery. His personage also encompasses the metaphorical image of Mary "the nurturing mother," with whom he has a history of visionary experiences. Some congregants told us about Cosimo's reputed ability to bilocate. These rumors, as well as the many reported healings associated with the shrine, add to his reputation as a vessel for the Divine.

Although we found no adequate scientific or clinical data supporting the healing phenomena, these stories are prevalent in the lore surrounding Fratel Cosimo and Madonna dello Scoglio. Many people who pray and consult privately with Cosimo appear to achieve some degree of emotional comfort and alleviation of distress. Because psychological dispositions are concomitant in somatic states, the "lifting" of distress can have positive physical affects, and vise versa.

Bertha told us that she has collected several cases of healings attributed to the Madonna. Two of these involved severe medically diagnosed heart disease. One case was a boy with a deformed spinal column. Another was a woman whose mental condition had not responded to 13 years of psychotherapy. One was a woman with multiple sclerosis who is now able to walk.[4] The final case was a personal friend of Bertha's, a man who had been injured in a fitness center. Allegedly, he made a complete recovery following a visit to the shrine.

During the first of our two visits to the shrine, a member of our group "won" the lottery and was able to meet privately with Fratel Cosimo. He talked with Cosimo about his daughter who was suffering from a congenital disease, and also asked Cosimo to bless a medal of St. Christopher. Our colleague was dealing with his own health problems at the time and when he mentioned this, Cosimo gave him a personal blessing. After the meeting, our colleague was tearful but expressed a sentiment of deep relief. Six months later, his health problem had become more severe and diagnosed as degenerative. On the other hand, his daughter's condition steadily improved. He also related that his niece had taken the St. Christopher's medal to her boyfriend's father who was hospitalized for a terminal disease. Apparently, he began to feel better after receiving the medal, and the nurses were surprised by his rebound. However, this improvement was only temporary.

The growing visibility and popularity of Fratel Cosimo and his work at Madonna dello Scoglio can be examined with respect to the broader issues of modernization and social change in Calabria. The region is one of the poorest in Italy, and has only recently embraced modernization. We often heard complaints from adults and elderly people in the small villages of the Calabrian interior, that young people were moving to coastal towns and cities marked by better jobs and "more action." We also learned that new immigrants were arriving illegally in Calabria

---

[4] The woman left her wheelchair in a special room at the shrine that houses reminders of the previously disabling conditions of worshippers.

from Eastern Europe, Africa, and South Asia. These changes, among others, contribute to the escalating uncertainties and anxieties about life, family, and community, and about the changing ideas and practices that new populations entail.

New religious movements often play a significant role in allowing people to find ways to cope with the changes that immigration catalyzes. The Madonna dello Scoglio is not a new religious movement, but may be best seen as a Christian renewal, deeply rooted in traditional Catholic faith. On the one hand, it offers a strong and growing spiritual following that is reinvigorating community and communal networks in the face of the fragmentation of traditional communal life. On the other hand, belief, practice, and faith alone remain familiarly and intelligibly Catholic, yet also have been disassembled and recreated into a more simplified system in a resonant and relevant form.

One possible interpretation points to the emphasis that Cosimo places on suffering, devotion, and transformation. Cosimo and his message exemplify these pillars of the human experience; that suffering is important for spiritual growth, prayer is the vehicle for opening one's heart, and transformation and healing are the potential results of prayer. These are basic themes in the lives of people amidst change, and Cosimo embodies them, possibly in ways not articulated in mainstream venues of religious practice. The fact that Roman Catholic authorities in the Vatican do not recognize Cosimo as a visionary has not impeded the growth of the community.[5] Rather, we got the sense that the immediacy and relevance of interacting with Fratel Cosimo was a significant attraction for the congregants at the shrine.

After both of our visits to Madonna dello Scoglio, we were fortunate to be included in a small group of people who were invited to have a private audience with Cosimo. On one occasion, he blessed a crucifix worn by a member of our group. He began to weep, saying that he was aware that the owner of the crucifix endured considerable suffering. On the other occasion, he was told that a member of our group visited and wrote about folk healers and visionaries in various parts of the world. He asked, "Did you find that these people had anything in common?" Our colleague responded, "They all spoke of the common bonds that unite humanity, despite their different worship practices." Fratel Cosimo immediately replied, "That is my belief as well."

Conclusion

Edward Lear, the humorist, was a notable visitor who adored Calabria. He wrote, "No sooner is the word uttered than a new world arises before the mind's eye—torrents, fastness, all the prodigality of mountain scenery—caves, brigands...horrors and magnificence without end" (in Noland, 2001, p. 69). Our group found communion with Lear's comments, especially after interviewing townspeople who still practice folkloric healing, participating in the Feast Day of Cosimo and Damian, and spending two evenings with Fratel Cosimo. Perhaps the land itself is origin of the healing, for which the folkloric remedies and religious rituals are credited.

---

5 Upon our return to the United States, a member of our group found Fratel Cosimo listed on a website titled, "Dangers of False Apparitions," apparently put together by a devoted but conservative Roman Catholic "defender of the faith."

References

Arrigotti, J. (2003). Universita Degli Studi di Padova SEM: The feast of the Saints Cosimo and Damiano in Riace. Musical performance and a changing rite within an intercultural tradition of Southern Italy. ATMI, CMS, SEM Annual Meeting, Miami.

Binde, P. (1999). *Bodies of vital matter: Notions of life force and transcendence in traditional Southern Italy.* Gothenburg, Sweden: University of Gothenburg.

Crawford, F.M. (1901). *Rulers of the South: Sicily, Calabria, Malta* (2 vols.). London: Macmillan.

Danubio, M.E., Piro, A., & Tagarelli, A. (1999). Endogamy and inbreeding since the 17th century in past malarial communities in the Province of Cosenza (Calabria, Southern Italy). *Annals of Human Biology, 26,* 473-488.

De Giacomo, G. (1899). *Il popolo di Calabria [The people of Calabria].* Trani, Italy: Ed. Vecchi.

Douglas, N. (1915/2001). *Old Calabria.* London: Phoenix Press. (Original work published 1915).

English, S. (1993). Effects of mass emigration on the social ecology of Calabrese territory: Anthropological changes and psychopathological symptoms (in Italian). In V. Micco & P. You (Eds.), *Boundary passages, ethnopsychiatry, and migrations* (pp. 53-67). Naples: Liguori.

English, S. (2000). The rite, the part, and the belief: Reflections on the Sacred One in the Calabrese collective imaginario (in Italian). In C. M. Helium, S. Ferraro, & S. English, *A long journey a year: Between belief and pity in the Calabria of the Jubilee* (pp. 221-233). Catanzao, Italy: Instant Editions.

Freeman, L. (2004). *Mosby's complementary & alternative medicine: A research-based approach.* St. Louis, MO: Mosby.

Galante, R. (Producer), Galante, R. (Director). (2007). A Devotion with a Dance Step / Una devozione a passo di danza [Short film] Production Company: Galante, Producer: Galante, Executive Producer: Galante, Director: Galante. Camera: Galante, Editor: Galante, Author: Galante.

Genovse, F. (1924). *La malaria in La Provincia di Reggio Calabria* [Malaria in the Province of Reggio Calabria]. Florence, Italy: Ed. Vallecchi.

Hufford, D. (1995). Cultural and social perspectives of alternative medicine: Background and assumptions. *Alternative Therapies in Health and Medicine, 1*(1), 53-61.

Keates, J. (2001). Introduction. In N. Douglas, *Old Calabria* (pp. 7-13). London: Phoenix Press. (Original work published 1915.)

Laurentin, R. (1988). *Learning from Medjugorje: What is the truth?* Gaithersburg, MD: Word Among Us Press.

Lindholm, C. (1992). Charisma, crowd psychology, and altered states of consciousness. *Culture, Medicine and Psychiatry, 16,* 187-310.

McGinn, B. (1985). *The Calabrian Abbot: Joachim of Fiore in the history of Western thought.* New York: Macmillan.

Noland, D. (2001, June). Lear—ing. *Sky,* pp. 63-69. (Original work published 1956.)

O'Connor, B.B., Calabrese, C., Cardena, E., Eisenberg, D., Fincher, J., Hufford, D.J., Jonas, W.B., Kaptchuck, T., Martin, S.C., Scott, A.W., & Zhang, X. (1997). Defining and describing complementary and alternative medicine. *Alternative Therapies in Health and Medicine, 3* (2), 49-57.

Orlando, A. (1998). *In Calabria.* Soveria Manelli: Arti Grafiche Rubbettino Editore.

Ramage, C.T., & Clay, E. (1987). *Ramage in south Italy. The nooks and highways of Italy: Wanderings in search of its ancient remains and modern superstitions.* Chicago: Academy Chicago.

Simorto, P. (1990). *The evil eye and the horn.* Rome: Laruffa Editore.

Traditional medicine fact sheet updated by WHO. (2003). *Alternative Therapies in Health and Medicine, 9* (5), 21.

White, A.D. (1898). *Warfare of science with theology.* New York, NY: Appleton.

Fading Non-empirical Healing

The Reemergence of the Mending Mind

Carl M. Hild

Indigenous circumpolar peoples have a long shamanic history. Many aspects of these traditions continue to the current day in the form of traditional healers and Tribal Doctors, as they are known in Alaska. This article reviews the indigenous people of northwestern Alaska, Inupiaq, shamanic traditions for diagnosing conditions and healing. In addition, it reviews the attributes of Places of Ancient Traditional Healing (PATH). PATH indicated specific places and times for the collection of herbs and plants specifically for healing. Certain animals were taken and specific parts used. Journey quests for self-healing included going to particular locations and gather-

---

Carl M. Hild, PhD is Associate Professor of Health Services Administration at Alaska Pacific University. Over the past four decades, he has researched Inupiat traditional knowledge and skills to foster programs that improve health and well-being among northern peoples. He is focusing his energies on community-based participatory health research under an endeavor he calls "Multicultural Engagement for Learning and Understanding." He is currently working on a second award from the National Library of Medicine on documenting the knowledge and skills of Inupiat healers.

This article was supported in part by the National Center for Minority Health and Health Disparities Grant R24 MD000499 while Dr. Hild was the Associate Director of the Institute for Circumpolar Health Studies at the University of Alaska Anchorage.

Inupiat drummers at dance in Barrow, Alaska.

ing special plants or materials. Some places are believed to be sites at which other forms of knowledge or healing songs could be obtained for advancing well-being. The Tribal Doctors continue to visit these PATHs to advance healing.

A community-based action research approach resulted in a process of multicultural engagement for learning and understanding (MELU), guided by the intention of documenting the advantages of utilizing Inupiaq traditional healing techniques to complement and integrate with modern allopathic health services. The use of other ways of knowing, spirit support, body manipulation, behavioral restrictions, and the extraction of bodily materials are all used to improve well-being. The documentation and assessment of these skills and knowledge for their beneficial aspects for healing indicate an ancient awareness of practical means to improve well-being. These ancient-based ways may lead investigations into further insights as to the various forms of healing that are currently not utilized or understood by contemporary medicine and science.

The author has lived in Alaska and worked with the indigenous people of northwestern region of the state over the past forty years. He has produced, in partnership with indigenous collaborators, educational materials that have offered opportunities for MELU for improved well-being. By learning about these ways of enhancing or restoring health, the allopathic medical community can gain new insights into the healing attributes of indigenous peoples.

Inupiat

The *Inupiat* (plural), the indigenous people of northwest Alaska, perceive a world that is more than just interconnected pieces, it is seen as one (Fair, 2004). The Inupiat see the whole through the spirit of *Inua* that is everything (Fitzhugh & Kaplan, 1992). By knowing who they are, they know the whole and therefore understand its aspects. They perceive and relate to the world in wholeness through respect and sharing. They do not see themselves as a part or as being separate from the whole. They know all as one.

A central aspect of *Inupiat* cognition

is *Inua*. Parallels within occidental and oriental philosophies are the Holy Spirit and *chi*. These parallels include a common element that flows through living things. In the Holy Spirit it may be limited to moving among humans only, or perhaps only from God to individuals. Chi moves from plants and animals as well as from energetic physical sources such as crystals, magnets, sun, wind, and rivers into people (Narby, 2006; Rossbach, 1983). Sacred places are either rich in chi or well-balanced with the *male* and *female* aspects. The study and application of the movement of chi is known as *feng shui* (Rossbach, 1983). The sacred sites of the Catholic Church are sources of the Holy Spirit because of God's perceived presence, not due to any natural or earthly flow of enthusiasm. Enthusiasm is defined as a stimulating sense, which comes from the Greek meaning "full of the spirit" or "inspired by God."

Inua is more than both of these concepts. It is wholeness or oneness. There is no movement of *Inua* from person to person, as they are one. There is no shift from rivers to people, as they are one. It is an understanding of oneness that pervades *Inupiat* actions and beliefs. The concept is one of "In the beginning God…" and if it could be appropriately stated, *Inua* is everything at once. *Inua* changes its form but does not change itself. Everything is made up of *Inua* and everything makes up *Inua* (Ellanna & Sherrod, 2005).

Inua is more than a life spirit. It is more than a perception of self. It is a well grounded sense of oneness that goes beyond the concept of just being part of a whole.

The oneness is not just a physical, three dimensional understanding. It includes the concept of time. *Inua* provides for ancestors to be present. This is done through the recognition that the knowledge being used currently was first learned by the ancestors. They shared that information in the form of stories. The stories provide the application of the information to demonstrate the understanding, which comes from the practical use of wisdom. What is learned today will benefit the future generations that are already here within the reproductive capacity of those who are now alive. Knowledge resides in *Inua* and can be called upon. That knowledge may be of things past, things future, or of things unseen in this physical world.

Within the *Inupiaq* (singular) culture there are healers who actively work simultaneously with the mind, body, and spirit to improve well-being. The *Inupiaq* name for this healer is *anatguk* (Burch, 1971, 2006; Ganley, 1996). Each *anatguk* is capable of providing a combination of a wide spectrum of skills. The *anatguk* uses experience, knowledge, and insight to provide care. This can be accomplished by working with the physical body for lacerations, cuts and broken bones as well as with the need to reestablish relationships with natural bodily functions through manipulation of the organs or skeleton. It can be through talking and raising questions to discover factors of individual behavior or attitudes. It can also be through spirit journeys and working at a different plane with helpers in a parallel world. The *anatguk* gains insight or information that is retrieved from non-physical sources (Deloria, 2006; Eliade, 1974; Halifax, 1979; Heinze, 1997; Kalweit, 1988; Schwartz, 2005; Talbot, 1991; Targ & Katra, 1999, Turner, 1989, 1996). Western European and American research literature classify the Inupiaq healing tradition as shamanic. Throughout this paper the citations to shamanic practices are used to elucidate the activities of the *anatguk*.

Traditional Healing Practices

The *Inupiat* perceive a world that is more than just interconnected pieces, it is seen as one (Bielawski, 1995; Burch, 1971; Carpenter, 1980; Ellanna & Sherrod; 2005; Fitzhugh & Kaplan, 1982; Freeman, Morgan & Farquhar, 2001; Nuttal, 2000; Osborn, 1990; Saylor, Burgess & Hild, 1998; Turner, 1989, 1996; Vitebsky, 2008; Weyer, 1932). They cannot separate themselves from the *Inua*, the spirit that is all. They talk to and with the animals, plants, water, wind, rocks and earth. Their healers call upon supernatural knowledge to understand not only the condition to be treated, but also the underlying cause of the problem. Not being well is an indication that a person's relationships to all aspects of life that support her or him need to be corrected (Saylor et al., 1998). When a person does not actively do her or his part to engage and respect the world that provides sustenance, then there cannot be wellness.

The *Inuit*, the transnational indigenous people's group of which the *Inupiat* are a member, produce images that are considered perceptually challenging in that they combine multiple facets into one object in what is called a "visual pun" and has been termed "simultaneous reality" (Carpenter, 1980; D. Benyshek, personal communication, June 14, 2006). Inuit art is festooned with complex figures expressing their simultaneously multifaceted worldview (Fitzhugh & Kaplan, 1982). Often Inupiaq art includes temporal and spatial scales that are outside of the physical eye view. The art incorporates what is not only capable of being seen, but what is known, what has been and what is taking place elsewhere. A scene may depict a hunter standing alone on distant ice, as well as show the ocean beneath the ice, the fish and seals swimming there, and a family far away, albeit very present, sitting needing the nourishment of the food that will be given by the animal. Inuit art reflects an understanding of the oneness of the world and the ability for life to transmute itself into combined or alternative forms. Wolves and orcas shift form, and regularly do, as they are perceived by the Inupiat as the same being (Dikov, 1999; P. Sovalik, personal communication, March 1972; Vitebsky, 2008).

The *Inupiaq* regularly utilize symbols that have multiple meaning. The title of this work was selected with a verbal pun as a visual cue. Fading in this paper has two perspectives. First, as time goes by there are fewer people who really do practice traditional healing with plants, manipulation, behavior, and through accessing non-local consciousness that has been classified as non-empirical. Second, as time goes by the non-empirical aspects of what the mind can do are being demonstrated in repeatable verifiable experiments, thereby removing them from such a classification. So while the non-empirical indigenous healing art is disappearing, the practice is being empirically documented as valid. Therefore traditional healing is fading in two ways. The hope is that the traditional ways can be preserved through practice and be well documented to serve as examples for future investigation and sharing for the larger well-being.

Where

Alaskan ethnographies report traditional healers going to special sites marked with stones or large bones to gather medicinal materials and/or engage in spirit communication as part of the ritual journey to well-being (Ganley, 1996; Lowenstein, 1994; Milan, 1964). A term used is "*itiuyaaq*" or "spirit shelter." Sites that are known to have been used may now have limitations to their access due to land "ownership" policies. Seeing and knowing that the world around them is healthy is integral to the perception of Inupiat personal well-being. Places of Ancient Traditional Healing (PATH) are becoming resources for continuing well-being among the *Inupiat*.

Historically the traditional healer utilized many local resources for plant, animal, and mineral based medicines; the spiritual components of each was honored, respected, and engaged for improving health (Burch, 1971, Craig, 1998; DeLapp & Ward, 1981; Dixon & Kirchner, 1982; Dixon, Myers, Book & Nice, 1983; Eliade, 1974; Ellanna & Sherrod, 2005; Ganley 1996, 2002; Garibaldi, 1999; Ramoth, 1976; Saylor et al., 1998; Turner, 1989, 1996). The healers sometimes traveled throughout the region in search of these healing resources and appropriate spiritual attributes. *Anatguk* used a breadth of resources to assist an individual in achieving health and supporting the community.

The magico-religious significance of place can be physically perceived in a number of ways, and a personal sense of place can enhance well-being. Place can also be a site of ritual, and in a culturally agreed upon set of beliefs, engendered with healing attributes that may trigger psychological and physiological benefits in the nature of psychoneuroimmunology (Freeman, 2004; Halifax, 1982; Krippner & Welch, 1992; Locke & Colligan, 1986).

Who

Among the *Inupiat* the most well known shamanic type is the *anatguk* (Burch, 1971, 2006; Ganley, 1996). This is the *Inupiaq* term for shaman, healer, or medicine person. These individuals worked in an open, public process that was often quite flamboyant in nature. They became powerful and were feared as they set taboos and regulated behavior (Burch, 1971; Fortuine, 1988; Ganley, 1996).

Most *anatguk* worked as specialists. Few had advanced healing skills in all practices, not unlike physicians today. There are reports of *anatguk* performing eye surgery in the 1800s to remove growths such as pterygium (DeLapp & Ward, 1981). They reportedly used a human louse suspended on human hair to scratch away the tissue, or through the use of a fine jade knife to cut away the material that was interfering with vision. There are accounts of the removal of tumors and of healing major wounds with just hands and songs (Anonymous, personal communication, Winter 2007; Turner, 1996). Their skills were remarkable for many of the services that they provided.

> Most shamans have undergone prolonged periods of physical, emotional, intellectual, and spiritual training during which their ego becomes service oriented so that they can become the vehicles and translators of transcendental knowledge....Shamans also stress that their training never ends because they keep receiving instructions from the "higher" source. (Heinze, 1991, p. 156)

There are also accounts of *anatguk* traveling physically and spiritually to other places to gain knowledge and skills to help improve the process of attaining well-being, as well as finding locations and insights to be able to perceive healing songs of tremendous power (Anonymous, personal communication, Winter 2007; Eide; 1952; Turner, 1996).

There was a second and relatively unknown historic shaman as well, the *ilisiilaq* (Burch, 1971, 2006; Ganley, 1996). This is the *Inupiaq* term for a sorcerer. The *ilisiilaq* worked in private and stayed out of the limelight that was so desired by the *anatguk*. The *ilisiilaq* was not considered malevolent in most areas, whereas the *anatguk* was

> Often Inupiaq art includes temporal and spatial scales that are outside of the physical eye view.

associated with fear and setting taboos. The *ilisiilaq* worked quietly, behind the scenes conducting spiritual journeys for interventions so that individuals could be successful in providing for their family and community. The *ilisiilaq* was considered clairvoyant in her or his ability to know about what was taking place, as well as being a healer of the spirit or a person adroit at reestablishing proper *Inua* relationships. It is the *ilisiilaq* who would foretell the outcome of a birth, hunt, or a season's weather pattern. They knew who would die in the near future, and "would often warn them to make things right with those they loved" (Anonymous, personal communication, Winter 2007). The *ilisiilaq* was a diviner.

The *anatguk* conducted trance sessions with little or no clothing (Eide, 1952; Eliade, 1974; Ellanna & Sherrod, 2005). They were adept at creating a vivid demonstration of the battle with spirits in requesting to be tied, in being able to provide a sense of other beings' presence with unusual noises, and through what now are considered "sleight of hand" feats (Eide, 1952; Eliade, 1974; Burch, 1971; Ganley, 1996). They also used masks to bring forth the spirit in question (Eliade, 1974; Ellanna & Sherrod, 2005, Fitzhugh & Kaplan, 1982). The *anatguk* did not always use a drum or rattle to initiate the trance. The *anatguk* and *ilisiilaq* both utilized song to gain knowledge and to provide care.

> When possessed by their familiar spirits, shamans could see and communicate with such phenomena, but

no one else could unless the particular entity involved chose to make itself visible. Even some features of the landscape were endowed with mystical power. If a person fell asleep in the wrong place, for example, or looked at a forbidden topographic feature, that person died. (Burch, 2006, p. 320)

The *ilisiilaq* did not utilize the drum or dramatic practice, but was able to secure other information through an intentional state to access nonlocal consciousness (Ganley, 1996). Both the *anatguk* and the *ilisiilaq* are reported to have gone to sacred sites that were marked with stones or bones to communicate with *Inua*, often traveling underground, under the sea or to the moon (Ellanna & Sherrod, 2005; Ganley, 1996; Milan, 1964; Ripinsky-Naxon, 1993).

The *anatguk* would conduct spirit retrievals to reestablish relationships that are required for well-being. Today the Tribal Doctor starts off each healing session with a fervent prayer calling upon the spirit of God in the name of Jesus to aid with the treatment. Often patients are also implored to pray so that the Tribal Doctor can best perform her or his duty and restore the person to health. This engagement of both the spirit and enlisting the patient fully in her or his own healing is part of what is demonstrated in the practice of psychoneuroimmunology (Freeman, 2004). The efforts to gain knowledge from the ancestors and nonlocal consciousness have been studied by scientists for over a century (Blum, 2006; Mayer, 2007).

The *ilisiilaq* was the clairvoyant and would see information. This was sometimes used for diagnosis and may have been based on training as a keen observer. This is not unlike any expert who can use insight and experience to glean apparently unknown information. A review of renowned surgeons demonstrates that they too rely on this insightful knowing to conduct their work (Mayer, 2007). Also the *ilisiilaq* would use spirit travel to access information. The declassification of US Central Intelligence Agency materials indicate that governmental programs have trained and utilized such skills for national defense (Katra & Targ, 1999; Targ & Katra, 1999). Studies by Targ have even shed light on advanced knowing, so that not only is space not a factor in perceiving subsequent distant events, but to a limited extent time is no longer the barrier it was once believed to be (Targ & Katra, 1999).

It appears that the *Inupiat* had found ways to learn that are not based on our current academic practices. It appears also that they had found ways to go beyond space and time, which only now our quantum physics is explaining on a subatomic level, and governmental sources have acknowledged making use of similar techniques for national defense (Targ & Katra, 1999).

What

The most common skills reported being used by Inupiat healers were in three general categories (Burch, 1971; Ganley, 1996). One was manipulating or poking the body's joints, organs and blood system to provide a physical advantage to healing—not unlike an osteopathic physician or acupuncturist. One was working with medicinal plants and animals to provide chemical or spiritual/*Inua* advantages in healing—not unlike a pharmacist with a physician prescribing pills (Garibaldi, 1999). One was working with spirits of ancestors, animals and the non-physical world to provide a spiritual/*Inua* advantage to reestablishing required relationships for healing and well-being—not unlike a psychologist, religious leader or faith healer.

Over the last half of the twentieth century a new form of traditional healer emerged (Ganley, 1996). The English name is that of a traditional healer or tribal doctor. The term shaman is not used, and is actively avoided, as its connotation is still closely associated with taboos, the evil *anatguk*, and the Christian concept of the devil. This new healer was formed as a composite of some of the more acceptable aspects to the new dominant culture of both the *anatguk* and *ilisiilaq*. The physical body manipulation, poking, and ethno-botanicals were combined with the private delivery of service and information under the guidance of Christian prayer by both the patient and the healer. The term *hand-healer* also is used for these individuals (Turner, 1996).

The *Inupiaq* term for this healer of composite skills is *ilnuunniaqti* which is close to meaning "traditional doctor." Such a healer performs various tasks such as: *kapi* – "poking" or draining a small amount of bloody fluid from sites where it has "pooled" and that are somewhat similar to acupuncture points; *ilusiiq* – setting joint dislocations; and *uniiuqtit* – the manipulation of organs and deep vessels to allow the for easing of perceived blockages to their normal functioning (Dixon & Kirchner, 1982; Eide, 1952; Ganley; 1996; Kirchner, 1982; Lucier & Van Stone, 1987; Lucier, Van Stone & Keats, 1987; Turner, 1989, 1996). The *ilnuunniaqti* also prepare poultices, wound dressings, and infusions. The current level of traditional knowledge of ethno-botanicals (plants), ethno-zoonotics (animals), ethnogeotics (water and minerals), is held by these individuals. Hospitals and clinics have requested that these ethno-pharmaceuticals not be used until there is a greater understanding of their potential drug interactions (DeLapp & Ward, 1981; Dixon et al., 1983; Garibaldi, 1999)). Likewise, allopathic practitioners have advised the halting of the manipulation of organs and poking, as they are perceived to be risky behaviors (Eby, 1994, 1998). The work of the allopathic system assessing traditional practices based on its own metrics is now more frequently viewed as inappropriate and culturally insensitive. However, as there is a desire to incorporate or make traditional practices integral in the hospital setting, there are discussions, but the dominant allopathic structure appears unyielding to date.

There are some common themes among the traditional healing being conducted by the Inupiat at the end of the twentieth century. These hold some parallels to the four fundamentals of healing mentioned above. They also provide an overview of the way that healing is conducted.

1. A different level of perception ("clairvoyance").
2. The existence and help of a healing spirit (here it is always "the Good Lord," Jesus); the life entity of the sufferer.
3. The concept of disease as a thing, a substance, that can be drawn out.
4. The hands as the instruments of cure, their special faculty.
5. The connectedness of healer and sufferer, the "conversation of bodies."
6. Correct positioning of the bodily organs – a fundamental concern of Inupiaq healing.
7. Therapeutic readiness, "healability." (Turner, 1989, p. 16)

If a hospital or clinic were to be distilled and condensed into its healing essence and put into one person there would be a similarity to the *anatguk*. The pharmacy is made up of plants, animals, water, and minerals gathered at specific places known to have healing attributes. The physical therapy department is located in the hands of the healer. The psychology department is incorporated in the taboos that were traditionally implemented to advance healing and reestablish relationships. Surgery and Emergency Room services are the methods employed to stop bleeding and stabilize the patient until a full healing ceremony can take place that will employ a full diagnosis and treatment that may entail the entire extended family or community. X-ray and laboratory are focused on all of the senses of the *anatguk* and are not limited to merely what the basic five can determine. Like ultrasound, X-ray, Magnetic Resonance Imagery (MRI) there are tools beyond those typically used every day, which on occasion can be put into practical use, such as magnetic sensors in the brain (Baker, 1984).

We must close our eyes and invoke a new manner of seeing… a wakefulness that is the birthright of us all, though few put it to use. Plotinus (seventeen centuries ago) (Katra & Targ, 1999, p. 61).

Slowly the *anatguk's* skills, while being modified and provided in a subtle manner in private, are being revived (Craig, 1998, Hild, 2007; Maniilaq, 2005). The Maniilaq Association has supported a Tribal Doctor Program since 1975 (Maniilaq, n.d.). The Norton Sound Health Corporation based in Nome, Alaska initiated the Tribal Healer Program in 2006. Those who have practiced quietly, in ways viewed as complementary to the dominant medical and religious understanding, have been able to continue. In three communities in Alaska, there are now formal traditional healing programs associated with clinics and hospitals. These programs also have apprenticeship programs that are preparing the next generation of traditional healers. There are plans in place to expand these types of programs to other areas of the state.

At One in a Changing World

Currently, the *Inupiat* have grave concern about the state of the environment. The climate has changed dramatically in the Arctic in just the past few decades. A phrase used is that "the earth is faster now" (Krupnik & Jolly, 2002). The reports of contaminants coming to the Arctic are making the *Inupiat* question their personal well-being (Arctic Monitoring and Assessment Programme [AMAP], 2002). If the seal eats the same foods as the Inupiat and it is found to have high levels of contaminants and is seen to have reproductive or immune system problems, how possibly can the *Inupiat* be advised to continue to eat a subsistence diet (Borre, 1994)? If the land is contaminated with global and local pollution, how can its spirit nourish the *Inupiat* (Borre, 1994; Hild & Stordahl, 2004)?

A century ago there were other challenges. After the industrial whalers had introduced diseases and decimated the marine and terrestrial animals, the *Inupiat* were struggling and starvation was rampant (Ellanna & Sherrod, 2005). The Christians, who first proselytized northwestern Alaska, were the Pastoral Religious Society of Friends, the Pastoral Quakers. Prior to their arrival there was an indigenous prophet and prognosticator who spoke throughout the region. *Maniilaq*, an Alaska Native, set the stage for the *Inupiat* of this region to embrace Christianity (Burch, 1994; Crowley & Crowley, 2000; Haile, 2003; LLT Productions, 1998, Maniilaq, n.d.; NANA, n.d.). He broke taboos that had been set by the *anatguk*, suffering no harm. He predicted a number of events that soon came to pass including the arrival of a new spirit and the arrival of a new material that would be written upon that was thinner than birch bark. The Bible was seen as the expression of his prophecies. Maniilaq is seen as being the Alaskan embodiment of John

The "Wolf Dance" of the Kaviagamutes, Eskimo of Alaska.

the Baptist and Nostradamus.

The Quakers came to this area of northwestern Alaska as married couples, which made for social interface much more readily than the single male clergy who did not fit with *Inupiat* family systems (Burch, 1994; Crowley & Crowley, 2000). The Friends' Church replaced an individual who set taboos and was feared, by having a more democratic and inclusive institution to take on the role of establishing behavioral standards for the community.

> Their denomination also had another advantage over more clerically based churches in that the lack of Quaker hierarchy matched the Inuit's own social structures. Once converted, no priests were needed and the Inuit could hold their own services. Each new convert could become an advocate for the new belief. Other Quaker ideas could be matched with Inuit ideas. The idea that shamans had inner warmth and light that attracted spirits could be equated to the Quaker idea of developing the Inward Light of the Divine in everyone. The Inuit need for public admission of wrongdoing was accommodated by public confession in Quaker services. (Crowley & Crowley, 2000, p. 131)

In a matter of just a few years at the beginning of the twentieth century, the *anatguk* were gone from sight and in about twenty years the Christian faith had become strongly entrenched (Burch, 1994; Eide, 1952; Ellanna & Sherrod, 2005; Ganley, 1996; Turner, 1989). Most health services were provided by the Bureau of Indian Affairs and later the Indian Health Service. In the 1970s, the Congressional Laws 93-638, Indian Self-Determination and Education Assistance Act, and 94-437, Indian Health Care Improvement Act, allowed for the local provision of health care. The community is once again determining how health services are delivered, and in a very Quakerly context.

How

Though challenged by the domineering influence of external cultures, some of the ancient healing practices continue to this day. Traditional healers are working within hospitals and clinics providing services, often for conditions not easily addressed in the contemporary medical model. They regularly call on the spirit, now through Christian prayer, to assist in their diagnosis and treatment of patients, while the patient takes on the role of requesting divine guidance for the healer (Maniilaq, 2005; tribal doctors, personal communications, Spring 2006). The inclusion and promotion of Alaska Native traditional healing, which is based soundly on the old *anatguk* and *ilisiilaq* traditions of the western Arctic, is viewed as a key element in the continued well-being of the people of northwestern Alaska.

Taboos, while instituted by the *anatguk* in the past, are now provided by the hospital or clinic (take these pills three times a day on an empty stomach), government (do not smoke in public buildings or around children), and religious groups (do not drink alcohol, do not have sex outside of marriage). These taboos, like those of old raise awareness of relationships and initiate behavioral change through setting acceptable activities for well-being. The area of the power of suggestion and placebo effect has been shown to have a great deal of influence on healing (Freeman, 2004; Locke & Colligan, 1986).

"*Kapi*" or "poking" is a form of *Inupiaq* treatment that combines acupuncture and historic blood-letting to release bad humors. Unlike the old blood-letting *kapi* is used at very specific locations to release fluids that are not blood. Using sterile techniques the Tribal Doctors use their hands to diagnose where old blood has collected and is no longer serving its purpose. It breaks down and needs to be removed. A small, shallow incision is made, now with just the point of a hypodermic needle and the area massaged. From personal observation what comes from the body is not blood. The fluid can be used for further diagnosis as it can range from close to a clear watery liquid to what appears to be nearly black tar, with a number of viscosities.

"*Ilusiiq*" or realigning joints and reducing dislocations is typically the work of an orthopedic with subsequent support from physical therapists. In the physically active and rigorous life of hunting on the Arctic ice pack rubble, and regular moving entire households throughout the year following migratory routes over the unmarked tundra, falls, sprains, and strains were common. The skill level in addressing these injuries was advanced. Films of 25 years ago showing traditional treatments have been evaluated by a doctor of Osteopathy and the techniques used are considered the state of the art in 2009 (Hild & Schenck, 2009; Maniilaq, 2005). Knowing the subtleties of how to reduce such joint injuries with minimal pain is a skill that would be very worthy of study. There has been interest in looking into the chronic pain management techniques that are used, as the local doctors admit that the *inuunniaqti* appear to have greater success at times than they do at the hospital.

"*Uniiuqtit*" or deep manipulation of the muscles and body organs is another practice that has been observed and for which additional knowledge is desired. This technique includes addressing low energy, gastrointestinal problems, conception, complex births, back pain, and high blood pressure (Maniilaq, 2005). The Tribal Doctors use their hands to probe down to the backbone and then reestablish the correct positions of arteries, organs, and muscles so that they work as they should. Watching a back massage given from the front and seeing the patient walk out smiling and upright is remarkable considering that when the healer had arrived the person was bed ridden only a short time before. What can the clinicians and investigators learn from these ancient skills?

The *anatguk* is reported to have used song specifically for healing. Sometimes this was done with drumming. Altered states of consciousness have been associated with the use of drumming as it establishes patterns and brainwave harmonics (Freemen, 2004, Freeman et al. 2001; Heinze, 1997). In addition the very low vibrations can establish infrasound that allows for a sensed presence (Tandy, n.d.). The use of drumming may enable the healer to access knowledge required for enhancing well-being, and it may position the patient to be more suggestible to what information and behavior is shared. Again the combination of the various aspects of healing are traditionally offered in a holistic manner rather than the silos of care provided so typically in allopathic settings.

How the *antaguk* enters a receptive and active state of non-local consciousness is an art work investigation. Inupiaq song can be a chant that requires a regular breathing pattern. This may be quiet and calm, but most often is energetic. Inupiat practice throat singing in which the harmonics of two chanting individuals produce what sounds as a third voice that pulsates with the others. Stanislov Grof has investigated the use of breathing patterns to achieve altered states of consciousness and has called this holotropic breathwork. In 1995 he produced a list of potential areas for research using this technique and it included "Documentation of Experiences that Challenge Newtonian-Cartesian Paradigm" (Grof, 1995, para. 7). Music, song, solitude, and suffering are additional recognized methods that have been used to enter altered states of consciousness:

> Song and music undeniably are the most ancient means of bringing man into harmony with himself, his environment, and nature…. And if a song or melody reaching us from without is capable of healing, why should not the wisdom of our body, in an endeavor to heal, produce its own song from within? …If, as we have seen, the song of power is a song of joy, this surely must be the joy at being reunited with our higher nature. (Kalweit, 1988, p. 156)

True wisdom is only to be found far away from people, out in the great solitude, and it is not found in play but only through suffering. Solitude and suffering open the human mind, and therefore a shaman must seek his wisdom there.

> This that I am telling you now, I dare to confide to you, because you are a stranger from a far away country, but I would never speak about it to my own kinsmen, except those whom I should teach to become shamans. [Quote from Igjugarjuk a Canadian Caribou Inuit] (Halifax, 1979, p. 69)

It is through the engagement of the indigenous people that their knowledge can be incorporated into new management practices. The desire is to have a sustainable approach to assuring the land has all of its attributes for the well-being of future generations. While the *Inupiat* have a set of cultural, historical, and contemporary events with which to deal, there are other indigenous peoples facing similar situations around the globe.

Multicultural Engagement for Learning and Understanding

The *Inupiat*, as Parran et al. (1954) reported, were generally viewed as being above average intelligence and in light of their worldview concept of *Inua*, self-report that they regularly access knowledge that they did not learn from empirical experience and then put that information into practical use (Anonymous, personal communication, Winter 2007; Burch, 1971). They also knew the land and the healing properties that it contains as they have watched and learned from the animals. They knew the body as they regularly saw how it and a bear are similarly structured. They had the capacity long ago to know how to provide healing. They still have that capacity.

Twentieth century science and investigations have found that indeed the human body is capable of detecting very subtle changes in the geomagnetic field, ion levels, smells of the soil and water, as well as the behavior of animals. Humans are keen observers of their environment, and are particularly sensitive when they are not physically insulated from the natural world by the anthropogenic materials that create interference to natural abilities. There is indication that humans can, at will, allow their minds to know more than is physically suggested. People can enter a state of consciousness, during which they can perceive knowledge that is not regularly available to them through the predominant five senses. The *Inupiat* have used more than the Western defined five senses in their relationships of knowing their world. They acknowledge that much more can be perceived and understood than the information that comes in through seeing, touching, hearing, smelling and tasting their environment. Through this elevated consciousness, which can be stimulated or enhanced at special places, there is a personal relationship to the earth and alternative level of other knowing.

The indigenous peoples of the Far North have faced centuries of challenges to the utilization of their places of ancient traditional healing. They are well aware of what might be lost if they are not diligent. They are well aware of the current environmental challenges that are facing humanity. There is a belief that the ability to reinitiate the conversation with the earth is held among those circumpolar indigenous people who can sense the healing resonance of the earth and sing the songs that it provides.

What does the information that has been collected mean? What will the proposed actions initiate? What are the next steps that will need to be outlined and researched? Who will foster the processes? What follows are the musings of the investigator upon reflection of the information that has been gathered.

First, there is the cultural perception of what information is and what takes place when it is utilized. Knowing information is not applying wisdom.

> Knowing in part may make a fine tale, but wisdom comes from seeing the whole. (Asian proverb)

> To fear the Lord that is wisdom, but to depart from the way of evil is understanding. (Job 28:28)

> Round about the accredited and orderly facts of every science there ever floats a sort of dust-cloud of exceptional observations of occurrences minute and irregular and seldom met with, which it always proves more easy to ignore than to attend to….Anyone will renovate his science who will steadily look after the irregular phenomena. And when the science is renewed its new formulas often have more of the voice of the exceptions in them than of what were supposed to be the rules. (attributed to William James)

> In the struggle for scientific progress, new facts are less of an obstacle than obsolete concepts. (Reich, 1973, p. 74)

> The Tribal Doctors use their hands to probe down to the backbone and then reestablish the correct positions of arteries, organs, and muscles.

Information is not wisdom, neither is it understanding. Information is fact in context. The investigator believes that how a fact is interpreted and utilized depends upon the filters through which it is received as communication. Just as a television set is adjusted to the local channels, people coming to a new cultural or social milieu may need to adjust their interpretations in order to better perceive community values. Those filters may be ones of spatial, temporal, cultural, or other parameters that forge the foundations of concepts for how the communications are understood and utilized. Therefore, how anyone interprets facts is based on her or his frame of reference.

Not only are facts seen through the filter of one's own experience, but the emotions that are present when those experiences take place and when the information is gained, can be imprinted into the very cellular matrix of the entire body.

These discoveries over the last twenty years have led [Candice] Pert to propose a theory that *emotions are the key element that effects the conversion of mind to matter in the body.* Emotions are not just in the head or the brain: They are part of the body, and we can no longer make clear distinctions between the brain, our mind, and our body. In fact, Pert refers to white blood cells as "bits of the brain floating around the body." ...

There is no such thing as a purely psychosomatic or purely physical illness: *Diseases are conversations, or events involving the exchange of information among cells within a living system.* And scientists have documented that mind and information travel throughout the body, not just in the brain or nervous system. (Targ & Katra, 1999, p. 252-253)

"This is the greatest error in the treatment of illness, that there are physicians of the mind and physicians of the body

Exorcising Evil Spirits from a Sick Boy.

and yet the two are indivisible," (attributed to Plato). "The whole history of scientific advancement is full of scientists investigating phenomena the Establishment did not believe were there" is attributed to anthropologist Margaret Mead in an address to the American Association for the Advancement of Science.

This of course raises the question of what else we should have been paying more attention to, rather than putting off the amazing skills of the shaman as the "work of the devil" and "sleight of hand magic." The continued use of *Inupiaq* traditional healing is now even more imperative than before. There is more substantiation in that there is scientific rationale behind its practice and success. The questions still remain as to how this is done, but without the continued practice of these skills there will be no future opportunity to investigate the answers.

What is being provided by the *Inupiat* as a thread to be followed is that some places allowed the shaman's abilities to flourish.

Cultural traditions of thought strongly influence scientific theories often directing lines of speculation, especially (as in this case) when virtually no data exists to constrain either imagination or prejudice. (Gould, 1980, p. 225)

The *Inuit* worldview allows transformations to take place when required. The wolf and orca are one and morph as needed. Shape-shifting oneness is a holographic universe concept. *Inuit* expressions including visual puns and simultaneous reality provide examples of their ability to perceive multiple concepts. Incorporating those worldviews to advance humanity's well-being can be achieved through the MELU process – multicultural engagement for learning and understanding.

References

Arctic Monitoring and Assessment Programme. (2002). *Arctic pollution 2002.* Oslo, Norway: AMAP.

Baker, R. (1984). *Bird navigation: The solution to a mystery?* New York, NY: Holmes and Meir.

Bielawski, E. (1995). Inuit indigenous knowledge and science in the Arctic. In D. L. Peterson & D. R. Johnson (Eds.), *Human ecology and climate change: People and resources in the far north* (pp. 219-227). Washington, DC: Taylor and Francis.

Blum, D. (2006). *Ghost hunters: William James and the search for scientific proof of life after death.* New York, NY: Penguin.

Borre, K. (1994). The healing power of the seal: The meaning of Inuit health practice and belief [Electronic version]. *Arctic Anthropology, 31*(1), 1-15.

Burch, E. S., Jr. (1971). The non-empirical environment of the Arctic Alaskan Eskimos. *Southwest Journal of Anthropology, 27*(2), 148-165.

Burch, E. S., Jr. (2006). *Social life in northwest Alaska: The structure of Inupiaq Eskimo nations.* Fairbanks, AK: University of Alaska Press.

Carpenter, E. (1980). If Wittgenstein had been an Eskimo. *Natural History,* (2), 72-77.

Craig, R. (1998). Traditional healing among Alaska Natives. *International Journal of Circumpolar Health, 57*(1), 1-12.

Crowley, V., & Crowley, C. (2000). *Ancient wisdom: Earth traditions in the twenty-first century.* London, UK: Carlton Books.

DeLapp, T., & Ward, E. (1981). *Traditional Inupiat health practices.* Barrow, AK: North Slope Borough Health and Social Service Agency.

Deloria, V., Jr. (2006). *The world we used to live in: Remembering the powers of the medicine men.* Golden, CO: Fulcrum.

Dikov, N. N. (1999). *Mysteries in the rocks of ancient Chukotka: Petroglyphs of Pegtymel.* Report NPS D-8. July 1999. Anchorage, AK: US Department of the Interior, National Park Service, Shared Beringian Heritage Program.

Dixon, M., & Kirchner, S. (1982). "Poking," an Eskimo medical practice in northwest Alaska. *Etues/Inuit/Studies, 6* (2), 109-125.

Dixon, M., Myers, W. W., Book, P. A., & Nice, P. O. (1983). The changing Alaskan experience: Health care services and cultural identity. *Cross-cultural Medicine, 139* (6), 917-922.

Eby, D. (1994, October). *Traditional healing, technological biomedicine, compacting – How do they fit together?* Unpublished paper presented at the American Public Health Association National Conference.

Eby, D. (1998). Traditional healing and allopathic medicine: Issues at the interface. *International Journal of Circumpolar Health, 57* (1), 62-66.

Eide, A. H. (1952). *Drums of Diomede: The transformation of the Alaska Eskimo.* Hollywood, CA: House-Warven.

Eliade, M. (1974). *Shamanism: Archaic techniques of ecstasy.* Princeton, NJ: Princeton University Press.

Ellanna, L. J., & Sherrod, G. K. (2005). *From hunters to herders: The transformation of earth, society, and heaven among the Inupiat of Beringia.* Anchorage, AK: US Department of the Interior, National Park Service, Alaska Support Office.

Fair, S. W. (2004). Names of places, other times: Remembering and documenting lands and landscapes near Shishmaref, Alaska. In I. Krupnik, R. Mason & T. W. Horton (Eds.), *Northern ethnographic landscapes: Perspectives from circumpolar nation* (pp. 230-254). Washington, DC: Smithsonian Institution, Museum of Natural History, Arctic Studies Center.

Fitzhugh, W. W., & Kaplan, S. A. (1982). *Inua: Spirit world of the Bering Sea Eskimo.* Washington, DC: Smithsonian Institution Press.

Fortuine, R. (1988). Empirical healing among the Alaska natives: An historical perspective. *Arctic Medical Research, 47* (1), 296-302.

Freeman, L. W. (2004). *Mosby's complementary and alternative medicine: A research-based approach.* St. Louis, MO: Mosby.

Freeman, L. W., Morgan, R., & Farquhar, T. (2001). Traditional peoples and the circle of healing. *Complementary Health Practice Review, 7* (1), 5-15.

Ganley, M. (1996).The role of anatguk in northwest Alaska: Historic transformation *NOAS, 12* (1-3), 5-19.

Garibaldi, A. (1999). *Medicinal flora of the Alaska Natives.* University of Alaska Anchorage, Environment and Natural Resources Institute, Alaska Natural Heritage Program.

Gould, S. J. (1980). *The panda's thumb.* New York, NY: W.W. Norton & Co. Inc.

Grof, S. (1995). *Suggestions for Research Projects Involving Holotrophic Breathwork.* Retrieved from the Association for Holotropic Breathwork International on 16 February 2009 at http://static.ning.com/holotropicbreathwork/research/grof1995.pdf

Haile, S. (2003). *Maniilaq: Eskimo prophet.* Springville, UT: Bonneville.

Halifax, J. (1979). *Shamanic voices: A survey of visionary narratives.* New York, NY: Penguin.

Halifax, J. (1982). *Shaman: The wounded healer.* New York, NY: Crossroad.

Heinze, R. I. (1997). *Trance and healing in Southeast Asia today.* Berkeley, CA: Independent Scholars of Asia, Inc.

Heinze, R. I. (1991). *Shamans of the 20th century.* New York, NY: Irvington.

Hild, C. M., & Stordahl, V. (2004). Human health and well-being. In N. Einarsson, J. N. Larsen, A. Nilsson, & O. R. Young (Eds.), *Arctic Human Development Report* (pp. 155-168). Akureyri, Iceland: Stefansson Arctic Institute.

Hild, C. M. (2007). Places of Arctic traditional healing. In R. I. Heinze (Ed.), *Proceedings of the 22nd Annual International Conference on the Study of Shamanism and Alternative Modes of Healing* (4 pages). Berkeley, CA: Independent Scholars of Asia, Inc.

Hild, C. M. (Producer), & Schenck, A. (Writer/Director). (2009). *Understanding the healing hands of the Maniilaq Tribal Doctor* [(abridged 30 minutes) Motion picture]. Retrieved http://www.arctichealth.org/tm.php)

Kalweit, H. (1988). *Dreamtime & inner space: The world of the shaman.* Boston, MA: Shambhala.

Katra, J., & Targ, R. (1999). *The heart of the mind: How to experience God without belief.* Novato, CA: New World Library.

Kirchner, S. (1982). Andrew Skin Sr.: Eskimo doctor. *Alaska Medicine, 24* (6), 101-105.

Krippner, S., & Welch, P. (1992). *Spiritual dimensions of healing: From native shamanism to contemporary health care.* New York, NY: Irvington.

Krupnik, I., & Jolly, D. (Eds.). (2002). *The earth is faster now: Indigenous observations of Arctic environmental change.* Fairbanks, AK: Arctic Research Consortium of the United States.

LLT Productions. (1998). *Maniilaq: The Eskimo prophet* [Motion picture]. Angwin, CA: LLT Productions.

Locke, S., & Colligan, D. (1986). *The healer within: The new medicine of mind and body.* New York, NY: E.P. Dutton.

Lowenstein, T. (1994). *Ancient land: Sacred whale, the Inuit hunt and its rituals.* New York, NY: North Point, Farrar, Straus and Giroux.

Lucier, C. V., & Van Stone, J. W. (1987). An Inupiaq autobiography. *Etudes/Inuit/Studies, 11* (1), 149-172.

Lucier, C. V., Van Stone, J. W., & Keats, D. (1987). Medical practices and human anatomical knowledge among the Noatak Eskimos. *Ethnology, 10* (3), 251-264.

Maniilaq Association. (2005). *Della Keats' collection.* University of Alaska Anchorage, Consortium Library Archives, Alaska Moving Images Preservation Association. (Accessed with written permission from the Maniilaq Association through Bertha Jennings secured July 10, 2005).

Maniilaq Association. (n.d.). *Company information.* Retrieved January 7, 2006 from the Maniilaq Association Web site: http://maniilaq.org/companyInfo.html

Mayer, E. L. (2007). *Extraordinary knowing: Science, skepticism, and the inexplicable powers of the human mind.* New York, NY: Bantam.

Milan, F. A. (1964). The acculturation of the contemporary Eskimo of Wainwright, Alaska. *Anthropological Papers of the University of Alaska, 11* (2), 1-95.

NANA – formerly the Northwest Alaska Native Association. (n.d.) Retrieved January 7, 2006 from the NANA Web site: http://nana.com

Narby, J. (2006). *Intelligence in nature: An inquiry into knowledge.* New York, NY: Jeremy P. Tarcher/Penguin.

Nuttall, M. (2000). Indigenous peoples' organizations and arctic environmental cooperation. In M. Nuttal & T. V. Callaghan (Eds.), *The Arctic: Environment, people, policy* (pp. 621-638). Amsterdam: Overseas Publishers Association.

Osborn, K. (1990). *The peoples of the Arctic.* New York, NY: Chelsea House.

Parra(1954). *Alaska's health: A survey report to the United States Department of the Interior.* PA: University of Pittsburgh, Graduate School of Public Health.

Ramoth, R. (1976). *Timimun Mamirrutit.* Kotzebue, AK: Mauneluk Cultural Heritage Program.

Reich, W. (1973). *The cancer biopathy.* New York, NY: Farror, Strauss & Giroux.

Ripinsky-Naxon, M. (1993). *The nature of shamanism: Substance and function of a religious metaphor.* Albany, NY: State University of New York Press.

Rossbach, S. (1983). *Feng shui: The Chinese art of placement.* New York, NY: Arkana/Penguin.

Saylor, B. L., Burgess, D. M., & Hild, C. M. (1998). *Bridges to the future: Traditional and local healing practices in Alaska.* University of Alaska Anchorage, Institute for Circumpolar Health Studies, prepared for the Southcentral Foundation.

Schwartz, S. A. (2005). *The secret vaults of time: Psychic archeology and the quest for man's beginnings.* Charlottesville, VA: Hampton Roads.

Talbot, M. (1991). *The holographic universe.* New York, NY: Harper Perennial.

Tandy, V. (n.d.) *Ghost sounds: A review and discussion of the infrasound theory and applications.* Retrieved May 6, 2004 from the University of Coventry Web site: http://heracles.coventry.ac.uk/cyberclass/vicweb/parapsychology.htm

Targ, R., & Katra, J. (1999). *Miracles of mind: Exploring nonlocal consciousness and spiritual healing.* Novato, CA: New World Library.

Turner, E. (1989). From shamans to healers: The survival of an Inupiaq Eskimo skill. *Anthropoligica, 31*: 3-24.

Turner, E. (1996). *The hands feel it: Healing and spirit presence among a Northern Alaskan people.* DeKalb, IL: Northern Illinois University.

Vitebsky, P. (2008). *The shaman: Voyages of the soul, trance, ecstasy, and healing from Siberia to the Amazon.* London, UK: Duncan Baird.

Weyer, E. M., Jr. (1932). *The Eskimos: Their environment and folkways.* New Haven, CT: Yale University Press.

Current Issues

Julian Assange, WikiLeaks, and the Trickster: A Case Study of Archetypal Influence

Niko Whitmire

Why has Julian Assange captivated the world? Why is there such an emotional charge centered around him? Both U. S. Secretary of State Hilary Clinton and Vice President Joseph Biden have equated his leaking of secret information with terrorist activity. Mainstream journalistic circles have passively looked on rather than leaping to his defense as they have in the past with other exposés threatened by governmental legal reactions (Adler, 2011).

Julian Assange is a case study of the trickster archetype playing out in an individual. To explore this topic, I have used excerpts from interviews, online newspaper and magazine reporting, Assange's

---

Niko Whitmire, MA is a doctoral student in clinical psychology at The Wright Institute in Berkeley, CA. His current interests lie in the intersections of neuropsychology, psychoanalysis and culture, and his present research centers upon examining the symptom presentation of Stendhal's Syndrome using a neuropsychological lens. He graduated with a BA in Psychology from UCLA, and then went on to get an MFA in Writing and Poetics from the Jack Kerouac School of Disembodied Poetics at Naropa University in Boulder, CO. He also received an MA in Depth Psychology from Sonoma State University in 2011.

Assange Stencil, Liepzig.

personal blog and statements, and portions from two of the books written about him by others, Daniel-Domscheit-Berg's (2011) book *Inside WikiLeaks* and David Leigh and Luke Harding's book (2011), *WikiLeaks: Inside Julian Assange's War on Secrecy*.

Questioning the Source

There are some potential issues of bias with some of the source material in that, as Julian Assange said himself in an interview with Chris Anderson, he is "a very combative person" (Assange, 2010). As a result, he has had very charged interpersonal relationships. Assange's colleague at WikiLeaks, Daniel Domscheit-Berg, resigned fall of 2010 to open another information leaking website. Although his book brings a different perspective upon the inside functioning of WikiLeaks and Assange's personal mode of operating, he had a significant personal conflict with Assange to the degree that Domscheit-Berg (2011) quotes Assange threatening him with physical harm. This conflict ultimately led to Domscheit-Berg leaving WikiLeaks. Because of the limited number of people involved in the inner workings of WikiLeaks, Domscheit-Berg's insider knowledge is important in spite of the potential bias that he holds. For instance, he exposes some of the fictions that Assange enacted in the functioning of WikiLeaks, such as the inflated numbers Assange used in speaking to the size of WikiLeaks staff, and he describes Assange posing as different members of the WikiLeaks team during correspondences. Jay Lim, a legal expert for WikiLeaks, for example, was in actuality Julian Assange (Domscheit-Berg, 2011).

Assange's relationship with both *The New York Times* and *The Guardian* (who employs the reporters David Leigh and Luke Harding) fractured and was unilaterally terminated by Assange. *The*

New York Times relationship ended after they refused to link to the WikiLeaks website where Assange had unredacted material that *The New York Times* felt might be a danger to some of the individuals discussed in the Afghan material. Assange also felt that their piece on Bradley Manning, the individual that the United States military has charged with leaking classified documents, minimized his heroic nature (Gaviria & Smith, 2011). And finally, Assange felt insulted by a *New York Times* piece written by John F. Burns. The paper nonetheless received the cables due to a leak within WikiLeaks (Leigh & Harding, 2011). *The Guardian's* relations with Assange became damaged after he bypassed their previous agreement and released information to BBC's Channel 4 (Leigh & Harding, 2011). Along with those issues, Assange has been quoted as describing mainstream journalism as "a craven sucking up to official sources to imbue the eventual story with some kind of official basis" (Khatchadourian, 2010, para. 97). It is not too surprising, therefore, that many members of the established journalist community have reacted negatively to Assange. Furthermore, many journalists have expressed discomfort regarding Assange's overt agenda against governments and other institutions (Adler, 2011). All of these concerns should be held in mind when receiving information from these sources as they may have had a biasing influence in their reporting.

Splendide Mendax

Assange has created his own personal mythology which both underscores the difficulty of the case study but at the same time reinforces the identification with the trickster. Assange plays both deceiver and inventor of his own record, and his taking of the hacker pseudonym, *Mendax*, or splendidly deceiving, from Horace's *Odes* (Khatchadourian, 2010; Manne, 2011; Obrist, 2011), indicates an awareness of this attitude. The Greek god *Hermes* does much the same when he performs the first sacrifice and adds his name to the list of the established pantheon (Kerenyi, 1976). Assange (Dreyfus & Assange, 1997) quotes Oscar Wilde in the researcher's introduction to *Underground*, "Man is least himself when he talks in his own person. Give him a mask, and he will tell you the truth" (p. 9). Assange chooses his own

> Bugs Bunny and Wile E. Coyote can be seen as two sides of the trickster, the blindly hungry bumbling hunter and the cunning prey who switches the trap onto the predator.

masks and in the same way creates his own truth, a truth that is consistent with his heroic activist ideal.

Many reporters fall into Assange's trap of personal truth without a researched Assange biography to fall back upon. Robert Manne (2011) writes, "Journalists as senior as David Leigh of the *Guardian* or John F. Burns of the *New York Times* in general accept on trust many of Assange's stories about himself. They do not understand that their subject is a fabulist" (para. 4). Assange's autobiography remains unpublished as of this writing, but as Domscheit-Berg (2011) states, any biography written by Assange should be treated with some skepticism because "Julian…had a very free and easy relationship with the truth" (p. 65). He reports that Assange had told him "at least three different versions of his past and the origins of his surname" (p. 72). Assange had also told Domscheit-Berg that his hair had became white when he was 14 after he had created a reactor in his basement and reversed the poles (Domscheit-Berg, 2011). In the TED talk interview with Chris Anderson, Assange was asked about being a hacker when he was younger. Assange reframed the statement to be that he was a journalist-activist who was prosecuted for writing a magazine (Assange, 2010) which is inconsistent with reporting by others that he was arrested for hacking (Manne, 2011; Khatchadourian, 2010; Leigh & Harding, 2011). Hacking has been equated with people stealing from grandmothers, he said, and that isn't the story that he wants to be part of anymore (Assange, 2010).

Archetype

Archetype has been defined as instinctual unconscious images or networks of images that influence the conscious mind through symbolic material (Neumann, 1963). This symbolic material can be illustrated by the image of the tip of an iceberg rising above the water. Most of the iceberg is submerged and inaccessible to the viewer. Similarly, much of the archetype is inaccessible to consciousness although it still exists and moves underneath the surface of the conscious mind. The symbolic materials experienced in our consciousness are the stories that we tell ourselves about ourselves, or that our friends and families speak of in reference to us. The characterizations of personality, vocation, hobby and relationship all draw from the pool of archetype as do the characters in our entertainment.

Nose art on FB-111.

The image one sees when one thinks of a bully, a scholar, a banker, an athlete, or philanderer are all derivations of archetypal referents.

The roots of stereotype come from archetypal images as well. We use stereotype to organize our perceptions when we lack concrete information or direct experience. Assange's trickster mask allows the archetype to carry our personal reactions to the man that we don't see. We place our experiences with the trickster archetype upon Julian Assange's character and motivations, often idealizing or demonizing as the case may be. When we experience someone who triggers the image of the archetype within us, we respond to our own internal connections to that symbolic material that has accrued during our individual life experience. Someone who is very mothering for example can trigger very different responses in individuals based upon their own experience with both the personal and archetypal mother image.

Trickster

As for the trickster in particular, it is often described as amoral and often impulsive, on the hunt for the fulfillment of its desires. They cross boundaries and challenge stereotypes (Hyde, 1998; Radin, 1956). Bugs Bunny and Wile E. Coyote can be seen as two sides of the trickster, the blindly hungry bumbling hunter and the cunning prey who switches the trap onto the predator. The trickster is the laughing fool and the inept villain, but ultimately it is what moves culture when it finds itself stuck. It crosses borders, violates strictures, and suffers punishments. The trickster is amoral, self-centered, greedy, and lustful (Hyde; Radin). Its agendas don't usually mesh with tradition or with those who consider themselves to be the guardians or custodians of it.

The author Lewis Hyde speaks of the trickster archetype in this way:

> We constantly distinguish—right from wrong, sacred and profane, clean and dirty, male and female, young and old, living and dead—and in every case trickster will cross the line and confuse the distinction. Trickster is the creative idiot, therefore, the wise fool, the gray-haired baby, the cross dresser, the speaker of sacred profanities. Where someone's sense of honorable behavior has left him unable to act, trickster will appear to suggest an amoral action something right/wrong that will get life going again. Trickster is the mythic embodiment of ambiguity and ambivalence, doubleness and duplicity, contradiction and paradox." (p. 7)

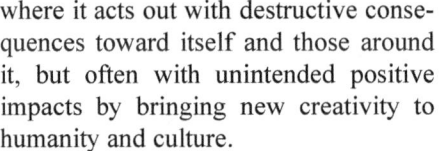
Coyote

The trickster is the clown and thief, seducer and fool, liar and prophet. It creates chaos and the opportunity for change. It opens up the space that allows something new to come into being. The tricksters is a particular archetype that often comes about when the world or society is stuck in a particular way of being and doesn't see or wish to see other possibilities. It can be viewed as the inadvertent revolutionary or creative hero in spite of itselves (Carroll, 1984). Its uncontrolled desires often put it into situations where it acts out with destructive consequences toward itself and those around it, but often with unintended positive impacts by bringing new creativity to humanity and culture.

However, this unrestrained desire is also the source of the trickster's transformative abilities, and so it becomes the source of its gift to humanity as well as its burden upon the culture and itself. *The Trickster Cycle of the Winnebago* (Radin, 1956) has an episode where the trickster sees some women bathing, so he (in this tale, the trickster is defined as male) sends his penis under the water to catch the chieftain's daughter and have intercourse with her. She is caught by him. It is only when the wise woman sticks an awl in his penis several times that he lets her go. It is this same penis that gets chewed up by a chipmunk when the trickster tries to send it into the rodent's den to punish him. Trickster picks up the pieces, after flattening the chipmunk, and plants them in the world to create useful vegetables that the people need: potatoes, turnips, the lily of the lake, among others. The trickster's inability to put off his desires provides the secondary benefit to society as a whole, and often to the detriment of the trickster himself in the course of these events. His unrestrained desire is what pushes him to cross the borders, to break through the antiquated boundaries which are impeding the growth of society.

The trickster often serves as an unconscious creator figure. The trickster's intended outcome usually strays from the path and provides something new and positive to the world in spite of its selfish intents. It takes on animal roles in many myths and that role reflects the instinctual nature of the trickster operation. Many times the regulation or damage mitigation of the trickster is provided by outside agencies. Or it requires suffering on the part of the trickster, sometimes depicted as a consumption of its desiring organs (Hyde, 1998). As you can see here in this Native American myth, Coyote inadvertently creates the sun, moon and stars after a childish tantrum. Coyote becomes the creator of the cosmos not through any conscious agency but rather through his following of childish whim to ruin the creation of others because of his exclusion.

Coyote and the sky – How the sun, moon, and stars began.

When they reached the other Animal People, Coyote was very angry that he had not been invited to come to the Fourth World. Coyote sulked behind a big rock so that no one could see him. When the Animal People opened the big bundle, they asked Badger to draw pictures of each animal on the yucca mat with the red-hot coals. Badger began to do so with a stick. All this time coyote was getting angrier and angrier. Suddenly he jumped out from his hiding place and grabbed one corner of the mat and flung it into the heavens! The coals became our stars. And if you look closely at the stars today, you can still see the outlines of the Animal People that Badger drew on the yucca mat. These are our constellations. In some places, the stars are in clusters, like in the Milky Way. This is where Coyote messed up Badger's drawings. Finally, Squirrel ran back to the Third World to tell Leader what Coyote had done. Leader decided to go up to the Fourth World.

When he got to the Animal People, he told Coyote that he had been bad and must leave the Fourth World. (Garcia, 2006)

Coyote unconsciously creates something new. It is one of the singular characteristics of the trickster that whatever the trickster creates couldn't come about in any other way. Chaos is required to shift the culture or cosmos into creation, and that chaos cannot come about through the conscious intent of any actor—for then it loses its chaotic character. Chaos is unexpected; intent is anticipatory. And so it is through this lens, however opaque, that I interpret the case of Julian Assange and his impact in our world.

Assange

What do we know about Julian Assange's background? In spite of his reticence to talk about his past there does seem to be a good amount of information available. He was born in Townsville in Queensland, Australia, and spent much of his childhood moving from town to town due to his parents' involvement in the theater (Obrist, 2011). Robert Manne challenges Assange's repeated assertion that he had attended 37 schools (Assange, 2010; Leigh & Harding, 2011), but even the more modest number of over 12 schools still reflects a transient upbringing. Assange stated that "[m]any of these towns were in rural environments, so I lived like Tom Sawyer—riding horses, exploring caves, fishing, diving, and riding my motorcycle" (Obrist, 2011, p. 2). His biological father, John Shipton, left his mother when he was about one year old, and he didn't have any connection to him until he was about 25. Julian speaks of his stepfather, Brett Assange, as his father, who only stayed with the family until Julian was about eight or nine. His mother's subsequent relationship with Keith Hamilton was another reason for Julian's transient childhood. Hamilton belonged to a cult which purportedly stalked Julian's mother through the use of government moles (Manne, 2011). Of his relationships with his peers, he wrote in his IQ blog on July 18, 2006 (Assange, 2006c), "we were bright sensitive kids who didn't fit into the dominant subculture and feircely [sic] castigated those who did as iredeemable [sic] boneheads" (para. 3). Assange identifies himself here as one who doesn't belong within the established boundaries of clique and culture. He, like the trickster, moves through the bonds of social norms and dwells outside of them.

As Assange grew older his explorations moved from caves to the online environments.

I was very curious as a child, always asking why, and always wanting to overcome barriers to knowing, which meant that by the time I was around fifteen I was breaking encryption systems that were used to stop people sharing software, and then, later on, breaking systems that were used to hide information in government computers. (Obrist, 2011, p. 2)

These activities culminated in a raid on his house in 1991 for his hacking activities. He ultimately pled guilty to the charges in 1996 and paid a fine (Leigh & Harding, 2011).

During the time between the raid and his trial, he became connected to the *cypherpunk* movement which espoused that politics in the age of the internet centers on the question of whether the state or anonymous individuals would triumph in a "battle for the future of humankind" (Manne, 2011). The cypherpunk ideology obviously resonated with Assange's beliefs to a large extent, although he was less interested in some of the right leaning libertarian attitudes that were held by members of the group. However, this rejection of the right wing ideologies doesn't mean that he was connected or identified with liberal or leftist constructs either. Manne notes that Assange was very anti-communist in his political ideology and often poked fun at the left. Assange believed that using truth to set people free held more social value that any particular political affiliation. He spoke of Voltaire, Galileo, and Gutenberg as "serial killers of delusion, those brutal, driven and obsessed miners of reality, smashing, smashing, smashing every rotten edifice until all is ruins and the seeds of the new" (Manne, 2011, para. 63). He also created during this time a program called Rubberhose, a cryptography software designed to protect human rights activists. With it he created a lively fictional posting announcement that was described by Robert Manne as revealing a "daring, wildness and a touch of genius" (para. 25).

The attitudes of conflict between state and individual continue in his posts on his IQ.org blog (Assange, 2006a) that lasted from July 2006 until August 2007. He quoted Alexander Solzhenitsyn speaking of his own arrest in the July 17th, 2006 post called *Jackboots* and spoke of what he referred to as the "mendacity of the state" (Assange, 2006b, para. 2). Assange theorized in this blog about what he called *conspiracies* that arise in governance. He conceptualized them as *conspiratorial webs* that become

A truck, driven by artist Clark Stoeckley, parked at the protest event Occupy Wall Street in New York City.

exclusive of the general populace. He believed these webs also develop attitudes that may not be aligned with the excluded majority group that remains outside of the governmental or corporate networks. He viewed these webs as networks working toward the maintenance of themselves above all other goals. The web network uses the component pieces—the individuals involved in the network—to maintain its existence, and expels those pieces that undermine these systems, or who do not act in a way that promotes the needs of their fellow individuals within the network. He saw these networks as undermining an organization's overt or articulated purposes. Only the releasing of the information hidden by the network will allow the people, both inside and outside of the network, to become free (Assange, 2006e). He saw in the creation of WikiLeaks the possibility of the undermining of state and corporate conspiracies, as he says "this is the good stuff" (Assange, 2006d; Manne, 2011). As Robert Manne (2011) succinctly says, "The revolution he [Assange] speaks of is moral" (para. 58).

And yet, with that releasing of information, Assange moves in areas outside of conventional morality. His moral principles in regard to what he views as conspiracy, and his imperative to have open access to information, trump all other ethical concerns. For example, his cavalier releasing of the names of civilians working with the United States military, and the publishing of military personnel Social Security numbers, showed a callous disregard for the risks that his disclosures can have upon the individuals involved.

WikiLeaks

The Why of It

WikiLeaks was created in 2006, and its first publication was in December (Domscheit-Berg, 2011; Leigh & Harding, 2011; Manne, 2011). This event followed the midterm elections in the United States where Democrats seized control over both houses of Congress, as they rode a wave of frustration over the continued war in Iraq and over the terrible tragedy of Hurricane Katrina. It was clear that the roots of the Iraq War had nothing to do with weapons of mass destruction or links to Al Qaeda, but rather hidden interests that can only be speculated about. CNN reported in January 2005 that nearly 9 billion dollars slated for Iraqi reconstruction went missing, and that part of the problem was the lack of transparency of the Coalition Provisional Authority in disbursing these funds (Cable News Network, 2005). The emergency response in the aftermath of Hurricane Katrina gave the impression of governmental organizations not only unprepared to help its citizens but also seemingly indifferent to its own incompetence. In October of 2006 the Abramoff scandal broke and revealed the depth and power of backroom influence in the United States legislature. The United States populace's trust in the Republican government was reeling from the opacity of its operating systems, and they looked toward the other party as an out. The choice of the Democratic Party—although understandable in its context—was perhaps naïve in its belief that significant change would be the result as both parties function within the same parameters of limited transparency.

Although Assange is Australian, the impact of the United States foreign policy was hitting him close to home. His essay *Conspiracy as Governance* (Assange, 2006e), written in December 2006 near the same time as his creation of WikiLeaks, seems to be a reaction to the Bush presidency. As Assange stated in his invitation to a member of the WikiLeaks board of directors, John Gilmore, WikiLeaks "will provide a catalyst that will bring down government through stealth everywhere, not the least that of the Bushists" (Manne, 2011, para. 77). He stated further that the new organization "has in its sights authoritarian governments, the increasingly authoritarian tendencies seen in the recent trajectory of the western democracies, and the authoritarian nature of contemporary business corporations" (Manne, 2011, para. 78).

> WikiLeaks has successfully taken advantage of the hydra nature of the internet: no matter how many heads you chop off, more will pop up.

What. How.

WikiLeaks is an anonymous whistleblower and information leaking venue. Assange has used the global aspect of the internet to evade the legal challenges that organizations (governmental, public and private) use to keep their secrets under wraps (Domscheit-Berg, 2011). Even the notoriously litigious Church of Scientology didn't use the courts to remove the information that WikiLeaks posted on the web, where previously the courts had helped them keep their skeletons safe and cozy inside the opaque spheres of their inner circles (Domscheit-Berg, 2011). As Raffi Khatchadourian reported in his 2010 *New Yorker* profile of Assange:

> Assange's response was to publish more of the Scientologists' internal material, and to announce, "WikiLeaks will not comply with legally abusive requests from Scientology any more than WikiLeaks has complied with similar demands from Swiss banks, Russian offshore stem-cell centers, former African kleptocrats, or the Pentagon." (para. 5)

WikiLeaks made itself immune to libel, copyright, and other legal recourses through the use of the same techniques that have served multinational corporations—cherry picking the world for the most conducive legal structures for their institution. Assange worked with the Icelandic parliament to create the Icelandic Modern Media Initiative. The IMMI is designed to make Iceland a "free haven for the media" (Domscheit-Berg, 2011, p. 134) by enacting the strongest media protections for investigative journalists. But even before that, they made sure that the main WikiLeaks servers were located in Sweden which has, outside of the newly created IMMI, very extensive free speech legislative safe guards in place.

But even more important than this technique has been the multiplicity of identical webpage sites. They have back up servers located elsewhere, so if one country takes down the website by shutting down the computers physically located within their borders, identical material can be posted from another site located in another country. This redundancy requires companies or governments to hire lawyers in different countries, file suits, and then go through with the legal procedures—only to have to repeat it somewhere else when the material moves to another location. When the Julius Bar Bank won their suit in California to have leaked material removed from the domain that had been originally created in that state, the court initially ruled in their favor and demanded that it be shut down (Domscheit-Berg, 2011). Immediately following the shutdown of the server located in California, myriad other identical pages popped up in its place (Domscheit-Berg, 2011). WikiLeaks has successfully taken advantage of the hydra nature of the internet: no matter how many heads you chop off, more will pop up. The repeated legal challenges only serve to increase the publicity of the leaked material through the news coverage of the suits (Domscheit-Berg, 2011).

WikiLeaks provides a safe place so that others may place their information there anonymously. Then WikiLeaks picks up the information, uses it, and disseminates it as it sees fit. The need for this anonymous-mechanism lies in our intense legal constriction of information. We have two things happening at once: a surge in information through the increased utilization of technology and the internet; and a reactionary attack by copyright concerns, governments, and other institutions to try and restrict that flow of information through the legal systems. WikiLeaks bypasses the legal threats, and allows for the information to get out. Assange has claimed to want "to make the world more civil" (Calabresi, 2010, para. 8) by undermining the secrecy of the state and corporate entities that seek to keep information out of the hands of others. WikiLeaks is designed to create that opportunity by using the internet to allow the information out and by allowing open access.

In addition to the two leaks listed above, WikiLeaks released countless documents through their portal and in conjunction with other media partners. WikiLeaks published a report by the Oscar Legal Aid Foundation which documented political killings perpetrated by the Kenyan police force; this news led to a 10 percentage point electoral shift in the subsequent elections in Kenya. WikiLeaks was subsequently honored with the Amnesty International Media Award.

WikiLeaks also received video footage from an Apache helicopter action. They then edited and released it in April 2010 as a video that they named Collateral Murder—it depicted the assault on a group of men by United States military. The military action resulted in the killing of two Reuters journalists, and the video revealed military personnel firing upon unarmed men trying to evacuate the wounded (Domscheit-Berg, 2011; Leigh & Harding, 2011; Khatchadourian, 2010). Domscheit-Berg reports that, contrary to Assange's statements, the film did not cost $50,000 to produce and that they had a password to the encrypted video. The video catapulted WikiLeaks even further into the world stage as the controversial footage was played countless times.

WikiLeaks followed the release of the video with the Afghan War Diaries in July of 2010, a release made in conjunction with *The New York Times*, *The Guardian*, and *Der Spiegel*. It contained confidential reports from United States military personnel in Afghanistan. And in October 2010, they released the Iraq War Logs which, among other things, revealed the hidden numbers of civilian casualties in Iraq. It showed that senior United States officials had lied when they proclaimed that they had no data on these deaths (Leigh & Harding, 2011). The last major leak of 2010 was the release of the United States diplomatic cables which was done in conjunction with two newspapers, *El Pais* and *Le Monde*. Some see these cables at the roots of the uprisings of the Muslim Spring, especially in regard to the revolutions of Tunisia and Egypt (Walker, 2011)

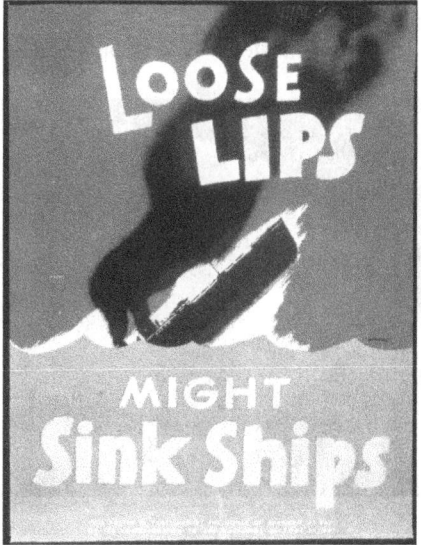

Loose Lips Might Sink Ships, 1941-1945.

Julian Journalistbane

During these last two releases, Assange's relationship with both *The New York Times* and *The Guardian* became strained. Assange was frustrated with *The New York Times'* reporting on him and Bradley Manning, and disputes about who was in on the information release. In addition, Assange came under fire from the United States government for releasing its confidential information. The mainstream journalist community was seemingly reticent to support him even amid talk of his being charged with espionage. Organizations, such as the American Society of Magazine Editors and the National Association of Broadcasters, did not make any statements on the subject of Assange being prosecuted under the Espionage Act (Adler, 2011). This attitude is in contrast to other large governmental leaks, and appears con-

> Julian Assange's erratic behavior when he tried to collaborate with the mainstream press reinforced their feelings toward the professional standards that they feel support a higher level of quality and integrity.

trary to their traditional stance of defenders of the first amendment. Ben Adler of *Newsweek* attributes this attitude to a variety of reasons, but principally to the negative reaction that most journalists have toward Assange's purpose and methods. They dislike his overt mission to disrupt governments—in specific, his agenda in regard to the United States—and his overt advocacy agenda which runs outside of the traditional idea of objective journalism (Adler, 2011). They also find fault in his lack of discretion in dealing with information that may put people at risk of harm, in particular, with his reticence to edit sensitive and potentially life threatening information (Adler, 2011).

However, their dislike of his methods and orientation may have its roots in their own connection to business as usual. Newspapers and broadcast news organizations have had to shift the way that they reach their audiences, but they have done so slowly and only after losing many of their viewers and their corresponding advertising revenue to more informal internet journalistic entities. There have been numerous articles and news pieces about the death of the newspapers and magazines and print media altogether. The growth of the blog and the amateur reporter has threatened the traditional system of reporting, and there have been highly charged negative reactions about the veracity and professionalism of such material and sources. These reactions are juxtaposed next to the growth of the Fox News Network which has deigned to make only the thinnest of accommodations to that journalistic norm of objective reporting.

WikiLeaks represents another threat in the changing world of information dissemination. Julian Assange's erratic behavior when he tried to collaborate with the mainstream press reinforced their feelings toward the professional standards that they feel support a higher level of quality and integrity (Leigh & Harding, 2011). However, most of the major media outlets have created their own leaking portals similar to the WikiLeaks model in order to access whistleblower information and possibly jump onto the bandwagon that WikiLeaks has initiated.

One Hundred Dollar Banknotes.

Disloyalty, Insubordination and Destabilization

Tricksters are trapped by their own unregulated and unrestrained desire, and Julian Assange has not escaped this difficulty. In August of 2010, an arrest warrant was issued for him in Sweden for sexual crimes perpetrated against two Swedish women. After Assange turned himself in to the authorities in the U. K., Assange's lawyer responded to the allegations as being a plot to discredit Assange made by "dark forces" (Davies, 2010, para. 4). His statement that "the honeytrap has been sprung" (Davies, 2010, para. 4) referred to the allegations being contrived in order to discredit Assange and the WikiLeaks organization. Assange himself referred to the charges as "dirty tricks" (Davies, 2010, para. 26) in a tweet, and ascribed the allegations as being the product of the United States intelligence services. Statements made by the two women in the allegation were then leaked to the press in December 2010, to the consternation of Assange and his legal team. Some of what was said is that Assange refused to wear a condom and tore the condom intentionally, initiated sex with a sleeping woman, and then when confronted by the women about getting an STD test, he refused (Davies, 2010). Assange, like the trickster, doesn't consider the needs or desires of others when under the compulsive drive of his own.

Also during the fall of 2010, Daniel Domscheit-Berg and a person only referred to as The Architect left the organization. This exodus effectively halved the permanent staff of WikiLeaks. The Architect was the individual who designed the platform and infrastructure that enabled the leakers to submit their information anonymously. The stated reason for their exodus was that Assange was becoming unstable and tyrannical (Domscheit-Berg, 2011) among other reasons. The Architect reportedly said that he was tired of dealing with amateurs (referring to Assange) (Domscheit-Berg, 2011). Domscheit-Berg was accused by Assange of "Disloyalty, Insubordination and Destabilization in Times of Crisis" (Domscheit-Berg, 2011, p. 200), words derived from the Espionage Act of 1917.

Gimme the Money

On the positive side, WikiLeaks with its increase in notoriety was making economic gains as well. Once it began to go after the US, the money from donations dramatically increased. The WikiLeaks organization paid Julian Assange a salary of $86,000 in 2010, and the Guardian reported that he signed a book deal for about 1.3 million dollars (Lewis, 2010). WikiLeaks also drew in another 1.3 million dollars in donations in 2010, according to the December 24th article in *The Wall Street Journal* (Crawford & Whalen, 2010). There is another financial account soliciting donations specific to his legal defense as well, but I am not aware that there have been any clear announcements on the size of that fund as yet. Domscheit-Berg believes that there are many unanswered questions as to the financing and disbursement of funds from WikiLeaks supporters and donors.

Trickster Assange

Assange clearly views himself as a trickster. He has named himself a trickster in print more than once (Assange, 2006d; Manne, 2011), and this is significant in that it reflects the story in which he sees himself. He views himself as the lively trickster breaking through the stultifying mass of antiquated systems and freeing those who are oppressed by them as well. His referring to himself as

Tom Sawyer resonates with the trickster; Twain's novels of *The Adventures of Huckleberry Finn* and *The Adventures of Tom Sawyer* are all about the adventures of two trickster boys. His hacking pseudonym, Mendax, speaks to his trickster identity, and later in 2006, he wrote on his OkCupid website that he was thinking about "Changing the world through passion, inspiration and trickery" (Manne, 2011, para. 72). Also in 2006 he wrote in his blog this statement about what he saw as the power of the trickster:

> Additional freedom is granted alone to the trikster [*sic*], who through adopting the manner and dress of the establishment may fool the agents of the state into deference. (Assange, 2006d, para. 8)

It is significant that at the same time that he created WikiLeaks, he spoke of himself as a trickster and of the power of the trickster as an opposition to the established and constricting systems. Even on a conscious level, Assange believes that the means to attain his social and political goals is through the activation of the trickster.

The trickster theme of boundary crossing is prevalent throughout Assange's life. His early interest in hacking is all about crossing the artificial borders and boundaries that have been put up by others. The judge presiding at his trial stated that it appeared that Assange had acted out of "intellectual inquisitiveness" (Leigh & Harding, 2011, p. 44) which echoes Assange's statement about his childhood and "barriers to knowing" (Obrist, 2011, p. 2). Assange appears to feel compelled to overcome these boundaries, to open the shut doors that he sees in front of himself.

The unrestrained desiring nature of the trickster and the darker side of the need to overcome boundaries both traps the trickster and subjects those around him to his unrestrained desire. This side could be reflected in the sexual allegations filed by the two women against him. I wonder if he also sees the condom as a boundary that needs bypassing. I suggest that it was the trickster acting in him to resist any semblance of restraint. The boundary crossing of Assange is also manifested when he gender-bends.

Assange has been reported to have dressed up in disguise, sometimes as an old woman, which echoes the gender bending theme that Lewis Hyde (1998) refers to in his description of the trickster as a crosser of established norms and stereotypes.

Another principle theme of the trickster is theft and thieving. One of the more captivating trickster figures in the Western European tradition is *Hermes*, the Greek god of thieves and merchants (Kerenyi, 1976). He guides the newly dead to the underworld, and travelers left him offerings along the roadside at piles of stone called *herms* in order to insure a safe passage. Other travelers would take these offerings in the spirit of the god of

Wikileaks Rally, IV, Sydney, Australia.

thieves and opportunity. I see WikiLeaks as functioning like a herm in that it allows the anonymous dropping off of information to be picked up and used by the organization. Assange facilitates the theft of information through insuring the anonymity of the leakers. He doesn't steal the information, but he disseminates it. *New York Times* writer Christian Caryl (2011) comments:

> In practical terms it seems to boil down to a policy of disclosure for disclosure's sake. This is what the technology allows, and Assange has merely followed its lead. I don't see coherently articulated morality, or immorality, at work here at all; what I see is an amoral, technocratic void. (para 3)

Caryl additionally notices "the scale is unprecedented. So, too, is the intent – or, more precisely, the lack thereof" (para. 2).

Lewis Hyde (1998) also speaks of the trickster in terms of his hunger and what he calls the "trap of appetite" (p. 17). Assange has not been successful in eluding the trap of appetite that his possession by the trickster has created. He desires more and more, and he traps himself in it. Hyde looks at the Native American Coyote figure as well as the Greek god Hermes in his study of the development of the trickster through his struggle with appetite. With Coyote, the restraining of appetite happens through the consumption of his own desiring organs, his intestines and his penis. He has to eat himself before he may restrain his urges. Hermes, in contrast, restrains his own hunger for meat (Kerenyi, 1976). After stealing Apollo's cattle, he stifles his personal hunger in order to use two of the cows as a sacrifice to the gods, and with this sacrifice, as I noted earlier, he places his own name among those to be worshipped. He holds back his hunger in order to satisfy an even greater hunger, the hunger for a place among the deities (Hyde, 1998; Kerenyi, 1976). I see Assange holding back his desire when he speaks formally in interviews. He becomes the otherworldly being (Khatchadourian, 2010) who speaks thoughtfully and slowly. With Assange, the unrestraint can be seen through the allegations of his sexual acting out, but also in his impulsive accusations and actions toward those he sees undermining him. His ostracizing of pivotal members of the WikiLeaks staff and his lack of restraint in dealing with media partners is much like Coyote eating up his own intestine or burning his own anus for failing to wake him when animals were stealing his food. This impulsivity contrasts itself with the collected and cool Assange he portrays in most of his interviews.

The trickster is known as the cunning fool. He traps and is trapped, often by his own desires. Assange can be viewed as the trapper in how he leaks information, and how he uses the legal outreaches of the documents' originators as a means of verification, or in the case of Julius Bar Bank, promotion of the leaked material.

> The fear that leaked information will come out seems to have caused the government to take proactive steps toward disclosure so that they can have some semblance of control.

However, he has been leaked from as well, accidentally and intentionally. And here we see him trapped by himself. He once released all of the names of his donors through an email and had it submitted to his site as a leak (Domscheit-Berg, 2011). When he was struggling to keep *The New York Times* out of the deal he had made with their editors and *The Guardian*, he was foiled by the leaking of the information by one of his own volunteers who released the material to a freelance journalist (Leigh & Harding, 2011). And finally, the details of the statements against him in the criminal proceedings were leaked out and his lawyers protested this leaking as being a scheme to further discredit Assange before his extradition hearings (Davies, 2010).

The trickster image is seen in Assange's presentation and deportment as well. *The New York Times* reporter Eric Schmitt (Keller, 2011) described him as looking "like a bag lady walking in off the street" (para. 8) at one of the meetings at *The Guardian* offices in London. He also stated that Assange once interrupted a conversation midsentence to skip ahead. He then stopped to continue the conversation as if nothing odd had happened (Keller, 2011). These eccentricities feed into the trickster characterization. In addition to referring to Assange as "having a bit of Peter Pan in him" (para. 13), Bill Keller states:

I came to think of Julian Assange as a character from a Stieg Larsson thriller — a man who could figure either as hero or villain in one of the megaselling Swedish novels that mix hacker counterculture, high-level conspiracy and sex as both recreation and violation. (para. 29)

The story characters used to describe Assange reflect the archetypal nature of how he comes across to others. He is more archetype than individual. He becomes an ambiguous character (both hero and villain) out of a novel or a children's fantasy book. Ravi Khatchadourian (2010) describes Assange as "a rail-thin being who has rocketed to Earth to deliver humanity some hidden truth" (para. 6). Jack Shafer in his article, *The 1,000 Faces of Julian Assange* (2011), adds this description to explain how frustrating Assange can be in relation to mainstream journalists:

> Assange bedevils the journalists who work with him because he refuses to conform to any of the roles they expect him to play. He acts like a leaking source when it suits him. He masquerades as publisher or newspaper syndicate when that's advantageous. (para. 3)

It is this shapeshifting nature that comes into play with his paradoxical relationship with the truth as well. On one hand, he promotes a rigid interpretation of what should be released. He has said that the names of civilians who worked with the United States military shouldn't be redacted because they were collaborators, and that it was important to release the social security numbers of military personnel for historical purposes (Leigh & Harding, 2011). As Robert Manne (2011) noted, Assange plays with the truth when it comes to himself. Domscheit-Berg (2011) stated that when Assange's autobiography is released it should go into the fiction section.

Assange as the trickster breaks through barriers and crosses borders. He shapeshifts and resists conformity. He traps and is trapped by desire. He is the patron of thieves and whimsical eccentrics. He comes across as amoral, but he also opens the space that allows for something new to come into being.

Apocalypse

Assange as trickster has accomplished some incredible things. Robert Manne (2011) states, "There are few original ideas in politics. In the creation of WikiLeaks, Julian Assange was responsible for one" (para. 71). Others have echoed this statement (Osorio, 2011). Esther Dyson (2010) says that WikiLeaks resolves two needs. The first is that it uses the internet's ability to spread information as a means for establishing "a better balance of power between people and power" (para. 15). And the second is that it provides a new openness that makes those in power behave better and that openness allows us to trust them more. When governments and corporations are forced to consider how things will look if a leak occurs, that also forces them to self-regulate rather than to rely on cover ups or disinformation.

In the past several years, there has been an explosion of leaking portals similar to WikiLeaks. Most of the major media outlets have created their own, and Domscheit-Berg's OpenLeaks is just one of the numerous independent organizations that have popped up as well. Assange has provided the individual a counterpoint to the increasing corporate and governmental opacity and consolidation of information and power. The irony is that WikiLeaks has become so large that "some of its secrets are no longer its own to control" (Stelter & Cohen, 2011, para. 1). This phenomenon is just the trickster energy continuing its natural path regardless with which entity it is involved.

Assange and WikiLeaks opened a way, and although that may have not been the original intent of the organization, it has provided benefit through not only its specific leaking system, but also through the opportunity of opening up information to be better accessed by the general public. In addition, benefits have been noted as a result of the specific information that has been provided to the world. Some of the information that has come out through the diplomatic cables added impetus to the protests in Tunisia and Egypt (Walker, 2011), though many will argue about the significance of that information in the context of all of the other factors involved. However, it cannot be denied that information about the abuses of tyrants lends power and drive to the people suffering under that yoke. They see the imbalance in print and discussed by others and that adds a push toward the wish for change. The trickster character in all of this is that the original intent of releasing the information was to engage and undermine the United States government and its foreign policy. It is Assange's antagonism toward the United States foreign policy that enabled the United States to reap rewards of a previously stagnant reliance on autocratic rulers in the Middle East who have often embarrassed the United States with their autocratic and anti-democratic policies.

I would add to this that WikiLeaks has caused changes in other governmental policy. In an article on the Osama bin Laden raid in *The National Journal*, Marc Ambinder (2011) writes that "Some senior JSOC [Joint Special Operations Command] officers are prepared to deal with a future that includes more openness about their operations" (para. 9). The fear that leaked information will come out seems to have caused the government to take proactive steps toward disclosure that they can have some semblance of control. These steps have involved dialogue with reporters about what is viable to be released, such as the names of participants involved. This new transparency is reflected in the comment by Col. Roland Guidry (retired), one of JSOC's founding members, "Why did the administration not respond like we were trained to do 30 years ago in early JSOC by uttering two simple words: 'no comment'" (Ambinder, 2011, para. 17)? This statement is further evidence of the impact of the advent of the leaking website. These impacts are not static, obviously. They should be noted as a reflection of the specific nature of how an archetype can become involved in our social systems through the actions of a single individual.

Julian Assage in Berlin.

Archetype affects not only our individual psyches, but they also can impact the culture as a whole through their manifestation in the individual. This aspect of archetypal action contextualizes individual behavior and societal needs. Human motivations are complex systems and often we find ourselves simplifying those systems in order to place the individual in question into a simpler moral container. In examining how the archetype impacts us, we can regain a fresh awareness of the gray areas in human behavior and how it can have unforeseen effects, both positive and negative, upon our cultural and group systems and identities. Furthermore, the expression of the archetype is part and parcel of the emotional charge that can be held within celebrity and other public figures. We are triggered by archetypal symbols. They leap up into our conscious minds from their depths and move us through intense emotional outpourings. By looking at the symbolic content that lies beneath these emotions and by seeing the story that lurks underneath our personal motivations, we may broaden our understanding of the deep, unconscious forces that are in play culturally. And hopefully, we may work towards a more conscious way of interacting on a group and cultural basis.

References

Adler, B. (2011, January 4th). Why Journalists aren't standing up for WikiLeaks. Retrieved from: http://www.newsweek.com/2011/01/04/why-journalists-aren-t-defending-julian-assange.html.

Ambinder, M. (2011, May 13th). Government fears too much disclosure in bin Laden raid will jeopardize future missions. Retrieved from: http://www.nationaljournal.com/government-fears-too-much-disclosure-in-bin-laden-raid-will-jeopardize-future-missions-20110513.

Assange, J. (2006a, June 22nd). Don't cross the tracks before putting on your shiny shoes [Blog post]. Retrieved from http://web.archive.org/web/20071020051936/http://iq.org/#Don%27tcrossthetracksbeforeputtingonyourshinyshoes.

Assange, J. (2006b, July 17th). Jackboots [Blog post]. Retrieved from http://web.archive.org/web/20071020051936/http://iq.org/#Jackboots.

Assange, J. (2006c, July 18th). Doing the Mont Park shuffle [Blog post]. Retrieved from http://web.archive.org/web/20071020051936/http://iq.org/#DoingtheMontParkshuffle.

Assange, J. (2006d, November 22nd). State and terrorist conspiracies [Blog post]. Retrieved from http://web.archive.org/web/20071020051936/http://iq.org/#Stateandterroristconspiracies.

Assange, J. (2006e, December 3rd). Conspiracy as governance. Retrieved from http://web.archive.org/web/20070829163014/iq.org/conspiracies.pdf.

Assange, J. (2010, July). *Julian Assange: Why the world needs WikiLeaks/interviewer: Chris Anderson.* [Video interview]. Retrieved from: http://www.ted.com/talks/julian_assange_why_the_world_needs_WikiLeaks.html

Cable News Network (2005, January 30th). Audit: United States lost track of $9 billion in Iraq funds. Retrieved from http://articles.cnn.com/2005-01-30/world/iraq.audit_1_iraq-reconstruction-stuart-w-bowen-iraqi-money/2?_s=PM:WORLD.

Calabresi, M. (2010, December 2nd). WikiLeaks' war on secrecy: Truth's consequences. Retrieved from: http://www.time.com/time/world/article/0,8599,2034276,00.html.

Carroll, M. (1984). The trickster as selfish-buffoon and culture-hero. *Ethos 12 (2)*, 105-131.

Caryl, C. (2011, January 13th). Why WikiLeaks changes everything. *The New York Times*. Retrieved from http://www.nybooks.com/articles/archives/2011/jan/13/why-WikiLeaks-changes-everything/

Crawford, D. & Whalen, J. (2010). WikiLeaks Spending Ballooned, Data Show. *The Wall Street Journal*. Retrieved from http://online.wsj.com/article/SB10001424052748703548604576037623559323348.html?KEYWORDS=assange

Davies, N. (2010, December 17th). 10 days in Sweden: the full allegations against Julian Assange. *guardian.co.uk*. Retrieved from *http://www.guardian.co.uk/media/2010/dec/17/julian-assange-sweden?INTCMP=SRCH*

Domscheit-Berg, D. (2011). *Inside WikiLeaks: My time with Julian Assange at the world's most dangerous website*. London: Jonathan Cape.

Dreyfus, S. & Assange, J. (1997). *Underground: Hacking, madness and obsession on the electronic frontier*. Retrieved from http://suelette.home.xs4all.nl/underground/Underground.pdf.

Dyson, E. (2010). Assange is a jerk, so what? Retrieved from: http://www.slate.com/id/2277764/.

Garcia, E. Sh. (2006). *Coyote and the sky – How the sun, moon, and stars began*. Albuquerque, NM: University of New Mexico Press.

Gaviria, M. & Smith, M. (Producer) & Gaviria, M. (Director). (2011). *WikiSecrets: The inside story of Bradley Manning, Julian Assange and the largest intelligence breach in United States history*. [Video]. Retrieved from: http://www.pbs.org/wgbh/pages/frontline/WikiLeaks/

Hyde, L. (1998). *Trickster makes the world: Mischief, myth, and art*. New York, NY: Farrar, Strauss and Giroux.

Keller, B. (2011, January 26th). Dealing with Assange and the WikiLeaks secrets. Retrieved from: http://www.nytimes.com/2011/01/30/magazine/30WikiLeaks-t.html?_r=1&hp.

Kerenyi, K. (1976). *Hermes: Guide of souls*. Putnam, CT: Spring Publications, Inc.

Khatchadourian, R. (2010, June 7th). No secrets: Julian Assange's mission for total transparency. *The New Yorker*. Retrieved from http://www.newyorker.com/reporting/2010/06/07/100607fa_fact_khatchadourian

Leigh, D. & Harding, L. (2011). *WikiLeaks: Inside Julian Assange's war on secrecy*. New York, NY: Public Affairs.

Lewis, P. (2010, December 26th) Julian Assange to use £1m book deals for legal fight. *guardian.co.uk*. Retrieved from http://www.guardian.co.uk/media/2010/dec/26/julian-assange-book-deals?INTCMP=SRCH

Manne, R. (2011, March). The Cypherpunk revolutionary Julian Assange. Retrieved from http://cryptome.org/0003/assange-manne.htm.

Neumann, E. (1963). *The great mother: An analysis of an archetype*. Princeton, NJ: Princeton University Press.

Obrist, H. U. (2011, May). In conversation with Julian Assange, part I. Retrieved from: http://www.e-flux.com/journal/view/232.

Osorio, A. M. (2011, May 16th). How cloud computing will change the nature of life and the gathering of information. The cases of Craig Venter and Julian Assange. Retrieved from: http://english.eluniversal.com/2011/05/16/clouds-of-the-future.shtml.

Radin, P. (1956). *The trickster: A study in American Indian mythology*. New York, NY: Philosophical Library.

Shafer, J. (2011, January 6th). The 1,000 faces of Julian Assange. Retrieved from: http://www.slate.com/id/2280157/.

Stelter, B. & Cohen, N. (2011, April 26th). In WikiLeaks' growth, some control is lost. Retrieved from: http://www.nytimes.com/2011/04/27/world/guantanamo-files-WikiLeaks-loses-control-of-some-secrets.html.

Walker, P. (2011, May 13th). Amnesty International hails WikiLeaks and Guardian as Arab spring 'catalysts'. Retrieved from: http://www.guardian.co.uk/world/2011/may/13/amnesty-international-WikiLeaks-arab-spring.

Book Reviews

The Somatic Revolution:
The Emergence of Somatic Psychology and Bodymind Therapy by Barnaby B. Barratt

Palgrave Macmillan, Paperback Edition, 2013

Reviewed by Samuel Arthur Malkemus

The field of somatic psychology is beginning to establish itself as a coherent discipline. Now with North American graduate programs at the *California Institute of Integral Studies*, *Naropa University*, *Meridian University*, and a new specialization at *Pacifica Graduate Institute* and *John F. Kennedy University,* somatic psychology is emerging as the psychological discipline of body life. Yet while it may be pre-emptive to characterize somatic psychology as a coherent discipline due to the diversity of perspectives that comprise it, Barratt's book is a fine contribution towards fortifying the roots from which this discipline is emerging. Available in paperback (2013) at a significantly reduced price from the initial hardcover publication (2010), from $80 to $25, this recent edition is more widely available to a general audience.

The Emergence of Somatic Psychology carries forward the first systematic overview of somatic psychology. It defines the field and method, and will no doubt become a benchmark for somatically oriented theoreticians and practitioners. Its central thesis is that somatic psychology is uniquely characterized by its investigation of psychic life *from* the living ground of bodily experience. Unlike a multitude of contemporary approaches *about* the body—from holistic medicine to cultural anthropology—the uniqueness and transformative potential of the somatic perspective is that it allows the body to speak *from* itself and *for* itself. In Barratt's words:

> Somatic psychology is the psychology of the body, the discipline that focuses on our living experience of embodiment as human beings and that recognizes this experience as the foundation and origination of all our experiential potential. (p. 21)

In this way, somatic psychology is defined as a unique psychological discipline while bodymind therapy is defined as the general praxis of that discipline. Barratt presents *bodymind therapy* as an umbrella term used to encompass all those embodied modes of healing that call forward the wisdom of bodily life. As such "body mind therapy is healing practice that is grounded on the wisdom of the body and guided by the knowledge and vision of somatic psychology" (p, 21).

To expand upon these definitions, Barratt provides a number of brief therapeutic case studies that exemplify bodymind therapy (chapter 3) and engages a detailed study of the ancient and contemporary sources of somatic psychology and bodymind therapy (chapters 6-12). By defining somatic psychology as the discipline, and bodymind therapy as the praxis of that discipline, Barratt provides a perspective that serves to unite the various academic

---

Samuel A. Malkemus, PhD, teaches graduate courses in psychology at the California Institute of Integral Studies and John F. Kennedy University. Together with Marina T. Romero he is the founder and director of the Institute of Holistic Transformation in Berkeley, CA. A fifth generation Californian, he leads courses and seminars in holistic sexuality and transformative education both internationally and in the San Fransisco bay area. With a private practice in embodied psycho-spiritual counseling his research interests involve exploring the role of embodied awareness in psycho-spiritual transformation, articulating a transpersonal understanding of sexuality and the sexual shadow, as well as developing somatic approaches to education and psycho-spiritual growth. The author of numerous articles he is currently preparing a book entitled *The Transpersonal Body.*

programs in somatic psychology with the broader therapeutic communities of the *European Association for Body Psychotherapy* and the *United States Association for Body Psychotherapy*.

On the one hand, Barratt's book is a rigorous and scholarly overview of the historical origins and contemporary advances of the field. Barratt draws on philosophical (chapter 8), socio-cultural (Chapters 8 & 15), spiritual (Chapters 11 & 16), depth psychological (Chapters 6 & 7), neuroscientific (chapter 12), and Asian religious (Chapter 10) perspectives to paint a broad historical and theoretical account of the discipline while articulating nuanced critiques of disembodied and socially oppressive perspectives. In doing so, it is his intention to provide a comprehensive research bibliography for other scholars.

On the other hand, his book is a revolutionary call for holistic modes of living and healing that are aligned with the bodily intelligence of a spiritually rich universe. His radical presentation of the discipline goes so far as to make the prediction that one day "psychology will become *somatic psychology* and psychotherapy will be *bodymind therapy*" (p. 21). To defend this prophetic and perhaps grandiose claim, as well as his additional assertion that it is "neither far-fetched nor whimsical," he presents an impressively erudite account of the conceptual history of Western culture (chapter 2). In it he explores how an ethics and epistemology of domination continue to perpetuate the "classism, elitism, racism (or ethnocentrism), gender-sexism, heterosexism, ageism, and ecocidalism" of the modern era, and shows how this modern worldview has "profoundly inscribed for all of us the condition of our alienation from the living experience of our embodiment" (p. 26). He also argues that contemporary psychology, and in particular cognitive behaviorism and psychoanalysis, has been adversely shaped by this oppressive history (chapter 1). Thus, his radical claim that psychology will one day become somatic psychology is supported by his assertion that the oppressive and disembodied ethos of the modern era is antagonistic to the holistic reality of bodily life and is in the process of internal collapse.

While *The Emergence of Somatic Psychology* is rich with Barratt's creative perspectives, which include his novel definition of healing (chapter 3) and what he terms *somatic sexology* (chapter 14) and *somatic psychodynamics* (chapter 7), I was most struck by his presentation of somatic psychology as both profoundly spiritual and socially transformative. It is rare to find these two domains so interwoven and I found Barratt's presentation of the spiritual and social implications of somatic psychology especially refreshing.

In particular, Barratt makes a radical call to somatic psychologists to not skirt the reality that somatic psychology is a "spiritual discipline," and that "the processes of returning to the awareness of our experiential embodiment are essentially a *spiritual* practice" (p. 174). Yet for Barratt it is crucial that somatic psychologists also recognize that such a process is also a "subversive act." This is because "listening to the voice of our embodied experience overcomes the alienation from our embodiment that is established in the course of our socialization and enculturation" (p. 175). In this view, somatic psychology ought to be antagonistic to psychologies of "cultural adaptation" and instead should aim to cultivate healing that brings the living voice of embodied spiritual wisdom to the critical analysis of culture and society.

This book is highly recommended to somatically oriented psychologists and bodywork practitioners. And while some readers may find it to be conceptually dense, and still others may be critical of the way that it meanders between an objective or scholarly presentation of the field and Barratt's own revolutionary agenda, I would argue that these features actually enrich this book by providing both a detailed and radical analysis of the field. This pioneering work is recommended for anyone looking to expand their understanding of the nature, history, and transformative potential of somatic psychology.

The Street Corner Ching: The Ancient Chinese Oracle in Plain English by Randy Handley

Open Books, 2010

Reviewed by Cristina Perea Kaplan

Cristina Perea Kaplan, M.A. weaves diverse fibers into her web of life. She is a Latina who writes poetry, essays, ethnoautobiography, and fairy tales. Her academic interests include hybrid identity, rites of passage, shamanism, and mythic stories. She teaches middle school English to immigrant students. She lives on Miwok land, and enjoys exploring the land's creeks as liminal spaces. She completed her graduate studies in depth psychology at Sonoma State University in 2013. With two fellow graduates, she recently founded the nonprofit, "Emerging Portals Collaborative," to bring depth practices to a diverse clientele including youth, women and men in transition.

The line from a song in the operetta, *Les Miserables*, "Little you know, little you care" comes into my mind as I begin this review of Randy Handley's (2010) interpretation of the ancient Chinese classic, *The I Ching or Book of Changes*. If you know nothing of this work, you may not care to read this review because it focuses upon a book that serves as an extension of the original. But if you have some interest in, or knowledge of, this mysterious guide, perhaps Handley's quirky approach to it may appeal to you. While I am not an avid user of *The I Ching* in any of its various translations, it is not for lack of curiosity. My husband owns a tattered copy of a 1970's workbook version of it (Wing, 1979), which I have consulted on a couple of occasions after encouragement from him with interesting outcomes.

I found myself alternately puzzled and pleased that this slim volume, *The Street Corner Ching* by Randy Handley (2010), had come into my hands for reading, reflection, and review. Yet having accepted the challenge, I felt that I could not fairly review this ambitious synthesis and interpretation without first dipping another toe into the mystery of the unabridged work as it has come to us in earlier English translations. Handley's purpose in writing this version was not to compete with these previous translations, but to render the original work more comprehensible to people of varying levels of education and background. He says that, "the *I Ching* is very much greater than a fortune telling oracle. In my opinion it is as great a source of traditional spiritual wisdom as any text known to man" (*p. xi*). That is a strong endorsement. Those of us seeking transformation in the world and in ourselves, as readers of *ReVision* necessarily seem to do could perhaps use Handley's window into a work that may or may not be a natural fit for a vast number of 21st century Western readers.

So I ask myself and all of you: Does any version of the *I Ching* have a place in the crowded bookshelves of people who came of age in the 20th century or even those now coming of age in the 21st century? Are its lessons, teachings, advice still pertinent to Western audiences thousands of years past its original conception as a "farming, fishing, and hunting almanac" (Wing, 1979, p. 8), and its later expansion by King Wen after he saw a vision and added commentary to make its wisdom applicable "for the worlds of commerce, politics, and social relations" (p. 8)? Jung (1950) spoke of its value

Xiantiantu, (Bagua, Diagram of Heaven)

in the English translation of Wilhelm's preface: "it is obvious that this book represents a long admonition to careful scrutiny of one's own character, attitude, and motives. This attitude appeals to me and has induced me to undertake this forward (p. xxiv)."

Jung's words would have been reason enough for me to take on this review, but I did not discover them until I read Handley's suggestion that readers of his book also acquire the Wilhelm translation with Jung's forward. For that advice alone, I see evidence of his wisdom and find his outlook sufficiently modest despite the immensity of the challenge he undertakes in condensing its "archaic, symbolic," and "flowery language" (Jung, p. xxxviii) into what he calls *The Street Ching.*

I cannot say that I love his title, nor all of his hexagram headings. One that bothers me is "A Backstreet Girl" (p.131) which Wing (1979) calls "Subordinate" (The Marrying Maiden). But in spite of these minor annoyances (I see the heading as flippant) I chose to approach this work with an open mind. I decided that I needed to make use of Handley's slim volume along with a copy of Wing's *The I Ching Workbook* by way of comparison. That is, I chose to consult it by throwing three coins (Handley, p. 19) before writing more than cursory impressions of the volume's merits. I was pleased to discover that Jung too had come to the same conclusion as I, and had thrown the coins himself. I discovered this soon after I threw coins on two related questions. Jung did so with the desire to know what the *I Ching* had to say about itself, its own worth, which was startlingly holistic and apt (Jung, 1950).

My questions related to the writing of this review, a maiden outing for me in this marvelous journal. Could I review the book fairly? Would a short effort be preferable to a long one? *The Street Ching's* answer to the first question was Hexagram 7, "The Military…no victory." Wing's answer seemed even more disheartening: "Collective Force (The Army)…misfortune." However, there were *moving* lines (Handley, p. 19) in my cast, so I was directed to Hexagram 46. *The Street Ching's* heading said: "Rise Above." It indicated it was "Time to grow, act, climb…Advance to fortune" (p. 115). The heading in Wing's version was subtly different: "Advancement (Pushing Upward)" (not paginated). Its advice was less glowing, but perhaps more encouraging: "Know what must be done and carry it out" (not paginated). When asked about the length of this review, *The Street Ching* answered with Hexagram 62, "Smallness" (p.147). Could that answer have been more to the point?

In conclusion, if you know and care about the complete translations of *The I Ching or Book of Changes*, this abridged and colloquial version might seem to you like a sacrilege. But if you are only toying with the idea of getting to know it, or if you are hoping to enjoy its great fruits of wisdom, but have found yourself confounded by its flowery language, Handley's *The Street Ching* may be just the ticket for your entrance into this fascinating and mysterious work. Furthermore, if you are a loyal user of *The I Ching*, and as such, cannot bear to leave it behind when traveling light, this slim volume might also fit your needs. In any case, you may find that some version of the *The I Ching* belongs in your bookshelf at this juncture when wise teachers cannot easily be found, or when found, may not be readily consulted.

References

Handley, R. (2010). *The street corner ching: The ancient oracle in plain English.* Bloomington, IN: Open Press.

Jung, C.G. (1950/1967). Forward to the I ching or book of changes. R. Wilhelm. (C. Baynes, Trans.). New York, NY: Princeton University Press.

Wilhelm, R. (1950/1967). *The I ching or book of changes.* (C. Baynes, Trans.). New York, NY: Princeton University Press.

Wing, R.L. (1979). *The I ching workbook.* Garden City, NY: Doubleday & Company, Inc.

Photo Index

Page	Artist, Source
1.	Paloma Cervantes, Wikimedia.
2.	Аркадий Зарубин, Wikimedia.
3.	Neil Oalmer, Wikimedia.
4.	Anonymous, Wikimedia.
5.	Marina T. Romero, provided.
6.	Ana Llamazares, provided, photo of mosaic mural made by students of the Profesor Luis Quesada School, province of Mendoza, Argentina, upon engravings by Luis Quesada.
9.	Taken from: Lewis-Williams, D. (2002). *The mind in the cave: Consciousness and the origins of art.* London, England: Thames and Hudson.
11.	Psyberartist, Wikimedia.
12.	Sketched by Nicolaas Witsen (1705). Taken from: Clottes, J. & Lewis-Williams, D. (1998). *The shamans of prehistory: Trance and magic in the painted caves.* London, England: Harry N. Abrams.
13.	Sketched by A. Breuil. Taken from: Laming, E. A. (1962). *La signification de l´Art Rupestre Paleolitique.* Paris, France: Picard.
14.	Alexander Nikolsky, Wikimedia.
15.	North American rock art. Taken from: Schaafsma, P. (1986). *Indian Rock Art from the Southwest.* Albuquerque, NM: University of New Mexico Press.
17.	Alexander Nikolsky, Wikimedia
19.	Prehistoric Rock Art, photography collection, Wikimedia.
21.	Ana Llamazares, provided, mosaic mural made by students of the *"Profesor Luis Quesada" School*, province of Mendoza, Argentina, upon engravings by Luis Quesada.
22.	Anonymous, Wikimedia, taken in Vancouver Island, British Columbia; wood.
24.	Novyaradnum, Wikimedia.
26.	Adrian Sampson, Wikimedia.
28.	Unknown Aboriginal Australian artist, c. 1860-1940CE, Griffith University, public domain.
31.	Anonymous, provided by Connie Grauds.
33.	Connie Grauds, provided.
35.	Connie Grauds, provided.
38.	Connie Grauds, provided.
39.	Connie Grauds, provided.
40.	Robert Tindall, provided.
42.	Anonymous, Wikimedia.
44.	Sascha Grabow, Wikimedia.

Page	Artist, Source
45.	Anonymous, National Institutes of Health, Wikimedia.
46.	Francesca Boring, provided.
49.	Anonymous, pencil and colored pencil, Black Hawk, c. 1880, public domain, Wikimedia.
50.	Fridtjof Nansen Archive, National Library of Norway, Siberia, 1913.
52.	Marina T. Romero, provided.
53.	Francesca Boring, provided.
54.	Denita Benyshek, watercolor, gouache, ink, collage on paper.
55.	Denita Benyshek, graphite on paper.
56.	Denita Benyshek, watercolor and ink on paper.
57.	Denita Benyshek, oil on canvas
58.	Denita Benyshek, watercolor, gouache, ink, collage, on paper
59.	Tomoniu N. Nicolae, of marble, 1938, by Constantin Brâncuşi, installed at the war memorial in Târgu Jiu, Romania, Wikimedia.
59.	Simiprof, of cast iron, 1938, by Constantin Brâncuşi, installed at the war memorial in Târgu Jiu, Romania, Wikimedia.
60.	Denita Benyshek, ink in sketchbook.
62-72.	All images provided by Michael Bova.
75.	Floyd Davidson, Wikimedia.
79.	Lomen Brothers, Nome, c. 1914, Library of Congress Prints and Photographs Division Washington, D.C.
82.	Frank Carpenter, of Yupik Shaman, Nushagak, Alaska, c. 1890, Wikimedia.
84.	Herder3, Wikimedia.
85.	National Archives and Records Administration ARC 6438338. Originally used by the B-24 Liberators of the 529th during World War II, Wikimedia.
86.	Wild coyote, Wikimedia.
87.	David Shankbone. Wikimedia.
89.	Office of War Information, National Archives and Records Administration ARC 51343, Wikimedia.
90.	Milad Mosapoor, Public domain, Wikimedia.
91.	Newtown grafitti, 2012, Creative Commons, Wikimedia.
93.	Andy McGee, Wikimedia
97.	Anonymous photographer, Wikimedia

New from ReVision Publishing

THE LIGHT IN THE DARK: THE SEARCH FOR VISIONS

Only $19.95
Includes shipping

264 pages

Ruth-Inge Heinze
Foreword by Stanley Krippner

Order from:
ReVision Publishing • PO Box 1855 • Sebastopol, CA 95473

SHAMANS OF EURASIA

New from
ReVision Publishing

$45.00
Pre-order Now

Mihály Hoppál

ReVision Publishing • PO Box 1855 • Sebastopol, CA 95473

www.ingramcontent.com/pod-product-compliance
Lightning Source LLC
Chambersburg PA
CBHW080406170426
43193CB00016B/2831